A HISTORICAL GUIDE TO
Ralph Waldo Emerson

The Historical Guides to American Authors is an interdisciplinary, historically sensitive series that combines close attention to the United States' most widely read and studied authors with a strong sense of time, place, and history. Placing each writer in the context of the vibrant relationship between literature and society, volumes in this series contain historical essays written on subjects of contemporary social, political, and cultural relevance. Each volume also includes a capsule biography and illustrated chronology detailing important cultural events as they coincided with the author's life and works, while photographs and illustrations dating from the period capture the flavor of the author's time and social milieu. Equally accessible to students of literature and of life, the volumes offer a complete and rounded picture of each author in his or her America.

A Historical Guide to Ernest Hemingway
Edited by Linda Wagner-Martin

A Historical Guide to Walt Whitman
Edited by David S. Reynolds

A Historical Guide to Ralph Waldo Emerson
Edited by Joel Myerson

A
Historical Guide
to Ralph Waldo Emerson

EDITED BY
JOEL MYERSON

New York   Oxford
Oxford University Press
2000

Oxford University Press

Oxford   New York
Athens   Auckland   Bangkok   Bogotá   Buenos Aires   Calcutta
Cape Town   Chennai   Dar es Salaam   Delhi   Florence   Hong Kong   Istanbul
Karachi   Kuala Lumpur   Madrid   Melbourne   Mexico City   Mumbai
Nairobi   Paris   São Paulo   Singapore   Taipei   Tokyo   Toronto   Warsaw

and associated companies in
Berlin   Ibadan

Copyright © 2000 by Oxford University Press, Inc.

Published by Oxford University Press, Inc.
198 Madison Avenue, New York, New York 10016

Oxford is a registered trademark of Oxford University Press.

Library of Congress Cataloging-in-Publication Data
A historical guide to Ralph Waldo Emerson /
edited by Joel Myerson.
p.   cm. — (Historical guides to American authors)
Includes bibliographical references and index.
ISBN 0-19-512093-0; ISBN 0-19-512094-9 (pbk.)
1. Emerson, Ralph Waldo, 1803–1882   2. Literature and history—
United States—History—19th century.   3. Authors, American—
19th century Biography.   I. Myerson, Joel.   II. Series.
PS1631.H45   1999
814'.3—dc21   99-13122
[B]

3 5 7 9 8 6 4 2

Printed in the United States of America
on acid-free paper

For Matthew J. Bruccoli

An institution is the lengthened shadow of one man . . . and all history resolves itself very easily into the biography of a few stout and earnest persons—
"Self-Reliance" (*CW*, 2:35–36)

Contents

Abbreviations

AW   *Emerson's Antislavery Writings*, ed. Len Gougeon and Joel
Myerson (New Haven, Conn.: Yale University Press, 1995).

CEC   *The Correspondence of Emerson and Carlyle*, ed. Joseph Slater
(New York: Columbia University Press, 1964).

CS   *The Complete Sermons of Ralph Waldo Emerson*, 4 vols.,
ed. Albert J. von Frank et al. (Columbia: University of
Missouri Press, 1989–1992).

CW   *The Collected Works of Ralph Waldo Emerson*, 5 vols. to
date, ed. Alfred R. Ferguson, Joseph Slater, and Douglas
Emory Wilson (Cambridge: Harvard University Press,
1971–).

EL   *The Early Lectures of Ralph Waldo Emerson*, 3 vols., ed.
Robert E. Spiller, Stephen E. Whicher, and Wallace E.
Williams (Cambridge: Harvard University Press,
1959–1972).

JMN   *The Journals and Miscellaneous Notebooks of Ralph Waldo
Emerson*, 16 vols., ed. William H. Gilman, Ralph H.
Orth, et al. (Cambridge: Harvard University Press,
1960–1982).

L   *The Letters of Ralph Waldo Emerson*, 10 vols., ed. Ralph L.
Rusk and Eleanor M. Tilton (New York: Columbia University Press, 1939, 1990–1995).

TN   *The Topical Notebooks of Ralph Waldo Emerson*, 3 vols., ed.

Ralph H. Orth et al. (Columbia: University of Missouri Press, 1990–1994).

W   *The Complete Works of Ralph Waldo Emerson,* 12 vols., ed. Edward Waldo Emerson (Boston: Houghton, Mifflin, 1903–1904).

A HISTORICAL GUIDE TO
Ralph Waldo Emerson

Introduction

Joel Myerson

R alph Waldo Emerson's reputation has never been as un-shakeable as it is today. Modern editions of his writings—letters, journals, notebooks, and published works—comprise nearly fifty volumes, with even more in preparation. In the last decade alone, nearly one thousand articles and books have been published discussing his life, ideas, and writings. He has been seen as beginning a line in American poetry that runs from him to Walt Whitman to Allen Ginsberg; his educational ideas were an important influence on Charles W. Eliot when he was president of Harvard; and he is viewed as the progenitor of a line of pragmatism in American intellectual life that was filtered through William James. In his own life he was a minister, a lecturer, a professional author, an agent for other authors (including Thomas Carlyle, Margaret Fuller, and Henry David Thoreau), and a traveler through America and Europe; modern studies of all these occupations mention Emerson as a serious and often important practioner of them. Every major critical trend in American literary study since 1900 has dealt with Emerson in some fashion. He is here to stay—and the bicentennial celebration in 2003 of his birth will undoubtedly set off another round of reevaluations of this seminal figure in American literature and thought.

A Historical Guide to Ralph Waldo Emerson presents materials that students of Emerson and American Romanticism will find useful in understanding the man and his times. Rather than attempting to duplicate the many bibliographic essays that attempt to survey the massive amount of scholarship written on Emerson, or the valuable and detailed chronologies and biographies of Emerson's life, or the numerous critical surveys that attempt to help us find ways to read Emerson's writings, this book presents historical essays designed to show us how Emerson was a product of his time.

Writers do not create their works in a vacuum. Among Emerson's contemporaries, for example, we can state with certainty that Nathaniel Hawthorne's *The Scarlet Letter* was as much about the author's dismissal from the Salem Custom House as it was about Hester Prynne, or that Herman Melville wrote as much about slavery as he did about seafaring. Emerson's long life (1803–1882) spanned an exceptional American century, as he observed and commented upon the War of 1812, Jacksonian democracy, the Mexican War, the antislavery campaign, the Civil War, Reconstruction, and, throughout his life, the tremendous growth of science and technology. *A Historical Guide to Ralph Waldo Emerson* places Emerson within that century by publishing essays that discuss him in the context of individualism, nature and natural science, religion, antislavery, and women's rights.

A Historical Guide to Ralph Waldo Emerson contains chronologies of both Emerson's own life and the major political, social, and literary events of his age. Here we can observe many interesting connections, such as how, in 1836, when Emerson published his first book, *Nature*, the Battle of the Alamo was fought, and William Holmes McGuffey published his first school reader; or, how, in 1873, when Emerson returned home to Concord from his last trip abroad, the first cable car was used in San Francisco, the first code of rules for football was drafted, Emily Post was born, and Mark Twain and Charles Dudley Warner published a book whose title became synonymous with the time, *The Gilded Age.*

Ronald A. Bosco's two essays, one on Emerson's life and the other on biographical studies of Emerson, show how we have appropriated Emerson and how this process began during Emerson's own age; that is, Bosco attempts to interpret and demonstrate Emerson's own proposition that "[a]n institution is the lengthened shadow of one man . . . and all history resolves itself very easily into the biography of a few stout and earnest persons."[1] Moreover, many of the essays in the book deal chronologically with Emerson's development, and help to flesh out the physical dimensions of his life. The general outlines of that life, as can be seen from the chronology in this book, are impressive but not, for someone of Emerson's reputation and class, very remarkable: he joined and then resigned from the ministry; he was a successful lecturer and writer; he suffered family losses but had a successful family life; he was a resident of Concord, Massachusetts, for nearly fifty years; he traveled a good deal as a lecturer, and made one trip to California and three to England or Europe; and he numbered among his friends or acquaintances nearly all the major literary and New England political figures of his era. Yet, of all the writers of his time, he has had the greatest legacy in the most areas of American life.

Emerson's life was lived against sweeping changes in a rapidly developing young nation. When he was born, America had not been a country for even three decades. In Emerson's youth, there were only about six million people in the country, and only six cities had populations in excess of ten thousand; the size of the United States, just prior to the Louisiana Purchase of 1803, was 236,826,000 acres; there were seventeen states; in 1830, the first year that such statistics were kept, forty miles of railroad tracks were built; and $28,000,000 was in circulation. At the time of Emerson's death there were over fifty-two million Americans, and 223 cities had populations over ten thousand; the size of the country was 1,837,763,000 acres; there were thirty-eight states; 84,866 miles of railroad tracks spanned from the Atlantic to the Pacific; and $1,409,398,000 was in circulation. The physical changes in America were, in a sense, just as great as the personal and intellectual changes in Emerson.

In "The Age of the First Person Singular: Emerson and Individualsm," Wesley T. Mott deals with a concept that is synonymous with the author of "Self-Reliance." By tracing the development of this idea in Emerson's own thought as well as in the culture around him, and in our present day, Mott helps us to better contextualize Emerson's thinking about and acting on this subject.

"Emerson, Nature, and Natural Science," by William Rossi, traces Emerson's development as a student and practitioner of this concept. After all, Emerson's first book was titled *Nature*, and one reason he moved to Concord, Massachusetts, in 1834 was to leave the city and live closer to the natural world. Rossi shows us how Emerson's study of natural science drew upon the works of contemporaries, and represented a serious intellectual inquiry, not just an attempt to capture a pastoral sense of romantic nature.

David M. Robinson, in "Emerson and Religion," reminds us that, just as Transcendentalism was first and foremost a religious movement, so, too, can Emerson's own beginnings be found within a religious context. He was, after all, a student at Harvard Divinity School and ordained a minister, served as pastor of the prestigious Second Church and Society in Boston, and wrote on the subject of religion his whole life.

In "Emerson and Antislavery," Gary Collison brings the picture of the "Sage of Concord"—as those who view Emerson as an abstract, philosophical writer tend to call him—back to reality by showing how concerned Emerson was with this, the great social campaign of the nineteenth century. Too often, contemporary readers of Emerson tend to think of him as far removed from daily life and concerns; Collison shows him absorbed and involved in the fight for freedom.

Armida Gilbert, in "Emerson in the Context of the Woman's Rights Movement," presents a topic not much examined until recently. With the growth of feminist studies, we have come to see just how important to Emerson's personal and intellectual development were such women as his aunt Mary Moody Emerson and his second wife, Lidian. Gilbert traces Emerson's views of women and women's rights from youth to old age, and also evaluates his ideas and language within the context of others writing on this subject during the period, and discusses the reaction of contemporaries to his comments on the subject.

Finally, I provide a bibliographic essay on the current state of Emerson's texts, followed by a comprehensive listing of the books written about Emerson and his times, grouped under the headings "Bibliographies," "Collections of Essays," "Biographies," "Religion," "Unitarianism," "Transcendentalism," "Concord, Massachusetts," "Philosophy," "Literary History," and "Books on Ralph Waldo Emerson."

Illustrations will help the reader to visualize Emerson and his surroundings. The images of Emerson range from those of him as a young man to a picture of him at his writing table a few years before his death. It is important to document and trace the physical changes in Emerson from a handsome young man to his strong middle age to his quieter later years because most images that are used in anthologies date from the later years of his life, when his declining creative powers (caused by old age and aphasia) are reflected in his features. The essays in this volume trace the development of Emerson's creative powers; the pictures should reflect how he appeared at these different stages of his career.

I thank T. Susan Chang for having the vision to create this series and the kindness to allow me to edit a volume in it. Robert Newman, Chair of the Department of English at the University of South Carolina, provided valuable support. I am grateful to Michael McLoughlin and Chris Nesmith for help in seeing the book through production. As usual, Greta indulged my obsession with Emerson.

NOTE

1. "Self-Reliance," in *CW,* 2:35–36. Especially valuable for following Emerson's daily life are the chronologies that begin each volume of *JMN*; and Albert J. von Frank, *An Emerson Chronology* (New York: G. K. Hall, 1994).

Ralph Waldo Emerson
1812–1892

A Brief Biography

Ronald A. Bosco

The study of Ralph Waldo Emerson's biography has long challenged both general readers and specialists in American literature. As the bibliographies printed in this volume indicate, Emerson, whose private and public writings alone now approach fifty printed volumes in modern editions, has been the subject of numerous book-length biographies. A recently published chronology of major events in his life extends to well over five hundred pages.[1] A person who engaged in complex personal and intellectual relationships with many persons in America and abroad, who had something to say about every important religious and philosophical controversy, political and social event, and scientific discovery that came to his attention between the 1820s and the late 1870s, and who nearly filled four notebooks with the titles of books he considered essential to read, Emerson defies easy summary.[2]

Divided into two parts, this essay is designed to introduce readers to the highlights of Emerson's life and thought. The first section, "Emerson's Personal and Professional Life," focuses on the details of his personal and professional development, concentrating on the 1830s as a defining decade for Emerson and, through an account of his principal publications and transformative events and relationships in his personal life, on the evolution of his idealistic philosophy. The second section, "Emerson and America's Coming of Age," focuses on the intellectual service Emerson performed for America through his lectures and writings and identifies him as a principal architect of American culture. Whereas the first section is largely descriptive, the second is interpretive; what links the two is my own interest in the processes of Emerson's intellect and imagination, as well as in the nature of his character and personality, as I have found them disclosed in the prose and verse of modern editions of his writings in which I have participated as an editor and a reader.[3]

Emerson's Personal and Professional Life

Ralph Waldo Emerson was born on 25 May 1803 in the parsonage of the First Church on Summer Street in Boston. His father, the Reverend William Emerson (1769–1811), who could trace his family's roots in America back to the first generation of New England settlement and was himself the product of several generations of ministers, was pastor of the prestigious First Church. His mother, Ruth Haskins Emerson (1768–1853), whose father was a wealthy distiller in Boston, came from a family that had made its name in the West India trade. Of eight children born to the Reverend Emerson and his wife, Ralph was the fourth and one of only five to survive to maturity.

Emerson's early years were spent mostly in school and in the company of his four brothers: William (1801–1868), Edward Bliss (1805–1834), Robert Bulkeley (1807–1859), and Charles Chauncy (1808–1836). Of these, William, Edward, and Charles eventually pursued careers in the law, although both Edward and Charles would die of tuberculosis at a relatively young age; Robert—or Bulkeley, as he was known in the family—was feebleminded and spent most of his adult years working for his room and board on farms outside of Concord, Massachusetts. With the death of Emerson's father in 1811, the family fortunes dwindled quickly. For many years his mother operated a succession of boardinghouses, and with the aid of her sister-in-law Mary Moody Emerson (1774–1863), who became the boys' principal educator and muse, she struggled to keep her family together and to provide her sons with respectable educations.

There was virtually no indication during his youth that Emerson would ever rise to make the mark on American life and letters with which he is credited today. He entered the Boston Latin School in 1812, when he was nine years old, and Harvard in 1817, when he was fourteen. Emerson's years at Harvard were generally undistinguished. Although he enjoyed his readings in the Latin and Greek classics, he performed no better than satisfactorily in either mathematics or philosophy. He eventually graduated thirtieth out of a class of fifty-nine. Between 1821, when he graduated from Harvard, and 1825, he grudgingly occupied himself as a teacher in and around Boston. His only pleasures during these years seem to have been an occasional walking tour, a few rude attempts at poetry, reading in any classical or modern studies of science, philosophy, and literary history which he could get his hands on, and engaging in an extended correspondence with his aunt Mary about the books he was reading and about knotty questions of philosophy or theology as he encountered them in his readings or in the sermons he heard that promoted the liberal brand of Christianity that would soon emerge as Unitarianism.

The years between 1825 and 1827 were promising but also difficult for Emerson. Periodically inclined to prepare for the ministry, he studied at the Harvard Divinity School in 1825 and 1827 but did not take a degree; between stints at Harvard he taught school in Chelmsford and Cambridge, Massachusetts, and on 10 October 1826, after he preached before the Middlesex Association of Ministers, he was approbated (licensed) to preach by the American Unitarian Association. Over the following month he preached in Waltham and in his father's old church in Boston. By the end of November, however, Emerson, who had been experiencing trouble with his eyes, joints, and lungs—early signs, as he knew, of tuberculosis—took the advice of his physician and traveled to Charleston, South Carolina, and St. Augustine, Florida, to improve his health.

Emerson returned to Boston in June 1827. On his way home from the south he preached in Washington, D.C., Philadelphia, and New York City. Not interested in a pulpit of his own, over the next year and a half he preached steadily in and around Boston, throughout the Connecticut Valley, and in New Hampshire. On 25 December, while preaching in Concord, New Hampshire, he was introduced to sixteen-year-old Ellen Louisa Tucker. Over much of 1828, he continued to preach wherever he was invited, but mostly in the vicinity of Boston or in Concord, New Hampshire, and he courted Ellen. After they were engaged on 17 December, Emerson began to think seriously of taking on a pastorate of his own.

Most of Emerson's biographers agree that the 1830s was a defining decade in his personal and professional life. But the decade actually opened for him in 1829, when he was ordained as the junior pastor of Boston's Second Church on 11 March, promoted to pastor of the Church on 1 July, and married Ellen on 30 September. Enjoying financial security and a degree of social prominence for the first time in his adult life, relishing the intellectual activity of composing weekly sermons in which he could draw out Unitarianism's humanistic qualities through reference to his extensive studies in biography, philosophy, and history, and delighting in a marriage in which he described himself as possessing "the luxury of an unmeasured affection for an object so deserving of it all & who requites all" (*JMN*, 3:149), Emerson comfortably settled into the dual role of pastor and husband. Drawing upon his readings in German Higher Criticism and the works of Samuel Taylor Coleridge and Victor Cousin, among others, in sermons before his congregation Emerson rehearsed many of the themes that would later characterize his teachings for the public in lectures and essays. Emphasizing self-culture and what he would later describe as "the infinitude of the private man," the moral authority of the individual intellect and conscience over the authority of religious or social institutions and even the Bible, and the liberation from its inherited past which the inventiveness and political freedom of the present offers the human race, Emerson's sermons from 1829 to 1832 anticipate the idealism of *Nature* (1836), "The American Scholar" (1837), and "The Divinity School Address" (1838).

In spite of their promise, however, the opening years of the 1830s delivered several successive blows to Emerson's personal life and professional ambition. Although he knew that Ellen had a tu-

bercular condition before their marriage, Emerson hoped that
rest and winter travel to warm climates would lessen the debilitating effects of her disease and, perhaps, provide an actual cure. But
Ellen's condition worsened immediately after their marriage; a recuperative journey to Philadelphia in the winter of 1830 and the efforts of several doctors, one of whom recommended a ten-year
relocation to Cuba or a comparable environment (*L*, 7:194), could
not stay the inevitable. Ellen died on 8 February 1831 at the age of
nineteen, leaving Emerson, as he explained to his Aunt Mary, balancing between relief that her suffering had finally ended and dejection at the prospect of life without her:

> My angel is gone to heaven this morning & I am alone in the
> world. . . . I have never known a person in the world in
> whose separate existence as a soul I could so readily & fully
> believe & she is present with me now . . . in her deliver-
> ance. . . . [But] I see plainly that things & duties will look
> coarse & vulgar enough to me when I find the romance of her
> presence . . . withdrawn from them all. (*L*, 1:318)

Two months before Ellen's death, Emerson's brother Edward,
who had been hospitalized for a physical and mental breakdown
in 1828, left Boston for Santa Cruz and, eventually, Puerto Rico,
having himself exhibited the symptoms of tuberculosis. Although he said little about his brother's departure, in the privacy
of his journals Emerson recorded Edward's death in 1834 with a
dark thought that echoed his dejection at Ellen's passing: "So falls
one pile more of hope for this life" (*JMN*, 4:325). Yet, devastating
as Ellen's death and Edward's illness must have been, perhaps the
most decisive blow to the stability of Emerson's life in the early
1830s occurred in 1832, when he found himself at odds with his
congregation over the meaning of the Lord's Supper, which he
considered an example of "worship in the dead forms of our
forefathers" (*JMN*, 4:27). After members of the Second Church
rejected his request that he be relieved of having to celebrate the
Lord's Supper with the bread and wine, Emerson resigned his
pastorate on 22 December, and on Christmas Day he set sail
from Boston for Europe aboard the brig *Jasper*.

Emerson's journey to Europe, which lasted from December 1832 to October 1833, was the first of three extended trips abroad, and it proved to be an ideal physical and psychological tonic. On this occasion he visited Malta, Sicily, Italy, Switzerland, France, England, and Scotland, and on virtually every page of the travel journals he kept during his journey, he described a new and unexpected delight (see *JMN*, 4:102–248). Like that of other Americans of this era such as Washington Irving and James Fenimore Cooper, who visited or lived in Europe, Emerson's provincialism was quickly worn away by the charm and historical significance he everywhere encountered in the European landscape. He roamed Palermo, Messina, Pompeii, and Naples as any tourist might, imagining the grand but silent histories that lay hidden behind their ancient walls and beneath their worn walks. Inspired by the architectural splendor of Italy's churches, the art of her great masters, and the simplicity of her many monastic orders, Emerson, whose resignation from his pulpit was a principled stand against ecclesiastic ritual, was unexpectedly attracted to, rather than repulsed by, the rituals of the season when he stayed in Rome during Easter week. In Florence, he visited the tombs of Machiavelli, Galileo, Dante, and Michel Angelo; attended a performance of Bellini's opera *La Straniera*, praising the prima donna as "a noble Greek beauty, full of dignity, & energy of action [and] . . . voice" (*JMN*, 4:171); and met with the English poet and essayist Walter Savage Landor.

Arriving in Paris in mid-June from Italy and a brief stay in Switzerland, Emerson was initially shocked by the character of the city. "I was sorry to find," he wrote, "that in leaving Italy I had left forever that air of antiquity & history which her towns possess & in coming hither had come to a loud modern New York of a place" (*JMN*, 4:197). His Yankee temperament was variously awed and tried by the opulence of the city's shops, the frivolity of the city's night life, and the high fashion sported by Parisian society. But Emerson's resistance to Parisian life passed quickly. Within a few days he was enjoying pleasant walks along the city's magnificent boulevards, visiting the Louvre and the Jardin des Plantes, and attending lectures on science at the Sorbonne and observing the seminars of Jean Baptiste Biot,

Dominique-François Arago, Antoine Laurent de Jussieu, and Louis Thénard, who were then France's leading men of science. On the Fourth of July, Emerson joined a large number of fellow Americans who had gathered to honor the Marquis de Lafayette, the hero of the American Revolution, at a dinner, and just before leaving Paris, he likely accompanied Jussieu on a botanical excursion in the countryside outside of the city.

Italy surprisingly but thoroughly captivated Emerson's imagination, and Paris eventually won him to her charms. In traveling to England and Scotland, however, Emerson carried with him a very definite set of expectations: He wanted to experience first-hand the roots and modern sites of Anglo-Saxon culture. Arriving in London on 21 July, he threw himself into an itinerary that included extended visits to Westminster Abbey, the House of Commons, the homes of the poet John Milton and the philosopher Jeremy Bentham, and the British Museum. He met with the economist John Stuart Mill, called on Coleridge in his home at Highgate, and saw the novelist Harriet Martineau. Leaving London on 9 August, he rode northward into Birmingham, Kenilworth, and Sheffield, stopping at Warwick Castle along the way, and he arrived at Edinburgh on 16 August. He toured Edinburgh with Alexander Ireland, who would become a lifelong friend and supporter and, eventually, one of Emerson's first biographers, and before leaving the city, he preached at the Unitarian Chapel. Between 21 and 26 August, he continued his travels northward into the Scottish Highlands, visiting Inversnaid, Dumbarton, Glasgow, and Dumfries before stopping at Craigenputtock, where he spent the night at the invitation of Thomas and Jane Carlyle. The lifelong friendship between Thomas Carlyle and Emerson which emerged from that first meeting sustained and, occasionally, irritated both men for the next forty years.

For Emerson, the virtue of meeting Carlyle in person on this occasion, and of mastering over time Carlyle's dense, volume-length excursions into English and Continental history, politics, and literary criticism, was that his newfound friend represented for him the voice and vision of Anglo-Saxon culture for which he had come to England and Scotland in the first place. Emerson's ride through the English Lake District and his long-awaited visit with William Wordsworth at Rydal Mount a few days after his stay with Carlyle seemed anticlimactic by comparison. Neither the landscape immortalized in English Romantic poetry nor the sage of Romanticism himself could fire Emerson's imagination or his desire to make something of his life in quite the same way that he had felt himself inspired during his overnight conversation with Carlyle. In effect, Carlyle had invited Emerson back into the world of the living; his counsel to the young American was, in so many words, "Seize and channel the power that resides within you." There is no small irony in the fact that after leaving Wordsworth and traveling to Manchester, Emerson made his final journey in England on a railroad. This was probably his first ride on a train, and the material power of the engine that carried him to Liverpool complemented the raw power represented by the names of railroad engines he saw in Liverpool's rail yards: the *Rocket*, the *Goliath*, and the *Pluto*. These served then as oblique, but nonetheless sure, emblems of the life that Emerson would make for himself back in America. On 4 September he boarded the brig *New York* for his return home, pausing the next day while sailing away from the coast of Ireland to make the following entry in the last of his travel journals: "I like my book about nature & wish I knew where & how I ought to live. God will show me" (*JMN*, 4:237).

"The call of our calling is the loudest call," Emerson wrote in December 1833, two months after his return to Boston from Europe (*JMN*, 4:252). He had, indeed, returned home a new man. Having left the traditional "call" of the pulpit, Emerson never looked back, although between 1833 and 1836 he occasionally served as a supply preacher for congregations in and around Boston. But his entire focus now was on determining his true calling—on deciding "how I ought to live"—and Europe had certainly widened his perspective on the possibilities available to him. In addition to the friendships he made with Ireland and Carlyle and the intellectual correspondences in which he could now engage with them, he became excited at the prospect of participating in the lyceum movement then sweeping America. He saw that the lecture hall could serve him as an easy site of transition away from the pulpit and, while providing him with a steady source of income, also afford him a congenial forum in which to test his evolving thoughts on philosophy, literary history, nature, and the human condition. Less than a month after returning from Europe, he delivered the lecture "The Uses of Natural History" before the Natural History Society in Boston; during 1834, he presented "The Relation of Man to the Globe," "Italy," and "The Naturalist," among other lectures, in Boston, New Bedford, and Concord, Massachusetts. By 1835, increasingly confident of his ability as a lecturer and self-assured in the timeliness and rightness of his ideas, he delivered two large lecture series in Boston. The first of these consisted of six lectures on biography and featured studies of Michel Angelo, Martin Luther, Milton, George Fox, and Edmund Burke. Emerson's second series, for which he received two hundred dollars, was sponsored by the Society for the Diffusion of Useful Knowledge. Devoted to English literature, this series consisted of eight lectures distributed among topics such as "Permanent Traits of the English National Character," "The Age of Fable," and readings on Chaucer, Shakespeare, Lord Bacon, and a number of other English poets and writers.

Although Emerson limited himself to local engagements between 1833 and 1835 and for several lectures drew topics from a relatively safe body of materials that included his experiences in Europe or subjects derived from his readings in and journal notes on biographical figures who he had formerly treated in his sermons, there can be no doubt that his early successes as a lecturer encouraged his conviction that the lyceum provided one important answer to his question about how he should live. Between the mid-1830s and the effective close of his career in the 1870s, Emerson delivered roughly fifteen hundred public lectures. More than any other activity in which he engaged, lecturing facilitated the growth of his reputation as an intellectual presence throughout America. Over the years he developed popular and profitable lecture series on philosophy, New England and American life, literary history, natural history, and cultural history, became a fixture at many college commencement exercises, and wrote a host of individual lectures on topics as diverse as temperance, personal ethics, women's rights, abolitionism, and what he variously called "the spirit of the times." With geographic expansiveness that corresponded to the expansion of his talents and reputation, he gradually traveled from New England's lyceums to lecture in New York, in the Middle Atlantic states and Washington, D.C., in newly established midwestern states, and in England; late in life, he traveled overland to lecture in California.

Emerson's renewed self-confidence in his professional life supported by his early successes as a lecturer was mirrored in a number of significant developments in his private and personal life. "I know," he wrote retrospectively in the essay "Experience" (1844), "that the world I converse with in the city . . . is not the world I *think*" (*CW*, 3:48). Although he had been a dutiful keeper of journals and notebooks since his college days, on his return from Europe Emerson began to regard his journals as a "savings bank" in which he had to make regular deposits of insights into "the world I *think*." Much like his letters and conversations with close friends, his brothers, and Aunt Mary, Emerson considered his journals and notebooks an extension of his private life. There—perhaps only there—he could be completely himself. In them, he recorded everything from his dreams and waking thoughts, to texts copied from his voluminous readings, to passages he translated from his favorite classical and modern writers, to snippets of correspondence he received from select friends, to modest prose drafts that were either original with him or syntheses—"assimilations," to use his term—drawn from one or more of the foregoing sources. Emerson quickly realized the value of his journals to his composition process; encouraged by their service to the lectures he gave between 1833 and 1835, he devoted increasingly large portions of each day to writing in them and devising elaborate indices to the thoughts they contained on a great variety of subjects.

Published during the last four decades of this century in nineteen substantial volumes, Emerson's *Journals and Miscellaneous Notebooks* (*JMN*) and *Topical Notebooks* (*TN*) are an extraordinary repository of the world he thought. They are private documents inasmuch as they collectively report his deepest engagements with his mind, imagination, and conscience. Beginning with the travel journals he kept in Europe in 1833, however, they also took on a public dimension as the first and most crucial stage of his composition process; for the remainder of his life, he would draw his lectures out of them, and with his lectures serving as a middle stage of composition, eventually the major essays on which his reputation rests today.

Several developments brought renewal to Emerson's personal life in 1834 and 1835. In May 1834, after settling a legal dispute with her family, Emerson received the first of two inheritances from Ellen Emerson's estate. The $11,600 he received at this time (he would receive another payment of $11,675 in July 1837) enabled him to pay off his debts, see to the security of his mother, who depended on him and his brother William for financial support, and leave Boston for Concord, the Emerson family's ancestral home. A few months earlier—probably in March—he had met Lydia Jackson of Plymouth, Massachusetts, and following a ten-month courtship, he proposed to her in January 1835. Whereas from first to last Emerson tended to idealize both the real life and his memory of Ellen, Lydia, whom he eventually renamed "Lidian" and sometimes called "Asia" in his journals and letters, was not a person he could so easily adapt into the mold of his ideal woman. He admired her for her spirituality and intellect, but even before their marriage he recognized that their life together would be one based on mutual respect for each other's intellectual and spiritual independence, not on the romantic love that characterized his marriage to Ellen. They were married in September 1835 and settled into a large home that Emerson had purchased and renovated in Concord. There, they raised four children: Waldo was born in 1836 but died from scarletina in 1842; Ellen Tucker, a daughter Emerson named for his first wife, was born in 1839 and cared for her parents during their later years; Edith was born in 1841 and, like her sister, occasionally served as her father's editorial assistant before and during the early years of her marriage to William Hathaway Forbes; and Edward Waldo was born in 1844 and eventually became a physician, married Annie Keyes of Concord, and performed a lasting service to his father's reputation by editing the Centenary Edition of his *Works* (W).

Emerson's journals and letters of 1835 reveal his sense that he had not completely answered the question of how he ought to live; nevertheless, established by the end of the year in Concord with his new wife, he could believe himself fairly well restored to sound professional and personal ground. He occupied himself with long stints of writing in his journals, where he drafted prose for potential use in new lectures. He took occasional day trips to Cambridge and Boston for new reading materials, and at home he left the solitude of his study for extended walks in Concord's woods or along her riverbanks. What nagged at him most in his moments of privacy in 1835 (as for some years afterward) was a belief that he had yet to bring to fruition one last dimension of his life in order to satisfy the loud call of his calling: He had to become an original author.

By 1835, Emerson had long been living through words: words written in his journals, words spoken from his pulpit and lectern, and words that, as he once confessed to Carlyle, cluttered and confused his private thoughts, dreams, daytime reveries, and conversation. "[M]y journals," he wrote to Carlyle on 30 June 1840, "which I dot here at home day by day, are full of disjointed dreams, audacities, unsystematic irresponsible lampoons of systems, and all manner of rambling reveries, the poor drupes and berries I find in my basket after endless and aimless rambles in woods and pastures. I ask constantly . . . whether life may not be poetic as well as stupid" (*CEC*, p. 272). The challenge before him in 1835 was to bring order to the formlessness of the words he had been gathering; they required a unifying theme, a unifying vision, to hold them together before they could achieve a degree of finality in print. As the year opened, he shared this thought with his brother William: "I think when I have done with my lectures which begin shortly I shall write & print a discourse upon Spiritual & Traditional Religion, for Form seems to be bowing Substance out of the World & men doubt if there can be any such thing as a spiritual nature out of the carcass in which once it dwelt" (7 January 1835; *L*, 1:430–31). By 20 June, however, he had discarded his idea of a discourse on *traditional* religion and was moving instead toward an announcement of the new, *spiritual* religion of the age, or, as he refers to it here, "the First Philosophy":

I endeavor to announce the laws of the First Philosophy. . . .
[T]heir enunciation awakens the feeling of the moral sublime,
& great men are they who believe in them. Every one of these
propositions resembles a great circle in astronomy. No matter
in what direction it be drawn it contains the whole sphere. So
each of these seems to imply all truth. Compare a page of
[Francis] Bacon with [Jonathan] Swift [or Lord] Chesterfield
. . . & see the difference of great & less circles. These are
gleams of a world in which we do not live: they astonish the
understanding. . . .
     There is every degree of remoteness from the line of
things in the line of words. By & by comes a word true &
closely embracing the thing. That is not Latin nor English nor
any language, but *thought*. The aim of the author is not to tell
truth—that he cannot do, but to suggest it. He has only ap-
proximated it himself, & hence his cumbrous embarrassed
speech: he uses many words, hoping that one, if not another,
will bring you as near to the fact as he is. (*JMN*, 5:50–51)

Language itself, as Emerson remarked at the conclusion of
the journal sequence just quoted, is "young & unformed" (*JMN*,
5:51). The unifying vision he required for his spiritual discourse
that would restore substance to the world and lives of ordinary
men would have to be constructed with words, but mortared
with thought. Only thought, not words, was eternal; only
thought could serve as the organizing first law of "the First Philosophy": all in the universe is related.
     During a visit on 13 July 1833 to the Jardin des Plantes in Paris,
Emerson spent the day wandering through the rooms of the
Cabinet of Natural History. His account of the thoughts that occurred to him as he studied case after case of specimens pre-
served in the museum makes clear that this was the day when the
unifying vision he required for his spiritual discourse—his "book
about nature," as he had described it when he sailed away from
England—was born. Here he witnessed for the first time in his
life the relational nature of all things in the universe. Nature was
suddenly and unexpectedly large and seemed to him thoroughly
organic; observer and observed became one as objects came to

life as extensions of the mind that beheld them and symbols of
the imagination that interpreted them:

> How much finer things are in composition than alone. 'Tis
> wise in man to make Cabinets. When I was come into the Or-
> nithological Chambers, I wished I had come only there. The
> fancy-coloured vests of these elegant beings made me as pen-
> sive as the hues & forms of a cabinet of shells, formerly. It is a
> beautiful collection & makes the visiter as calm & genial as a
> bridegroom. The limits of the possible are enlarged, & the
> real is stranger than the imaginary. . . .
>   I saw black swans & white peacocks, the ibis the sacred &
> the rosy; the flamingo, with a neck like a snake, the Toucan
> rightly called *rhinoceros*; & a vulture whom to meet in the
> wilderness would make your flesh quiver[,] so like an execu-
> tioner he looked.
>   In other rooms I saw amber containing perfect musqui-
> toes, grand blocks of quartz, native gold in all its forms of
> crystallization, threads, plates, crystals, dust; & silver black as
> from fire. Ah said I this is philanthropy, wisdom, taste—to
> form a Cabinet of natural history. . . . Here we are im-
> pressed with the inexhaustible riches of nature. The Universe
> is a more amazing puzzle than ever as you glance along this
> bewildering series of animated forms,—the hazy butterflies,
> the carved shells, the birds, beasts, fishes, insects, snakes,—&
> the upheaving principle of life everywhere incipient in the
> very rock aping organized forms. Not a form so grotesque, so
> savage, nor so beautiful but is an expression of some property
> inherent in man the observer,—an occult relation between the
> very scorpions and man. I feel the centipede in me—cayman,
> carp, eagle, & fox. I am moved by strange sympathies[;] I say
> continually, "I will be a naturalist." (*JMN*, 4:198–200)

"I will be a naturalist." Among the meanings attached to the
profession of naturalist in the nineteenth century was this: a naturalist was a person who, among other things, believed that spiritual truth derived from nature, not from miraculous or supernatural revelations, and that everything from the order of the
universe to the evolution of personal and cultural ethics could be

discovered through the close study of nature broadly construed. This brand of naturalism relied entirely on the intuitive capacity of the observer of nature, and the observer's ability to move from the factual to the metaphoric or relational meaning of objects, events, persons, ideas, and even words as he encountered them in nature. Intuition enabled the observer to see through the remoteness or ambiguity of words and things to the unifying source of all in the universe: thought. In stating that he would be a naturalist, Emerson meant that he would be a naturalist of this variety; he thereby staked a claim for himself as a cultural priest and visionary who would enlarge his recognition in the Jardin des Plantes of the relatedness of all objects in the universe into the organizing principle of his First Philosophy. He would put his personal "Cabinet of Natural History" on display not only through his lectures but also in the grand, penetrating sweep of the volumes he would publish. There he would write, as he renamed his First Philosophy in 1853, a "New Metaphysics" (TN, 1:134), and his New Metaphysics would be an analogic, not an analytic or theologically revealed, system of philosophy replete with its own internally consistent poetics, ethics, and history. His New Metaphysics would be a spiritual as well as a material biography of the human race, and he was confident that, as this biography gradually unfolded, he would remove all limits of the possible for mankind, liberate the spiritual content of human experience from the ritualized confinement of institutional religion and politics, and awaken in his fellows a feeling of the moral sublime. This, finally, was the call that Emerson heard loudest of all.

The year 1836 was one of tragedy, triumph, and renewal in Emerson's life. In May his brother Charles suddenly died from the disease that had earlier claimed both Ellen and his brother Edward. Emerson revealed his devastation at his loss of Charles, whom he variously described as his intellectual equal, muse, and truest companion, when he wrote to Carlyle, "[W]e made but one man together" (17 September 1836; CEC, p. 148). Between moments of despair over Charles's death, he continued to work steadily on the manifesto in which he would announce his First Philosophy to the world. *Nature*, which was published on 9 September, is Emerson's sweeping declaration of the divinity of human life and the universality of thought. Having assimilated much from his readings in Platonic and Neoplatonic thought, in Eastern philosophy and religion, and in natural history, Emerson proclaimed nature the resource through which individuals could restore "original and eternal beauty" to their world and achieve the redemption of their souls (*CW*, 1:43). In its appeal to intuition and the senses, its conviction that language, like any other material fact, is symbolic of a higher spiritual reality that governs the universe, and its song of the "Orphic poet," which reminds modern man that he is "the dwarf of himself," that is, the dwarf of a figure who before time began "was permeated and dissolved by spirit" and "filled nature with his overflowing currents" (*CW*, 1:42), *Nature* impressed many early readers as a highly progressive and idealistic text.

Emerson's extravagant and impressionistic style in *Nature* was consistent with his message. His opening description of himself as a "transparent eye-ball" in whom all egotism has vanished and the currents of "Universal Being" circulate was an apt characterization of the transformation he hoped to effect in human culture (*CW*, 1:10). Emerson's own personal transformation from the shell of the man he was when he left Boston for Europe in 1832 was completed with the birth of his son Waldo on 30 October 1836. Professionally, Emerson had hit his stride with the publication of *Nature*, and in the months just prior to its appearance, he joined a number of like-minded thinkers and writers to form a "symposium" in which they could discuss their radical ideas on philosophy and theology. In the Transcendental Club, which formally convened on 19 September, Emerson found his ideas reinforced by the beliefs and encouragement of others. Between its formation in 1836 and its dissolution in 1840, the Transcendental Club included Bronson Alcott, James Freeman Clarke, Convers Francis, Margaret Fuller, Frederic Henry Hedge, Theodore Parker, Elizabeth Palmer Peabody, and Henry David Thoreau among its members. The club's most lasting effects on Transcendentalism in America were that it lent cohesiveness, if not complete consistency in practice, to the movement's main principle that God was immanent in all aspects of the Creation, and it instigated the founding of the *Dial* as the movement's unofficial journal in 1840.

Fuller edited the *Dial* between 1840 and March 1842; Emerson assumed the editorship from her, but the journal, which was a convenient target for critics of Transcendentalism, failed for lack of subscribers in 1844.

In 1837, Emerson expanded on the themes of *Nature* in "The American Scholar," an address he delivered before Harvard's Phi Beta Kappa Society during commencement celebrations. In the address, he challenged America's future writers and professors to break with their dependence upon imitation of classical and European models in their own art and thought. Imitation, Emerson argued, made men and their intellects passive; he wanted, instead, active scholars, men of original thought who aspired to be something more than the mere "parrots" of other men's words and ideas. In 1838, Emerson reinvoked *Man Thinking*, the forceful image he introduced in "The American Scholar," to stir the imaginations of the young ministers who were then graduating from the Harvard Divinity School. In religion as in art, he said, imitation cannot move beyond its models, so the imitator dooms himself to hopeless mediocrity (*CW*, 1:90). Observing that the formalism of traditional Christian practices was a sign of "a decaying church and a wasting unbelief" that left worshipers thoughtless, defrauded, and disconsolate, he urged his audience to become "newborn bard[s] of the Holy Ghost[,] . . . acquaint men at first hand with Deity[, and] . . . rekindle the smouldering, nigh quenched fire on the altar" (*CW*, 1:88, 90, 92).

Among members of Emerson's expanding Transcendentalist circle, *Nature*, "The American Scholar," and "The Divinity School Address" were intellectually liberating performances; among members of the literary, educational, and religious establishment, however, the first two pieces represented the gibberish of a pantheistic romantic who had lost control of his ability to think and write clearly, while "The Divinity School Address" was simply the collected ravings of a heretic. In "The Divinity School Address," Emerson had indeed tested and crossed the line that the establishment traditionally drew between belief and unbelief, and he did so in the very seat of establishment power: Harvard. Yet by 1838 his position should have come as a surprise to no one. His attack on the forms of religion was an old complaint; when he said, "Miracles, prophecy, poetry, the ideal life, the holy life, exists as ancient history merely; they are not in the [true] belief, nor in the aspiration of society; but . . . seem ridiculous" (*CW*, 1:80), he was expounding on the teachings of German Higher Criticism about which he had preached earlier in the decade and enlarging on the issue of conscience that had occasioned his resignation from the pulpit in 1832. His stirring challenge to the young ministers that they "dare to love God without mediator or veil" followed directly from his appeals to individualism and *Man Thinking*, in *Nature* and "The American Scholar"; similarly, the counsel he offered them in the address drew upon his evolving doctrine of self-reliance, a doctrine he himself had followed for much of the 1830s as he worked out the details of his true calling: "Obey thyself. That which shows God in me, fortifies me. That which shows God out of me, makes me a wart and a wen" (*CW*, 1:82–83, 90).

Emerson appears to have been unfazed by the harangue to which he and his ideas were subjected by the establishment during the late 1830s and early 1840s. He knew that he had crossed a line, but it was one he believed he had to cross in order to awaken his contemporaries from their intellectual and imaginative stupor. "I have taught one doctrine, namely, the infinitude of the private man," he wrote at the opening of the 1840s, which "the people accept readily enough, & even with loud commendation, as long as I call the lecture, Art; or Politics; or Literature; or the Household; but the moment I call it Religion,—they are shocked, though it be only the application of the same truth which they receive everywhere else, to a new class of facts" (*JMN*, 7:342). Thus, he continued to write in his journals and create new lectures out of them. Between 1839 and 1841, he organized some of his lectures into essays for publication in a single volume. For all practical purposes, it would seem that writing, lecturing, and his first years of fatherhood kept his mind centered on his domestic life and his calling as controversy swirled around him.

The appearance of Emerson's *Essays*, published in America and England in 1841, enhanced his reputation at home and abroad. The volume contained twelve essays: "History," "Self-

Reliance," "Compensation," "Spiritual Laws," "Love," "Friendship," "Prudence," "Heroism," "The Over-Soul," "Circles," "Intellect," and "Art." Collectively, these essays demonstrated the
wide application to which various aspects of Emerson's idealistic
philosophy could be put. In "History," for instance, Emerson
drew his readers' attention to their share in the universality of
nature and the human condition through thought. As he himself
had realized at the Jardin des Plantes in 1833, everything in the
universe stands in a fundamental relation to everything else; all
is, as he then discovered, unified by thought or, as he wrote in
"History," mind:

> There is one mind common to all individual men. Every man
> is an inlet to the same and to all of the same. . . . What
> Plato thought, he may think; what a saint has felt, he may feel;
> what at any time has befallen any man, he can understand.
> Of the works of this mind history is the record. Its genius
> is illustrated by the entire series of days. Man is explicable by
> nothing less than all his history. (CW, 2:3)

And with man explicable by nothing less than all his history,
Emerson reduced history itself to an empty discipline which he
supplanted with biography:

> We are always coming up with the emphatic facts of history
> in our private experience, and verifying them here. All history
> becomes subjective; in other words, there is properly no His-
> tory, only Biography. Every mind must know the whole lesson
> for itself—must go over the whole ground. What it does not
> see, what it does not live, it will not know. (CW, 2:6)

The "infinitude of the private man," nature's organicism, and
the importance of the individual's realization that he is part of a
universe strung together by multiple relational threads are recur-
rent themes throughout *Essays*. In "Self-Reliance," which ranks
with *Nature* as one of his best-known works, Emerson merged
the Socratic ideal of "Know thyself" with the Stoic ideal he had
counseled the Divinity School graduates to emulate, "Obey thy-

self." Against these ideals, both of which represent rejections of imitation, the doctrine of self-reliance became an ethical construction that Emerson applied to realize the political impulses of democracy:

> Our reading is . . . sycophantic. In history, our imagination plays us false. Kingdom and lordship, power and estate are a gaudier vocabulary than private John and Edward in a small house and common day's work: but the things of life are the same to both: the sum total of both is the same. Why all this deference to Alfred . . . and Gustavus? Suppose they were virtuous: did they wear out virtue? As great a stake depends on your private act to-day, as followed their public and renowned steps. When private men shall act with original views, the lustre will be transferred from the actions of kings. (*CW*, 2:36)

Whereas in "Self-Reliance" he stressed the centrality of individual will and power to the personal and cultural ascendancy of the "private man," in "The Over-Soul" Emerson demonstrated that individual will and power must themselves yield to a force in nature that he variously described as "higher" and "greater" than they. That force is thought or, as he also called it in *Nature*, spirit. It is analogous to the one mind common to all individual men in "History," and it facilitates the transformative moment in *Nature* when the speaker becomes a "transparent eye-ball," although in "The Over-Soul" Emerson obliquely represented it as a "stream whose source is hidden," pouring moment by moment "being" into man. "Our being is descending into us from we know not whence," he wrote; but even as his being descends from an origin higher than he, "within man is the soul of the whole; the wise silence; the universal beauty, to which every part and particle is equally related; the eternal One" (*CW*, 2:159–60).

Three years after the appearance of *Essays*, Emerson published *Essays: Second Series* (1844). The volume contained nine works: "The Poet," "Experience," "Character," "Manners," "Gifts," "Nature," "Politics," "Nominalist and Realist," and "New England Reformers." Readers have sometimes critiqued this volume as the point in Emerson's life and thought where his idealism yields to realism and fatalism. An important fact about Emerson's life which lends credibility to this view is that as he wrote and compiled the essays for the volume he was immersed in an extended period of mourning over the death of his son and namesake Waldo in January 1842.

Emerson's journals and letters of the period from 1842 to 1844 show that he was beyond consolation at the loss of this son whose birth had signaled the reconstitution of the father's own intellectual and personal manhood. For months after Waldo's death, Emerson measured everything in his universe through the impression left on it by the boy's life and death. Nature, his own idealistic thought, and his relationships with friends and family, which formerly had been invigorated and unified by Waldo's presence, now struck Emerson as cold, empty, and foreboding his own doom. As the man of words tried to cope with his loss on paper, his sentences, many of them fragments, became emblems of his suddenly shattered existence:

> Yesterday night . . . my little Waldo ended his life. . . . What he looked upon is better, what he looked not upon is insignificant. The morning of Friday I woke . . . & every cock in every barnyard was shrilling with the most unnecessary noise. The sun went up the morning sky with all his light, but the landscape was dishonored by this loss. For this boy in whose remembrance I have both slept & awaked so oft, decorated for me the morning star, & the evening cloud, [and] . . . how much more with his lively curiosity every trivial fact & circumstance in the household. . . . For every thing he had his own name & way of thinking[,] his own pronunciation & manner. And every word came mended from that tongue. A boy of early wisdom, of a grave & even majestic deportment, of a perfect gentleness[.] . . . Every tramper that ever tramped is abroad but the little feet are still[.] . . . Sorrow makes us all children again[,] destroys all differences of intellect[.] The wisest know nothing[.] (*JMN*, 8:163–65)

Waldo's death, and Emerson's seeming inability to reconcile himself to his loss on any of the terms associated with his own idealism, unquestionably exerted a negative impact on his philosophy. The limitations of Emerson's Transcendentalist views on history, biography, and the "over-soul" are exposed throughout the essay "Experience," where in a world without Waldo, the doctrine of self-reliance, for example, is checked by "Illusion, Temperament, Succession, Surface, Surprise, Reality, [and] Subjectiveness." "[T]hese," Emerson now wrote, "are the threads on the loom of time, these are the lords of life" (*CW*, 3:47). Similarly, in "Gifts," Emerson treated optimism and brotherly love with sentiments bordering on contempt. Yet as a whole, *Essays: Second Series* does not justify the negative reading it has sometimes been given. In "The Poet," for example, Emerson moved his philosophy a significant step forward, identifying the poet as the "sayer," the "namer," the representative of beauty, who stands among "partial men for the complete man, and apprises us not of his wealth, but of the commonwealth" (*CW*, 3:4–5). The poet is the priest and visionary who, recognizing that the "[u]niverse is the externization of the soul," introduces his fellows to "the secret[s] of the world, . . . where Being passes into Appearance, and Unity into Variety" (*CW*, 3:9). There have always been great poets—Chaucer, Dante, Spenser, Shakespeare—but consistent with his views on the past in *Nature* and "History," in "The Poet" Emerson argued that since "the experience of each new age requires a new confession," his age required its own poet, who, by writing "his autobiography in colossal cipher, or into universality," would "draw [for] us with love and terror . . . the flowing vest [and] . . . firm nature," "chaunt our own times and social circumstance," celebrate "[our] bravery," and declare "[our] new religion" (*CW*, 3:7, 21).

As he did in "The Poet," in "Nominalist and Realist," another of the essays printed in *Essays: Second Series*, Emerson reaffirmed his idealism in the face of both personal adversity and the challenge to humanity which he found represented at this time by slavery. Although he had experienced great personal losses before which left him feeling dejected and fragmented, the feelings were momentary, not permanent, in the larger scheme of his life. In an autobiographical aside on the comfort he had always taken in reading and writing, he announced himself restored to the ideal:

"I am faithful again to the whole over the members" (*CW*, 3:137). Emphasizing the fluidity of nature and experience, in "Nominalist and Realist" he argued, "Nothing is dead": "It is the secret of the world that all things subsist, and do not die, but only retire a little from sight, and afterwards return again." "There is somewhat spheral and infinite in every man," he concluded; "every man is a channel through which heaven floweth. . . . Nature keeps herself whole, and her representation complete in the experience of each mind" (*CW*, 3:142–43).

Although Waldo's death and the appearance of *Essays* and *Essays: Second Series* were momentous events for Emerson during the 1840s, they do not entirely define either his personal or his profession life at this time. The good health and growth of his children Ellen, Edith, and Edward restored calm to his domestic life, while his extensive lecturing on the lyceum circuit further enhanced his visibility in America, enlarged his supply of new materials for eventual publication, and provided him with a substantial income. Reluctant to take up reformist causes during the 1830s, in the 1840s Emerson became an antislavery activist and announced his views in a forceful address, "Emancipation of the Negroes in the British West Indies," delivered at the Concord Court House on 1 August 1844. Having thrown himself into the political arena with this address, he became an influential spokesperson for abolitionism for the remainder of the 1840s and throughout the 1850s as he adapted his moral conviction of "the infinitude of the private man" into denunciations of the inhumanity of slavery and spoke repeatedly against the infamous Fugitive Slave Law after its passage in 1850.

At the end of the 1840s, Emerson made his second trip abroad. With Thomas Carlyle and Alexander Ireland making most of the arrangements, he undertook an extended lecture tour of Scotland and England, delivering sixty-four lectures between 2 November 1847 and 24 February 1848 in twenty-five cities and towns, and a series of six lectures entitled "Mind and Manners of the Nineteenth Century" between 6 and 17 June 1848 at the Literary and Scientific Institution in London. During his tour he visited extensively with Carlyle and met with many prominent scientists and naturalists, including Robert Chambers, Charles Lyell, and

Richard Owen, and with literary figures such as Wordsworth, Thomas De Quincey, Harriet Martineau, Thomas Macaulay, and William Makepeace Thackeray. He attended performances of Shakespeare's *King Lear* and Rossini's opera *La Cenerentola*, and he dined with Frederic Chopin. By all accounts, when he was abroad this time, Emerson cut a thoroughly cosmopolitan figure, and while his first journey to Europe had restored him personally and shown him the way to his true professional calling, he returned home from this trip an established international figure with an increasingly wide following.

One important result of this tour was that Emerson, ever the penetrating observer, came home with several journals full of insight into English history, manners, and character (see *JMN*, 10). He transformed the observations entrusted to these journals into "England," one of the most popular lectures of his entire career, a few lecture series devoted entirely to English culture, and *English Traits*, which, since its publication in 1856, has stood as the fullest expression of Emerson's thought on Anglo-Saxon culture. Another important result of the tour was that several of the lectures he delivered in the "Mind and Manners of the Nineteenth Century" series in London became the basis for his construction of a "Natural History of the Intellect." A law crucial to his First Philosophy or "New Metaphysics," in a lecture series entitled "Natural History of the Intellect," which he delivered on his return to America, Emerson established the authority of the intellect in a formal accounting of the mind which he developed through a scientific classification of its properties. Predictably, the properties that most intrigued him were genius, talent, memory, "self-possession," and the moral or ethical dimensions of the mind. Between the 1850s and the 1870s, he continued to work on this subject, elaborating on it in three substantial lecture series: "Natural Method of Mental Philosophy" (1858), "Philosophy for the People" (1866), and "Natural History of the Intellect" (1870, 1871).

A dimension of Emerson's development during the 1840s and 1850s which he considered as crucial to his personal and professional well-being as the love of his family and his increased stature in America and abroad was his participation in an ever-widening circle of intellectual friends and acquaintances. Early in his life, Emerson had relied almost entirely on his brother Charles, his Aunt Mary, and Ellen to serve as sounding boards for his ideas and ambitions. When they were not available, in his journals he turned to luminaries from the past—Plato, Proclus, Shakespeare, Montaigne, or Ben Jonson—for confirmation of ideas or feelings. However, with his growing correspondence with Carlyle and the formation of the Transcendental Club, Emerson began to rely heavily on the conversation, companionship, and intellectual rigor of intimates who over the years included not only Carlyle but also Alcott, the poets Ellery Channing and Jones Very, Fuller, Caroline Sturgis Tappan, Thoreau, and many others. Luminaries from the past could only partially fill his needs; as he explained in "Uses of Great Men," Emerson recognized that his own "infinitude" as a private man had to be nurtured, tested, and informed by flesh-and-blood relations:

> [I]t is hard for departed men to touch the quick like our own companions, whose names may not last as long. What is he whom I never think of? whilst in every solitude are those who succour our genius, and stimulate us in wonderful manners. There is a power in love to divine another's destiny better than that other can, and by heroic encouragements hold him to his task. What has friendship so signal as its sublime attraction to whatever virtue is in us? We will never think more cheaply of ourselves or of life. We are piqued to some purpose. (*CW*, 4:9)

Given the canonical stature that Emerson enjoys today, it would be natural for some to think of Alcott, Channing, Fuller, Tappan, or Thoreau as his disciples. However, there is no evidence that he ever thought of them in this way; instead, these were persons against whose ideas and feelings he measured the depth of his own and established his humanity. In fact, in his journals he explicitly rejected friendship as a disciple-making enterprise when he wrote: "The new individual must work out the whole problem of science, letters, & theology for himself. . . . The private soul ascends to transcendental virtue . . . but this liberty is not transferable to any disciple . . . nor to the man himself when he falls out of his trance & comes down from the tripod" (*JMN*, 7:202, 216). The value, then, that Emerson found in meeting and walking or talking with his friends confirmed one of his general rules about friendship and conversation: When they are best, they provide one with "a series of intoxications" that yield inspiration ("Inspiration," *W*, 8:292). As journal entries such as these about Alcott suggest, in the presence of his friends Emerson found his faith in the ideal justified, and he felt himself personally and intellectually enlarged:

> I think [Alcott] has more faith in the Ideal than any man I have known. Hence his welcome influence. A wise woman said to me that he has few thoughts, too few. . . . Well, Books, conversation, discipline will give him more. But what were many thoughts if he had not this distinguishing Faith, which is palpable confirmation out of the deeps of nature that God yet is? With many thoughts, & without this, he would be only one more of a countless throng of lettered men; but now you cannot spare the fortification that he is. . . .
>
> Alcott is a certain fluid in which men of . . . spirit can easily expand themselves & swim at large, they who elsewhere found themselves confined. He gives them nothing but themselves. . . . Me he has served . . . in that way; he was the reasonable creature to speak to, that I wanted." (*JMN*, 7:34, 11:19)

Just as he could rely on Alcott's "faith in the Ideal" to nourish and restore his own when necessary, so too Emerson could turn to Channing and Thoreau, the artist and the naturalist, for expansions of his own view of nature each time they served as his personal guides on walks through Concord's fields and woods or along its riverbanks. Without directly naming them, in "Country Life," a lecture first delivered in Boston in 1858, Emerson revealed his reliance upon the eyes and knowledge of these "professors" of nature:

> There are two companions, with one or other of whom 'tis desireable to go out on a tramp. One is an artist, or one who has an eye for beauty. 'Tis sometimes good to carry a tele-

scope in your pocket, specially for birds. And as you take a telescope, that you may see what your eyes cannot reach, so, if you use a good and skilful companion, you shall see through his eyes, and, if they be of great discernment, you will learn wonderful secrets. In walking with [him], you shall see what was never before shown to the eye of man. And as the perception of beauty always exhilarates, if one is so happy as to find the company of a true artist, he is a perpetual holiday, and ought only to be used, like an oroflamme or a garland, for feasts and may-days, and parliaments of wit and love. The other is a naturalist, for the reason that it is much better to learn the elements of geology, of botany, of ornithology, and astronomy, by word of mouth from a companion, than drily by book. There is so much, too, which a book cannot teach, which an old friend can.[4]

Because he stood to learn so much from his friends, Emerson was willing to expose his most hidden thoughts and feelings in conversations and correspondence with them. As remarked already, one of the most sustained relationships that Emerson enjoyed was with Carlyle. Their correspondence from 1834 to 1872 served Emerson as a testing ground for his ideas and as a site where, as in the case of his remark to Carlyle after Charles Emerson's death, he could openly express his feelings or, at other times, confess the inadequacies he feared his lectures and writings betrayed about his ability.[5] With Caroline Sturgis Tappan, he could express his most profound doubts about the efficacy of freedom against his perception of fate without fearing censure or rebuke. In a remarkable letter written on 22 July 1853, he described to her the nightmare world he thought he lived in when the "heavy cobweb" of "fate" that hung about seemed to close in on him: "Friends are few, thoughts are few, facts few—only one: only one fact, now tragically, now tenderly, now exultingly illustrated in sky, in earth, in men & women, Fate, Fate" (L, 8:374–75). Able to write out his feelings so freely to Tappan, Emerson could feel emancipated from his fears and restored to the ideal. He felt the same way about the effect his relationship with Fuller had on him. Once he called her "my audience" (JMN, 11:258), but the nature of their friendship was sufficiently interactive that she served variously as Emerson's alter ego, confessor, and conduit to the ideas and feelings of others as well. In *Memoirs of Margaret Fuller Ossoli* (1852), on which he collaborated with William Henry Channing and James Freeman Clarke after her death, Emerson remembered Fuller's roles and the satisfaction and enlargement he drew from them. In conversation and correspondence with her, he wrote, "[her] companion was made a thinker, and went away quite other than he came. The circle of friends who sat with her were not allowed to remain spectators or players, but she converted them into heroes."[6]

As the nineteenth century reached its midpoint, Emerson remarked in his journal:

> Culture, the height of culture, highest behavior consist in the identification of the Ego with the universe, so that when a man says, I think, I hope, I found,—he might properly say, the human race thinks, hopes, & finds,—he states a fact which commands the understandings & affections of all the company, and yet, at the same time, he shall be able continually to keep sight of his biographical *ego*. (1850; *JMN*, 11:203)

The necessity of the dual maneuvers represented in this passage of discovering and keeping true to one's own identity while also accepting that one's identity must always be constructed in relation to persons, events, and things outside of oneself in nature is an important lesson that Emerson found reinforced by the company of his friends. As a lesson, it brought forward into the 1850s the ideal laws of the First Philosophy Emerson had announced in *Nature*, and it effectively summarized one of the controlling themes of *Representative Men*, which he published in 1850, and *The Conduct of Life*, which appeared in 1860. As he had with *English Traits*, Emerson created both of these volumes out of lecture series. *Representative Men* has its origin in a popular series of the same title which he delivered in America and England between the mid-1840s and 1848; *The Conduct of Life* has its origin in a lecture series that he gave sparingly during the 1850s, although several of the essays in the volume—"Power," "Wealth," "Cul-

ture," "Worship," and "Beauty," in particular—were drawn from
lectures that performed extensive service outside of Emerson's
Conduct of Life lecture series.

Representative Men consists of seven chapter-length essays, or
"lectures," as Emerson called them: an introductory essay entitled the "Uses of Great Men," a two-part essay on Plato, and one
each on Swedenborg, Montaigne, Shakespeare, Napoleon, and
Goethe. Emerson underscored the representative quality of the
volume and the figures it treated by identifying each principal figure with either a quality that defined his character or a simple
statement of his profession. Hence, Plato is "the Philosopher,"
Swedenborg "the Mystic," Montaigne "the Skeptic," Napoleon
"the Man of the World," and Goethe "the Writer." But in a radical departure from his practice in 1835, when in his "Biography"
lecture series he developed Michelangelo, Martin Luther, Milton,
and others as exemplary, unblemished heroes, in *Representative
Men* Emerson did not portray heroes as such, but as men of un-
common ability whose lives also revealed a host of common
flaws inherent in human character and behavior: intellectual conceit, pettiness, and avarice, to name a few. For instance, Swedenborg, a philosopher who Emerson greatly admired, is portrayed
as possessing a narrow "theological bias"; overvaluing form, he
lacks "central spontaneity" and is unable to incorporate the "apparatus of poetic expression" into his philosophy (*CW*, 4:67–68,
74, 80). Swedenborg and his system are too cerebral; lacking in an
essential appreciation of nature (in the Emersonian sense of the
term), neither Swedenborg the person nor the philosophy he
promotes has "the power to generate life" (*CW*, 4:74–75). Similarly, although in Emerson's estimation Napoleon is "the incarnate Democrat . . . the idol of the common man, because he
had in transcendent degree the qualities and powers of common
men" (*CW*, 4:130–31), he too turns out to be a failure because of
his lack of moral sentiment. In a burst of rage, Emerson attacked
Napoleon's character, noting that he was "singularly destitute of
generous sentiments," lacked "the merit of common truth and
honesty," and was unjust, egotistic, monopolizing, and thoroughly unscrupulous. "In short," he concluded, "when you have

penetrated through all the circles of [Napoleon's] power and splendour, you [are] not dealing with a gentleman at last, but with an impostor and a rogue" (*CW*, 4:145–46).

Among Emerson's major works, *Representative Men* is one of the most difficult to account for as an expression of his idealistic philosophy. Featuring imperfect, defective men, it struck nineteenth-century readers, as it often does readers of today, as Emerson's concession to the inevitable failure of the ideal in the real world of real men. Put another way, the book seems to confirm one of Emerson's personal confessions in "Experience": "[T]he world I converse with in the city . . . is not the world I *think*." Yet this reading is at odds with both Emerson's meaning in "Experience" and his stated purpose in *Representative Men*. In "Experience," Emerson's "world I *think*" is the world of the ideal, and to the extent that the men who people and act in that world are idealized representations of human character and behavior, they provided Emerson with a goal, an ideal, to aspire to in his own thought and ethics. The men who write, think, and act in *Representative Men*, on the other hand, are from "the world I converse with in the city," or in history, Emerson would say. They are subjects still evolving toward ideal thought and action; in them, the ideal is nascent, not actualized, so that as persons, as men, they are less important in themselves than they are suggestive representations of the potential humans have to achieve the ideal. Emerson explained this point fully in his introduction to *Representative Men*:

> The genius of humanity is the real subject whose biography is written in our annals. . . . The history of the universe is symptomatic, and life is mnemonical. No man in all the procession of famous men is reason or illumination, or that essence we are looking for. . . . The study of many individuals leads us to an elemental region wherein the individual is lost, or wherein all touch by their summits. Thought and feeling that break out there, cannot be impounded by any fence of personality. This is the key to the power of the greatest men[: spirit] diffuses itself. . . . If the disparities of talent and position vanish . . . even more swiftly the seeming in-

justice disappears, when we ascend to the central identity of all the individuals, and know that they are made of the substance which ordaineth and doeth.

The genius of humanity is the right point of view of history. The qualities abide; the men who exhibit them have now more, now less, and pass away. . . . No experience is more familiar. Once you saw phoenixes: they are gone: the world is not therefore disenchanted. The vessels on which you read sacred emblems, turn out to be common pottery, but the sense of the pictures is sacred, and you may still read them transferred to the walls of the world. ("Uses of Great Men," CW, 4:18–19)

The idealistic vision Emerson ultimately advanced in *Representative Men* provided the necessary foreground for *The Conduct of Life*. In this volume, he enlarged on the theme he had developed in his journal in 1850: "[T]he height of culture [and] highest behavior consist in the identification of the Ego with the universe." Because that theme followed directly from the conclusion of "Uses of Great Men" quoted previously, it implied Emerson's recognition of the fact that, although "the height of culture [and] . . . behavior" had not yet been achieved, the world was not therefore "disenchanted." "The lesson of life," as Emerson had learned firsthand during the periods of devastating grief that followed the deaths of his first wife, brothers, and son, and explained in his treatment of Montaigne, "is practically to generalize, to believe what the years and the centuries say against the hours; to resist the usurpation of particulars; to penetrate to their catholic sense." To survive in the city, to survive in an evolving yet imperfect culture, the idealistic individual had to learn "to look for the permanent in the mutable and fleeting" and "to bear the disappearance of things he was wont to reverence, without losing his reverence" (CW, 4:104–5).

In writing and publishing *The Conduct of Life*, Emerson expected readers to recognize that his emphasis was still on reverence for nature and thought. Although he admitted repeatedly in the volume that the individual had to submit to the sway of myriad influences on his life, influences that ranged from fate, to culture, to the illusion and subjectiveness he had called "the lords of life" in "Experience," he held fast to his idealism. "If we must accept Fate," he asserted, "we are not less compelled to affirm liberty, the significance of the individual, the grandeur of duty, the power of character" ("Fate," *W,* 6:4). "Does the reading of history make us fatalists," he wondered; if so, "[w]hat courage does not the opposite opinion show," that the record of human thought and of men's expression of moral sentiment makes men free ("Fate," *W,* 6:28–29). Admitting that imbecility often seemed to be the key to all ages, "imbecility in the vast majority of men at all times, and even in heroes in all but certain eminent moments," Emerson countered with his belief that "Imbecility . . . gives force to the strong" ("Power," *W,* 6:53, 54). In an uncharacteristic rhetorical maneuver, he paused in the middle of his essay "Power" to state, "[H]ere is my point":

> [A]ll kinds of power usually emerge at the same time; good energy and bad; power of mind with physical health; the ecstasies of devotion with the exasperations of debauchery. The same elements are always present, only sometimes these conspicuous, and sometimes those; what was yesterday foreground, being to-day background;—what was surface, playing now a not less effective part as basis. . . . The faster the ball falls to the sun, the force to fly off is by so much augmented. And in morals, wild liberty breeds iron conscience; natures with great impulses have great resources, and return from far. In politics, the sons of democrats will be whigs; whilst red republicanism in the father is a spasm of nature to engender an intolerable tyrant in the next age. (*W,* 6:64)

The Conduct of Life echoed the idealistic certainty out of which Emerson had argued in "The Method of Nature" (1841), an often overlooked essay that he published from an oration he had delivered at Waterville College in Maine. "Things ripen, new men come," he proclaimed in that essay; he asserted, further, that as for man, "it is his attitude,—not feats, but forces,—not on set days and public occasions, but at all hours . . . as in energy" that makes him, through thought in which all men share, "formidable and not to be disposed of" (*CW*, 1:120, 127–28). In "Illusions," the essay that concludes *The Conduct of Life*, Emerson reaffirmed the idealism with which he continued to respect the power of man, his mind, and the efficacy of thought. In an extended conceit that depicted "[e]very god . . . sitting in his sphere" and a "young mortal . . . in the hall of the firmament [temporarily blinded by] snow-storms of illusions," he showed that once "the air clears and the clouds lift a little," two essentials remained: the young mortal still possessing the integrity of his will and thought, and the gods, who, as universal mind, sanction eternally moral man's will and thought (*W*, 6:325).

In the context of Americans' rising skepticism that accompanied foreshadowings of the Civil War in the 1850s, the terrifying reality of the war in the early 1860s, and Abraham Lincoln's assassination in 1865, Emerson reaffirmed that ideal yet again, first in a journal passage, and then in adaptations of the passage in his essay "Culture" in *The Conduct of Life* and the title essay of *Society and Solitude*, a volume of twelve essays published in 1870 that drew almost entirely from lectures:

> Nature has as seldom a success in her machines, as we in ours. There is almost never good adjustment between the spring & the regulator, in a man. He only is a well made man, who has a good determination. Now, with most men, it does not appear for what they were made, until after a long time. . . . [T]hey have a determination, but they ripen too slowly than that it should distinctly appear in this brief life. As with my Catawbas, the season is not quite long enough for them. (*JMN*, 11:197–98; cf. *W*, 6:134, 7:8)

This, Emerson might have agreed, would have sufficed as an apt closing commentary on his life and thought. Once he heard and heeded his call in the 1830s, he never strayed far from his mission to win his hearers and readers to the ideal, even though, as this passage suggests, he appreciated that the human race was not likely to convert to idealism any time soon. This is not to say that the last twenty years of his life were merely an extended anticlimax to either the intellectual ferment that characterized his early

career or the sense of urgency that drove him to write in his journals and later create from them lectures and essays for ever appreciative audiences. Far from it. He spent much of the 1860s lecturing throughout America, editing the papers of his friend
Thoreau, who died in 1862, collecting his poetry for a volume he
titled *May-Day and Other Pieces* in 1867, and editing a two-volume
collection of his *Prose Works* that appeared in 1869.

As the 1870s opened, the decade seemed to an aging but still
vigorous Emerson as promising as the preceding four decades
had been. His Yankee humor, not always apparent in his writings,
surfaced when he received an early sales statement for *Society and
Solitude*. "My new book sells faster . . . [than] its foregoers," he
remarked in his journal; "[t]his is not for its merit, but only shows
that old age is a good advertisement. Your name has been seen so
often that your book must be worth buying" (*JMN*, 16:175). He
gave his "Natural History of the Intellect" lectures at Harvard in
1870 and 1871 a mixed review, although students and others who
attended them gave them consistently positive notice.[7] In April
and May 1871 he traveled to California, and after his return he
spent the remainder of the year negotiating engagements for the
1871–1872 lecture season, working on *Parnassus*, an anthology of
his favorite poetry that he had been collecting for fifty years, and
arranging journal material and several lectures for another volume of essays he expected to publish. He was not, however, destined to complete either *Parnassus* or his anticipated volume of
essays by himself. On 24 July 1872 his house was substantially
damaged by fire, the short-range effect of which was to break his
inclination to write, while its long-range effect was to accelerate
the progress of what today might be diagnosed as either senile
dementia or Alzheimer's disease. Late in 1872, his daughter Ellen
accompanied him on a recuperative journey to Europe and
Egypt; lasting from October 1872 to May 1873, this trip abroad
provided Emerson with an occasion for one last meeting with
Carlyle and other friends and admirers in England, and for a return to some of the sites that in 1833 had restored his spirits. But
this time he returned home unrestored. Gradually accepting the
editorial services of his daughters, Ellen and Edith, and of James
Elliot Cabot who he named his literary executor in 1875, Emer-

son saw *Parnassus* into print in 1874 and *Letters and Social Aims*, the volume of essays he had begun earlier in the decade, in 1876. He died in Concord on 27 April 1882, having faced his last years with an equanimity foreshadowed in the closing lines of his poem "Terminus" (1867):

> As the bird trims her to the gale,
> I trim myself to the storm of time,
> I man the rudder, reef the sail,
> Obey the voice at eve obeyed at prime:
> "Lowly faithful, banish fear,
> Right onward drive unharmed;
> The port, well worth the cruise, is near,
> And every wave is charmed." (*W*, 9:252)

Emerson and America's Coming of Age

Moments after Emerson died on the evening of 27 April 1882, the bells of Concord's First Parish Church tolled seventy-nine times to mark his passing. His death was not unexpected. Approaching his seventy-ninth birthday, Emerson had lived a remarkably long, productive, and influential life by any standard. Over the nearly half-century since his first appearance on the American scene as an original voice of national faith in individualism, optimism, nature, and social reform, his words had moved his countrymen to aspire to an ideal level of human thought and action unimaginable to earlier generations of Americans. An intellectual and social doctrine that erased most vestiges of Calvinism and fatalism retained from the formative years of American settlement, Emerson's message conveyed his "instinctive faith" in possibility and in "a perfect system of compensations" founded upon the universality of these laws:

> That the mind is in its own place
> That exact justice is done . . .
> That the Soul is immortal . . .
> That the best is the true.

That the Mind discerns all things.
That the Mind seeks itself in all things
That truth is its own warrant. (*JMN*, 3:316–17)

Emerson's message was well known by the time of his death, and in spite of the lofty and occasionally abstract manner in which he articulated it, Americans easily found in it a place for themselves and their collective aspirations. His message resonated with their "instinctive faith" in themselves as individuals and as a people and in the possibilities of a great national future represented by the vast landscape of the North American continent. Delivered from the pulpit he occupied during his early years, from the lecture platform from which he spoke throughout his career, and in the printed essays and volumes that lent authority, if not finality, to his words, Emerson's message was progressively adapted into an American New Testament. To call it such is hardly an exaggeration, for in his own time as in ours, Emerson was respected as a cultural priest and visionary, and much as we might, his contemporaries, who first received his words, intuitively responded to their prophetic strains.

In ways that postmodern Americans will critique and resist, nineteenth-century Americans embraced Emerson's new American testament for the confidence it expressed in their individual power and for the absolute faith it held in the grand destiny of the American cultural experiment. Like him, they believed "that Revelation is not closed and sealed, but times of refreshment and words of power are evermore coming, . . . that neither is the age of miracles over and forever gone[—]that the Creation is an endless miracle as new at this hour as when Adam awoke in the garden" (*CS*, 4:246). They found that belief reinforced in the words of *Nature*, where after lamenting American dependency on the past and on the retrospective preoccupation of biography, history, and criticism that yielded so many "sepulchres of the fathers," Emerson counseled readers, "'Build . . . your own world'" (*CW*, 1:7, 45). America's future ministers and men of letters heard that counsel echoed in the themes of Emerson's "The American Scholar" and his address before the Harvard Divinity School in 1838. In the first address, Emerson extended his rejection of the past, challenging his audience to espouse a philosophy of "self-trust"—of trust literally in themselves as well as in the high spiritual causes working in the nascent national impulses of the day. Praising the opportunities for improving the human condition opened by new science, the virtue of the commonplace ("[t]he literature of the poor, the feelings of the child, the [ideas] of the street, the meaning of household life"), writing that is "blood-warm," not "cold and pedantic," and an intellectual life consonant with an environment "inflated by the mountain winds" and "shined upon by all the stars of God," Emerson asked his audience to channel their youthful enthusiasm into creating an elevated national consciousness. He imagined it to be a consciousness wherein "each believes himself inspired by the Divine Soul which inspired all men," wherein "[w]e will walk on our own feet; we will work with our own hands; we will speak our own minds" (CW, 1:67–70).

Emerson's new American testament was perfectly timed. Indeed, its spirit was in the air, for Americans already had hints of the elevated national consciousness for which Emerson called in J. Hector St. John de Crèvecoeur's exuberant definition of them: "The American is a new man, who acts upon new principles[,] . . . entertain[s] new ideas, and form[s] new principles." A new Adam transported into a new Eden from the corruption, "servile dependence, penury, and useless labor" of decadent European culture, his task was to carry on the work of Revelation and create miracles out of his own ideas, talents, and land.[8] Americans also had glimpses of the height to which this new consciousness called them in the verses of Philip Freneau, where all the promises of human culture first voiced in Asia, then in Europe, were portrayed as fully realized in the western movement of intellect, morals, and the arts to America:

> To western woods, and lonely plains, . . .
> Where Nature's wildest genius reigns,
> To tame the soil, and plant the arts—
> What wonders there shall freedom show,
> What mighty states successive grow! . . .

While virtue warms the generous breast,
There heaven-born freedom shall reside,
Nor shall the voice of war molest,
Nor Europe's all-aspiring pride—
There Reason shall new laws devise,
And order from confusion rise. . . .

Far brighter scenes a future age,
The muse predicts, these states will hail,
Whose genius may the world engage,
Whose deeds may over death prevail,
And happier systems bring to view,
Than all the eastern sages knew.[9]

And if Crèvecoeur's conception of the American or Freneau's portrayal of the laws of human nature being finally realized in America struck any as too abstract, Americans could find aspects of the ideal national consciousness to which both of these writers drew their attention personified in Benjamin Franklin's elevation of the pragmatic to the virtuous, in Thomas Jefferson's Renaissance-style personal life and professional career, and in Thomas Paine's revolutionary individualism so forcefully conveyed in his statement "My own mind is my own church."[10]

Emerson lived the major part of his public career from the 1830s through the 1870s. These were heady and hectic times. These were times in which the example of a Franklin, a Jefferson, or a Paine could be selectively invoked to bring an abstraction down to earth, but more important for Emerson's purposes, these were also times in which each discernible aesthetic, intellectual, political, or social advance seemed a new confirmation that the evolutionary track of American character and culture represented the final stages of a divinely inspired and guided national destiny. As one historian closer than we are to the prevailing sentiments of the age put it, Americans of this time harbored an ideal conception—a "dream"—of what they represented and were destined to accomplish, and that conception inspired and motivated the highest rank intellectual as well as the person on the street. Imagining the frame of mind exhibited by an American at the beginning of the nineteenth century, Henry Adams wrote that "his dream was his whole existence." And although the particulars of each American's dream certainly varied from one person to the next, Americans collectively dreamed of a "great democracy" that would "transmute its social power into the higher forms of thought," "provide for the moral and intellectual needs of mankind," "take permanent political shape," "give new life to religion and art," and produce "a higher variety of the human race."[11]

From Adams's historical perspective—he was writing at the end of the century—and from Emerson's immediate perspective, broad strokes of mid-nineteenth-century American experience not only confirmed their ideal conception of the ultimate end of this "great democracy" but also established the mythic terms that, now fully assimilated into American culture, intellectual historians and politicians invoke in modern contexts today. Those broad strokes of American social history included the opening of the American West and the discovery of unimagined natural resources along the way; the legitimation of political doctrines such as Manifest Destiny; the promotion of education, labor laws, sanitation and health care, and other reforms for the public good; the coming of age of the print industry in America, which coincided with the beginning of the lyceum movement as means to disseminate ideas, history, and art, as well as news and information, to the populace; the rise of a distinctively American literary class, which included Washington Irving, Nathaniel Hawthorne, Herman Melville, Harriet Beecher Stowe, and Walt Whitman, among many others, who addressed American subjects directly to an American audience; and the progress of experimental science and invention, which revolutionized industry, medicine, and agriculture in America and facilitated geographic expansion.

Yet almost as a counterpoint to each seeming advance of American culture, circumstances and events such as these raised serious questions about the extent to which the ideal could, in fact, be fully realized: the continual displacement and eventual eradication of entire native tribes; the persistence of institutions such as slavery, and the second-class citizenship accorded to

women and freed blacks; and the spoiling of the natural environment and the creation of a menial worker class to support industry, expansion, and trade, all in the name of progress. Confronting this dark side of nineteenth-century American life,
Adams found that the century's social history raised at least as
many unsettling questions about the ideal as advocacy for it appeared to answer. Given such circumstances and events, could
America consistently follow an enlightened course that elimi-
nated or, at least, lessened what seemed to be the inevitable
bloody results of human politics in Western culture: war and
class struggle? Could the American really create in himself and
his fellows a whole new mind, a whole new race? In sum, could
the American ideal ever be fully realized?

Adams, who died in 1918, was never able to answer these questions to his own or his readers' satisfaction. In 1891 he concluded
the ninth and final volume of his *History of the United States* by
stating that American "history required another century of experience" before answers could even be attempted.[12] But Emerson had no difficulty: His answers to all questions such as these
were consistently affirmative. As cultural priest and visionary,
he, as with most of his contemporaries, cared less about assessing the impact of particulars than he did about expressing
confidence in the ideal. Unless they happened to provide factual
support for the ideal or lent themselves to imaginative advocacy of the ideal through poetry or another art, the particulars—
circumstances and events, and persons as well—were only so
many finite steps along the way to the ideal. If those steps happened to be negative, as certainly slavery and the creation of a
low worker class were, they did not compromise the ideal;
rather, they showed the necessity of making broader generalizations in support of the ideal.

Although he occasionally skirted skepticism as he encountered
illustrations of the dark side of human nature and experience during his time, Emerson was steadfastly optimistic that all particular
negatives were capable of being eventually rectified by an enlightened race. Since "[m]ind seeks itself in all things" and "truth is its
own warrant," good—the ideal—would, he believed, inevitably

emerge out of, and prevail over, personal or cultural evil. With Walt Whitman, Emerson could insist that the particular was incapable of permanently offsetting or contradicting the ideal. Writing out his ideal conception of self, Whitman had to admit that human experience displayed as much variety in morals, thought, and action as there were individuals in the race. Facing that variety which exhibited evil along with good, he asked, "Do I contradict myself?" "Very well then," Whitman answered, "I contradict myself": "I am large, I contain multitudes."[13]

In the "multitudes," both Whitman and Emerson established their surest confidence in the eventual triumph of the ideal self and ideal culture over the personal or particular. In a sweeping romantic gesture, Emerson, effectively speaking for both, identified "the permanent," the ideal, in "the mutable and fleeting" ("Montaigne, or the Skeptic," *CW*, 4:105). Employing metaphors of nature's persistent evolution toward perfection as representations of the individual's and the culture's persistent evolution toward the ideal, he expressed confidence in the ideal both in print and in the privacy of journal entries such as this:

> We are idolaters of the old. We do not believe in the omnipotence of the Soul: We do not believe there is any force in Today, to rival or re-create that beautiful yesterday. We linger in the ruins of the old tent where the Soul gave us bread & shelter & organs[;] we cannot trust its power anew to feed[,] to cover & empower us. We cannot find again aught so dear, so sweet, so graceful. But the voice of the Almighty saith, Onward for evermore! We cannot stay amid the ruins. . . .
>
> The finite is the foam of the infinite. We stand on the shore & see the froth & shells which the sea has just thrown up, & we call the sea by the name of [its] boundary. . . . We do the like with the Soul. We see the world which it once has made, & we call that *God*, though it was only one moment's production, & there have been a thousand moments & a thousand productions since. But we are to learn to transfer our view to the Sea instead of the Shore, to the energy instead of the limitation, to the Creator instead of the World. (*JMN*, 7:202–3)

Rejecting idolaters and sepulchre-builders, persons who in seeing only the negative or limitation reinforced the intellectual and imaginative stupor of their time, Emerson proposed a new class that would think and write as prophets and priests, who would create the dear, sweet, and graceful in their fellows through reverence for the "force in Today" instead of through reference to "the ruins of the old tent," who would look to "energy instead of limitation," to the metaphoric "Sea instead of the Shore." Contrary to what we may infer from so much of the seemingly positive historical evidence presented by nineteenth-century American life, the "force" and "energy" for which Emerson wished to create a new sense of reverence in readers was not the material. For Emerson and others of the class he proposed, material progress alone could be neither the arbiter of a culture's values nor the measure of a culture's value. In "The Method of Nature" he took issue with cultures that measured their worth only through the material and that directed their complete attention to the "results of machinery, commerce, and the useful arts." These, he argued, inevitably produced a variety of "puny" and "fickle folk" whose lives revealed the spiritual impoverishment of their culture, not its devotion to the ideal (*CW*, 1:120). Such cultures, he said, "died by suicide," and the sure signs of their demise were first the decay, then the dissolution of thought ("The Man of Letters," *W*, 10:246).

Distinct from the material, then, the "force" and "energy" most revered by Emerson followed directly from his "instinctive faith" in the higher cause illuminated by American experience: the infinite capacity of "Mind" and "Soul." Confident of the infinite capacity of "Mind" and "Soul," Emerson could express unwavering confidence in immortality as a concept and a fact and in the ultimate triumph of the ideal over experience. In "The Method of Nature," he wrote that he shared his countrymen's delight in "the music of the water-wheel," felt with them "the pride which the sight of a ship inspires," and looked "on trade and every mechanical craft as education." But he also wrote that waterwheels, ships, and the like were, in the final analysis, just so many temporal, finite inventions that repeat themselves "a thousand times." Proclaiming, "I will not be deceived into admiring the routine," Emerson discerned something more "precious" in multiple acts of material invention: "the intellectual step," "the spiritual act," whereby inventions are initially made, then recreated and improved upon by succeeding generations or in different nations (*CW*, 1:120–21).

As suggested by his remarks in "The Method of Nature," for Emerson the "perfect system of compensations" represented in his journals required compartmentalization of life between experience (the finite) and the ideal (faith in the spiritual and infinite). One can read this essential dualism in religious terms and imagine the individual standing with his feet planted in this world of transition and of human care and woe, while his heart and eyes are fixed firmly on the permanence and salvific wonder of the next. One can also read this essential dualism in philosophical terms, where Platonism provides the model for understanding experience only as a temporal redaction of a higher realm of existence, where ideas, not the material, the practical, or the particular, are dominant. Yet however read, Emerson's "perfect system of compensations" always required absolute confidence in his culture's predisposition to aspire to and finally realize the ideal, and Emerson affirmed—and reaffirmed—that confidence throughout his career. For instance, in "Circles" he defined the universe and all it contained as "fluid and volatile," as entities in which "[p]ermanence is but a word of degrees," for events and individuals "always walk as prophecies of the next age" (*CW*, 2:179–81). If along the way to the next age an individual or a culture seemed stuck at a negative moral, social, or political impasse, that moment in time did not compromise the ideal: For Emerson, the ideal was larger than the individual or the culture. When pressed for proof, Emerson had only to turn to the example of nature to argue for the constancy of the ideal in spite of any apparent evidence to the contrary:

> And it seems as if nature, contemplating the long geologic night behind her, when at last in five or six millenniums she had turned out five or six men,—say, Phidias, Plato, Menu, Columbus, was nowise impatient of the millions of disgusting blockheads she had spawned along with them, but was well

contented with these few. These samples, she said attested the virtue of the tree, these were a clear amelioration of trilobite & saurus, and a good basis for further proceeding. The next advancements should be more rapid. With this artist time & space are cheap, & she is insensible to what you say of tedious preparation. (*JMN*, 11:167; cf. *CW*, 4:45)

The attractiveness of Emerson's conception of the relation between the finite and the ideal, like that of his conception of nature and its relation to life, is its elasticity: its capacity to find good emerging from evil, its confidence that with mind fixed on the ideal, each generation possesses and shares across the ages a "recuperative power" to "make the sons of the miscreants of today the benefactors [of] the next age" (*JMN*, 15:286; *TN*, 3:233). "The first lesson of history," Emerson often said, "is the good of evil. Good is a good doctor, but Bad is a better." Oppression, "savage forest laws," and despotism made possible "the inspirations of [a] Magna Charta"; in the nineteenth century, modern versions of the same make possible a great democracy's realization of its aspirations (*JMN*, 13:440, 458; *TN*, 3:125; "Considerations by the Way," *W*, 6:258). The "perfect system of compensations" upon which nineteenth-century American minds like Emerson's relied and the headiness of the times turned thus provided for genius alongside "blockhead" mediocrity, for unprecedented levels of individual freedom and power alongside institutions such as slavery, and for poetry alongside apparent cultural dissolution. Emerson was completely aware that even among the seemingly unqualified aspects of American promise and progress enumerated here—the opening of the West, advancements in industry and invention, and the like—misappropriations of power and the crudest forms of inhuman behavior could be found. But he believed that these abuses were transitory, not permanent, and that in America, as in nature, they would be ameliorated over the sure, progressive evolution of the culture.

"My . . . quarrel with America," Emerson once wrote after debating the merits of American culture against English culture with Henry David Thoreau, is "that the geography is sublime, but the men are not; that the inventions are excellent, but the in-

ventors, one is ashamed of; that the means by which events so
grand as the opening of California [and] Texas, . . . & the junc-
tion of the two Oceans, are effected, are paltry, the filthiest selfishness, fraud, & conspiracy." Without absolute confidence in the
ideal, the juxtaposition between the sublime and the shameful in
human affairs as Emerson developed it here would surely lead
one to despair of the value of progress or invention as those
terms were understood in the nineteenth century. Emerson's
immediate response to the opposition of the sublime and the
shameful on this occasion was to identify this compensation in
the example of nature: "As . . . we find in nature, that the ani-
malcule system is of ferocious maggot & hideous mite, who bite
& tear, yet make up the fibre & texture of nobler creatures; so all
the grand results of history are brought about by these disgraceful tools" (*JMN*, 11:284–85). As with poetry, which Emerson believed represented "faith" as well as "protest" in the "uproar of
atheism" that civilization could be (*JMN*, 13:239), nature, in this
case assisted by science, served as an indispensable lens through
which one could see through reality to the ideal. Here, by recognizing the "nobler creatures" and the "grand results of history"
that emerge out of "disgraceful tools," Emerson showed practically how to "transfer our view to the Sea instead of the Shore, to
the energy instead of the limitation." While "disgusting block-
heads," like "ferocious maggot[s] & hideous mite[s]," may appear to prevail in one generation, their power is momentary and
soon transformed by the enduring impact on the human race of
a great philosopher like Plato, of a revered lawgiver like Menu,
or of a discoverer of new worlds like Columbus. Emerson acknowledged as much in "Montaigne, or the Skeptic" in 1850,
when he admitted that there is always in this world a "chasm" between "the largest promise of ideal power" and "shabby experience": That, he said, is the reality of every person's life (*CW*,
4:104). A few years earlier, he had defined the shabbiness of experience: "Illusion, Temperament, Succession, Surface, Surprise,
Reality, Subjectiveness,—these are the threads on the loom of
time, these are the lords of life" ("Experience," *CW*, 3:47). However, in "Montaigne, or the Skeptic," Emerson showed that to
survive these "lords" one had only to accept that through "the

years and the centuries, through evil agents, through toys and
atoms, a great beneficent tendency irresistibly streams" with this
"lesson of life": "believe what the years and the centuries say
against the hours; . . . resist the usurpation of particulars"
(*CW*, 4:104).

At about the time that "Montaigne, or the Skeptic" appeared
in print, Emerson wrote in his journals, "We should kill ourselves if we thought men . . . could derange the Order of Nature" (*JMN*, 11:95). A decade later he reiterated that belief in
"Fate," developing it as an imaginative hedge against the anarchy
of material culture and the pessimism to which one would inevitably be drawn who ever lost faith in the constancy of the
ideal and in the good which that constancy implied for the
human condition: "If we thought men were free in the sense that
in a single exception one fantastical will could prevail over the
law of things, it were all one as if a child's hand could pull down
the sun. If in the least particular one could derange the order of
nature,—who would accept the gift of life?" (*W*, 6:48–49). Emerson's American New Testament, consistently idealistic and visionary, sustained his contemporaries in the work of establishing
a national identity and culture. The "order of nature" and the
constancy of the ideal were one and the same, and they moved
Americans to embrace "the gift of life" not only for themselves
but also, and more important, for the fulfillment of the promises
of the "great democracy" which, collectively, they had inherited.
In concert with nature, Americans could stand as individuals and
at the same time create out of themselves a culture exhibiting a
new mind and a new configuration of the race. Even the gross
barbarity of the Civil War did not deter Emerson's advocacy for
his new American testament. The war, the problems associated
with Reconstruction, and the rapid rise of a wealthy industrial
class that profited from the war and its aftereffects were not im-
pediments to the ideal but only, as he suggested in his lecture
"The Rule of Life" (1867), just a few more of "the very stairs on
which [the American] climbs" toward his realization of the ideal.
That ideal, he said, could be neither "profaned" by war or materialism nor "forced" into premature existence, for it followed
the slow but progressive "natural current" which he had earlier

defined in "Montaigne, or the Skeptic" as "a great beneficent tendency."

"I can be poor," Emerson wrote in "The Rule of Life," for

> a good soul has the art of being poor, [and] does not need fine cloths, nor sweet cake, and spiced food. . . . [I]n America, there need be no poverty to the wise. America is the glorious charity of God to the poor. If you go out west,—and you need not go very far west, you may find multitudes of men in America who bought last year a piece of land, and a house, and with their own hands raised a crop which paid for their land and buildings.

By their labor, Emerson's westward emigrants were slowly but surely bringing to closure the ideal America that Crèvecoeur and Freneau had once imagined and in which Emerson fully believed; through their labor, these Americans exercised personal power to "defy the cold patron, the official secretaries, and the conservative committees" that would otherwise deny them the opportunities afforded to independent men in a democracy. "The Rule of Life" was Emerson's final statement against the apparent primacy of the "the lords of life." In that lecture he envisioned a land in which "absolute justice" prevailed and men of "healthy perception" dominated. There, he said, "a new feeling of humanity infused into public action" would be found that would answer "the questions of the rights of women, the law of free trade, the treatment of crime, and regulation of labor."[14] Unlike Henry Adams, then, Emerson, writing out of his confidence in "the order of nature" and the constancy of the ideal, did not require another century of experience to believe that the America which he and his contemporaries envisioned would be realized.

In a remarkable display of the seamlessness between theory and practice, Emerson's new American testament also sustained him personally in those dark hours when he suffered the loss of family and friends, balanced between the justice of the Union cause and the horror of the Civil War, and endured the inevitable diminution of individual power that came with his own advancing age and infirmity. Over the last decade of his life, he appeared in public with some regularity, sometimes as a lecturer, but more often as a guest in the homes of friends, where he would converse on poetics, morals, political reform, and the American national character—subjects that, still dear to his heart, seemed to reinvigorate his mind. At other times, he could be found discharging his duties as a Harvard Overseer, attending ceremonial events in Boston or Concord, or participating in meetings of the Radical and Saturday Clubs. The public tributes he received during his journey to England and Egypt in 1872–1873 confirmed his already acknowledged international stature, and throughout the 1870s the sales of a steady stream of publications appearing over his name provided tangible reminders that, at home and abroad, his ideas commanded as much attention and exerted as much influence as they ever had. Yet over that same decade, Emerson's decisions to entrust his literary affairs to James Elliot Cabot and his business affairs to his son-in-law William Hathaway Forbes, and his increasing reliance on his daughter Ellen for his day-to-day needs, were visible concessions by him to the inevitable. To judge from his comments in the essay "Old Age," they were concessions he willingly made.

> When life has been well spent, age is a loss of what it can well spare. . . . But the central wisdom, which was old in infancy, is young in fourscore years, and, dropping off obstructions, leaves in happy subjects the mind purified and wise. I have heard that whoever loves is in no condition old. I have heard that whenever the name of man is spoken, the doctrine of immortality is announced; it cleaves to his constitution. The mode of it baffles our wit, . . . [but] the inference from the working of intellect, hiving knowledge, hiving skill,— at the end of life just ready to be born,—affirms the aspirations of affection and of the moral sentiment. (*W*, 7:335–36)

NOTES

1. See Albert J. von Frank, *An Emerson Chronology* (New York: G. K. Hall, 1994).

2. For Emerson's notebooks on books, see *JMN*, 8:442–79, 550–76, 16:325–46; *TN* 2:199–255. Emerson's actual reading has been reconstructed by Kenneth Walter Camerson; see *Emerson's Reading* (Raleigh, N.C.: Thistle Press, 1941; rev. ed., Hartford, Conn.: Transcendental Books, 1962); and *Emerson's Workshop: An Analysis of His Reading in Periodicals Through 1836* (Hartford, Conn.: Transcendental Books, 1964). For a reconstruction of Emerson's personal library, see Walter Harding, *Emerson's Library* (Charlottesville: University Press of Virginia, 1967).

3. The editions to which I refer are the *Journals and Miscellaneous Notebooks* (*JMN*), *Topical Notebooks* (*TN*), *Complete Sermons* (*CS*), *Collected Works* (*CW*), and *The Later Lectures of Ralph Waldo Emerson, 1843–1871*, ed. Ronald A. Bosco and Joel Myerson, forthcoming from the University of Georgia Press.

4. "Country Life," which Emerson first delivered on 1 March 1858 as the opening lecture in a series entitled "Natural Method of Mental Philosophy," will appear in full in the forthcoming *Later Lectures of Ralph Waldo Emerson, 1843–1871*.

5. For examples of the latter, see Emerson to Carlyle, 19 April 1853, where Emerson discussed his inability to bring his lecture "Fate" to an adequate conclusion, and Emerson to Carlyle, 17 June 1870 and 10 April 1871, where he judges his repeated efforts to bring order to his twenty years' worth of lectures on philosophy dismal failures (*CEC*, pp. 485, 570, 577–78).

6. *Memoirs of Margaret Fuller Ossoli*, 2 vols., ed. Ralph Waldo Emerson, William Henry Channing, and James Freeman Clarke (1852; Boston: Roberts, 1884), 1:213.

7. Unfortunately, the texts from which Emerson lectured at Harvard no longer survive; nevertheless, Emerson's performance in 1870 and the gist of his lectures have been recently reconstructed from the notes of two auditors. See Ronald A. Bosco, "His Lectures Were Poetry, His Teaching the Music of the Spheres: Annie Adams Fields and Francis Greenwood Peabody on Emerson's 'Natural History of the Intellect' University Lectures at Harvard in 1870," *Harvard Library Bulletin*, n.s., 8 (Summer 1997): 1–79.

8. J. Hector St. John [de] Crèvecoeur, *Letters from an American Farmer*, ed. W. P. Trent and Ludwig Lewishon (New York: Fox, Duffield and Co., 1904), p. 56.

9. Philip Freneau, "On the Emigration to America and Peopling

of the Western Country," lines 1, 3–6, 37–42, 55–60. See *The Poems of Philip Freneau,* 3 vols., ed. Fred Lewis Pattee (1907; New York: Russell and Russell, 1963), 2:280–82.

10. Thomas Paine, "The Age of Reason," in *The Life and Works of Thomas Paine,* 10 vols., ed. William M. Van der Weyde (New Rochelle, N.Y.: Thomas Paine National Historical Association, 1925), 8:5.

11. Henry Adams, *History of the United States of America during the Administrations of Jefferson and Madison,* 9 vols. (1891–1896; New York: Antiquarian Press, 1962), 1:173, 184.

12. Ibid., 9:242.

13. Walt Whitman, "Song of Myself," lines 1323–25. See *Leaves of Grass: A Textual Variorum of the Printed Poems,* 3 vols., ed. Scully Bradley et al. (New York: New York University Press, 1980), 1:82.

14. Emerson first delivered "The Rule of Life" on 12 May 1867 at Fraternity Hall in Boston; he delivered it again on 12 March 1871 at Horticultural Hall in Boston. The lecture, which has never been published, will appear in full in the forthcoming *Later Lectures of Ralph Waldo Emerson, 1843–1871.*

EMERSON IN
HIS TIME

"The Age of the
First Person Singular"

Emerson and Individualism

Wesley T. Mott

> To believe your own thought . . . —that is genius.
> Trust thyself: every heart vibrates to that iron string.
> Whoso would be a man must be a nonconformist.
> Suppose you should contradict yourself; what then?
> . . . live ever in a new day.
>
> "Self-Reliance" (*CW*, 2:27, 28, 29, 33)

"In all my lectures," Ralph Waldo Emerson wrote in his journal in April 1840, "I have taught one doctrine, namely, the infinitude of the private man" (*JMN*, 7:342). And he perceived that, for all his contemporaries' materialism and timidity, this was a kind of article of faith for "the Age." "A personal ascendency," he declared in his 1841 "Introductory Lecture on the Times," "—that is the only fact much worth considering" (*CW*, 1:169). Emerson was America's great philosopher-psychologist-poet of the Self as well as a keen observer of the characteristics of "the times." But his true gift to his contemporaries, and to later generations, was his ability to ignite in others an empowering sense of self-reliance. As twenty-eight-year-old Henry Thoreau wrote in his journal during the first winter of his Walden experiment, "Emerson has special talents unequalled— The divine in man has had no more easy methodically distinct expression." And he acknowledged his generation's gratitude to his mentor: "His personal influence upon young persons greater than any man's."[1]

Since the late 1830s, Emerson has been a dominant presence in American culture. He gave voice to the restlessness and idealism of his age, and a younger generation turned to him for inspiration. Even Nathaniel Hawthorne and Herman Melville, though they quarreled with his vision, could not ignore him. The countless thousands who read his books and attended his lectures— whether they were baffled, stirred, or merely curious, whether they thought of him as a dangerous heretic or the champion of a new age—approached him as a celebrity. And, eventually, when the passage of time smoothed out the edges of his early radical reputation, he came to be regarded as a national treasure, an oracle approached to reassure a sometimes troubled America that its self-image was true, its mission on track. Today, on the verge of the twenty-first century, invoked as often as Shakespeare or the Bible by politicians and social commentators, in television commercials and on uplifting greeting cards, Emerson remains, to use that much overworked term, an American icon.

Usually, invoking Emerson proves harmless. Quoting the Sage of Concord on the beauty of a snowstorm or a forest grove is innocuous enough. But the matter becomes stickier when we invoke him to endorse political or social agendas. It matters a great deal what Emerson *meant* when, for example, we quote him on virtues and qualities relating to moral value or national purpose. In the American experience, perhaps no abstract terms are more emotionally or ideologically charged than *self-reliance* and *individualism*, terms whose currency is generally credited to Emerson.

The perennial debate over the condition of the American body politic, and even the state of the national psyche—so often fought over the implications of "individualism"—inevitably comes back to Emerson. He is celebrated as an originator of our virtues, and damned for releasing our vices. Ironically, for a writer quoted to buttress so many self-images and ideologies, Emerson has often seemed a cracked mirror reflecting a con-

flicted culture's split personality. This should perhaps come as no
surprise, for critics have long observed that readings of Emerson
typically reflect his readers. Still, it is fair to ask why Emerson's
pronouncements on the "self" have inspired and empowered so
many while eliciting such a range of creative (mis)readings. Emerson often is thought to have desired through "self-reliance" to
transcend (read *escape*) the weight of time and history. But for
more than perhaps any other major American writer, history
may help to explain just what Emerson *meant*.

Uses of Emerson

"True genius," noted Emerson in "Uses of Great Men," "will not
impoverish, but will liberate, and add new senses" (*CW*, 4:11).
Emerson himself has been a liberating god to generations of
readers. Without his support and example, Thoreau probably
would not have found his voice, and Whitman might not have
risen to the call for a new and genuine American poet. In the
twentieth century he has influenced writers as diverse as
Gertrude Stein, Ezra Pound, Wallace Stevens, and Ralph Ellison.
More than any other major American writer except perhaps
Mark Twain and Thoreau (whose relevance to political and environmental issues in the second half of the twentieth century has
been striking), Emerson has spanned the gulf separating letters
and academia from popular culture, transforming countless
more obscure readers who have found in his message of individualism the strength to live their own lives. Edgar Lee Masters
once testified that Emerson spoke to a uniquely American search
for identity, reassuring us that "we had possibilities . . . that we
were potential geniuses, ready to expand wings and fly if we laid
our hands upon the springs of courage that were within us and
within the human breast everywhere."[2] As a Texas high school
and college student, Grammy Award–winning musician Don
Henley responded similarly. Because of his tireless efforts to save
historic sites in Walden Woods threatened with development and
to establish a Thoreau Institute to carry on educational programs
and research on the Concord writers, Henley is more readily as-

sociated with Thoreau. But "Emerson's essay 'Self-Reliance,'" he declares, "was one of the primary forces that motivated me to become a song writer. It gave me confidence in myself."[3]

Emerson has not appealed only to sensitive, searching souls, however. Legendary Ohio State football coach and military historian Woody Hayes—the same coach who in a nationally televised game lunged onto the field and slugged an opposing player as he scampered by the Ohio State bench with an interception—adored the mild Concord philosopher: "Emerson," declared Hayes in a lecture at Harvard during the 1982 centennial of Emerson's death, "he's on my starting eleven. In fact, he's my No. 1."[4] And other competitive types have found a soulmate in the Concord Sage. He was the favorite author, for example, of Henry Ford.[5] But if "self-reliance" could be employed to validate aggressive, entrepreneurial self-assertion, then, as many in the wake of the Great Depression came to think, Emersonian individualism must be a veil for economic Darwinism, an endorsement of wealth and privilege. Henry B. Parkes considered Emerson an optimist lacking a vision of evil who naively thought "success . . . a result of moral goodness."[6] Allen Tate concurred, mocking Emerson as "the light-bearer who could see nothing but light, and was fearfully blind," who, lacking a tragic sense, "unwittingly became the prophet of a piratical industrialism, a consequence of his own wordy individualism that he could not foresee."[7] Indeed, Emerson not only has been linked to the release of commercial impulses; he also has been *used in* commercials on television. A spot for Nike athletic equipment that ran during the early 1990s showed rapid-fire shots of supple, self-absorbed youths, as a muted voice-over intoned a series of one-line aphorisms from Emerson's "Self-Reliance," all culminating in Nike's crass trademark slogan designed for a narcissistic, attention-span-impaired generation: "Just do it." What "it" meant was less important than reassuring consumers that their fleeting impulses, however unreflective, must surely be worthy of acting on (all the better if a profit was to be made in the process!).

Although Emerson is cited to bolster mercantile and conservative values, he also inspires innovators, rebels, those making a stand for conscience. The essay "Self-Reliance" in this sense is both a stirring call to personal freedom of thought and expression, and the philosophical forerunner and underpinning of Thoreau's enormously influential "Resistance to Civil Government" ("Civil Disobedience"), which is usually regarded as a more experiential or practical application of Emerson's ideals, a ringing call for moral integrity instead of mere expediency in politics. Although it has more often been Thoreau who has fired the minds of reformers worldwide in the twentieth century— Gandhi in South Africa and India, Martin Luther King, Jr., in the 1960s civil rights movement in the United States, dissident Chinese youth at Tiananmen Square in 1989—Emerson, too, has been a beacon of individual liberty. Tolstoy considered him one of the world's great thinkers, and much of the world has come to regard Emersonian self-reliance itself as distinctively American.[8] American students, too, are occasionally "turned on" by Emersonian as well as Thoreauvian individualism. John Lydenberg once recalled a leader of the militant student organization Students for a Democratic Society declaring "that his actions made him feel 'like an Emersonian man.'"[9] Emerson even supplied the radical sixties with two of its trademark terms when, in "Historic Notes of Life and Letters in New England," he observed that "[t]here are always two parties, the party of the Past and the party of the Future; the *Establishment* and the *Movement*" (*W*, 10:325; emphases added). In this spirit Karl Keller, in the waning days of the interminable Vietnam War, found in the Emersonian Self a staunch counterweight to imperialism.[10]

Even as Emerson has been malleable to competing doctrines, however, he has often seemed strangely unapproachable. To many he seems denatured—an abstract, cool, remote marble bust of a figure. The widely held version of Emerson as a serene philosopher above the din of the world was constructed in the late nineteenth century, a period of extensive immigration and social unrest. Polite middle-class readers found comfort invoking the Waspish Sage of Concord—self-contained, peaceful, removed from the strife of an increasingly alienating, threatening world.[11] He was depicted during the 1903 centennial celebration of his birth as, in Len Gougeon's words, "a cross between a conservative Boston Brahmin and a captain of industry."[12] Similarly, against the Communist "menace" of the Cold War during the 1950s and

1960s, Emerson as optimistic individualist appealed to conservative minds as a rock-solid embodiment of "American" values. This
Emerson in twentieth-century popular mythology has become a
rhetorical symbol who, depending on one's politics, rose above, or
"transcended," the messy world of social unrest (the right-wing
figure), or wimped out while his counterpoint Thoreau heroically
went to jail for refusing to pay his poll tax as a protest against slavery and the war with Mexico (the left-wing straw man). "Henry!
Henry!" the Left supposes Emerson to have asked. "What are you
doing in jail?" To which Thoreau supposedly retorted, "Waldo!
What are you doing *out* of jail?" To Emerson's activist detractors it
is beside the point that this episode never happened.[13] Emerson
also has appeared in a *New Yorker* cartoon as a flaky, irrelevant idealist and inept egghead who pontificates, "The only thing in the
world, of value, is the active soul" even as his suffering wife Lidian
complains, "The roof is leaking." To which the obtuse poet Waldo
offers, "By the rude bridge that arched the flood." This is only a
more patronizing version of satire that started with Christopher
Pearse Cranch's famous 1839 caricature of Emerson's account in
Nature of a surprising moment of oneness with the universe, in
which he becomes "a transparent eye-ball" (*CW*, 1:10): Cranch's
rendering of a huge eyeball, sporting a hat and mounted atop
spindly legs, contemplating a landscape, remains a classic spoof of
the mystical streak in Transcendentalism.[14]

Add to these contradictory versions of Emerson the difficult
nonlinear quality of his prose, and today's "general reader" knows
Emerson less as an author to be read and enjoyed than as a pur-
veyor of platitudinous wisdom or as a benchmark for certain cultural values. But in academia, at least, Emerson has reemerged at
the twentieth century's end as a complex—even elusive—and continually stimulating writer. The proliferation of important new
editions and monographs inspired in part by the 1982 centennial of
his death shows no sign of abating, evidence of both the daunting
breadth of Emerson's work and the many ways in which he remains central to American culture. Emerson, finally, is not a pro-
pagandist but a thinker and artist whose prose is deliberately
provocative, fluid, contradictory[15]—a fact easily overlooked by
polemicists. Oliver Wendell Holmes long ago remarked on the

hazards of trying to appropriate his message: Emerson was "the poet whom some admired without understanding, a few understood, or thought they did, without admiring, and many both understood and admired,—among these there being not a small number who went far beyond admiration, and lost themselves in devout worship."[16]

And yet even in the academy, conjuring up the image of Emerson as a timid or smug defender of the status quo has remained rhetorically irresistible. The late president of Yale University A. Bartlett Giamatti told graduating seniors in 1981 that Emerson is the source of that ugliest American trait, a "worship of power." Emerson, he said, "freed our politics and our politicians from any sense of restraint by extolling self-generated, unaffiliated power as the best foot to place in the small of the back of the man in front of you." Emerson allegedly rejected the past, custom, and what Giamatti above all found lacking in American culture, civility. "To Emerson," he proclaimed, "we owe that spirit of Puritan America that has survived to today, the smug, abstract moralism that is distrustful of any accommodation, that is always certain of its righteousness because it is merely self-regarding, that is scornful of any flexibility of spirit because it has never looked over its shoulder."[17] Giamatti was a dynamic president, a charismatic baseball commissioner, and a respected scholar of English Renaissance literature. But he might have *read more* Emerson (his address was based on Emerson's essay "Power") before trading in one of the oldest polemical clichés in American literature. Giamatti's Emerson is an amoral monster who anticipates the meanness of economic boosterism and jingoism, of Nietzsche, Hitler, the Vietnam War.

Much of our eagerness to either appropriate or ridicule Emerson derives from our national anxiety over the very significance of "self" as both a social and an existential construct. Emerson's emphasis on the individual has been accused, for example, of destroying human bonds. Self-reliance, it has been alleged, makes too great a demand on friendship. Wilson Carey McWilliams in 1973 found Emerson's "radical individualism and privatism . . . so extreme that despite his own practice it could serve to moralize disloyalty and self-seeking"; in effect, Emerson's theory of friendship was nothing more than "a teaching of sublimation."[18] Moreover, self-reliance has been accused of disdaining the communal ties essential to religion and culture and of tending to anarchy in politics. Quentin Anderson memorably charged Emerson with constructing an "imperial self" that results in "a denial of history, membership in a generation, charity, reform, institutional means of every sort."[19] Indeed, Emerson has recently been blamed for the extreme forms of self-absorption, self-help, and self-therapies spawned during the selfish 1980s. In their best-selling sociological inquiry into the erosion of community in American life, *Habits of the Heart* (1985), Robert N. Bellah and his colleagues explained that "the current focus on a socially unsituated self from which all judgments are supposed to flow is a development out of aspects of American selfhood that go all the way back to the beginning." They note, however, that it was Emerson who "popularized" the term *self-reliance*, and "it still comes easily to the tongues of many of those to whom we talked." And Emerson comes in for much of the blame for perverting a concept he initially conceived as a challenge to conformity. "Most of us," Bellah and his team assert, "imagine an autonomous self existing independently, entirely outside any tradition and community, and then perhaps choosing one." The resulting moral vacuousness of what is derisively called the "Me Generation" they trace directly to Emerson's essay "Self-Reliance."[20]

What we make of Emersonian individualism, then, is no mere academic exercise but a matter central to our cultural identity. Does he call out our best instincts or justify aggressive competition? Does he champion human rights and justice or endorse institutional power? Is he a clueless philosopher or a sinister shill for vested interests? Emerson's use as a straw man often serves noble purposes. But in quoting Emerson, as with Shakespeare and the Bible, context is everything. *Self-reliance* and *individualism* being inherently abstract terms, the uses to which we put Emerson say more about us and our rhetorical needs than about him.

It is possible to reconstruct the world in which Emerson actually declared his doctrine of self-reliance. Much of the paradox of Emerson's legacy can be explained by the competing definitions of individualism that arose from tensions within European and American culture during the 1830s and 1840s, the period that saw the publication of his seemingly most affirmative (and until recently his most canonical) writings. The Emerson who emerges from this context is far richer and more challenging (if less handy as a rhetorical cudgel) than the self-canceling stereotypes of the champions and detractors we have just seen.

Emerson in His Time

"Just do it," the commercial slogan of the 1980s and early 1990s, exploited a trademark phrase of the defiantly idealistic 1960s— "Do your own thing." This phrase, in turn (ironically, considering its fate in American culture), may be traced to Emerson's ringing challenge in "Spiritual Laws" to "convert" "that thing you do" "into the obedient spiracle of your character and aims" (*CW*, 2:83). Emerson's own aim here is to call us to fulfill our highest "vocation," just as, in using a variation on the phrase in "The American Scholar" (*CW*, 1:64), he had called for ethical thought and action that partakes of the very divinity of creation. As Robert D. Richardson, Jr., has written, "[T]he central work of [Emerson's] life was to be uncovering and making available those sources of power that exist in people and in the world."[21]

But what *kind* of power? "It is said to be the age of the first person singular," Emerson noted in his journal early in 1827 under the heading *"Peculiarities of the present Age."* More than a generic observation that his contemporaries were newly preoccupied with private matters, this journal entry lists six other major manifestations of the times. Among these are the spread of the English language and the reform impulse, including the tendency to associate into societies "to promote any purpose." Particularly significant for our purposes are the fourth and sixth, in which Emerson observes both intellectual and economic forces transforming the age: "4. Transcendentalism. Metaphysics & ethics look inwards—and France produces Mad. de Stael; England, Wordsworth; America, Sampson Reed; as well as Germany, Swedenborg.—. . . . 6) The paper currency. / Joint stock compa-

nies" (*JMN*, 3:70–71). Other forces shaping Emerson's sense of
individualism might be noted here: the legacy of the American
Revolution, with its elevation of personal political liberty; the
emergence of Unitarianism, or "liberal Christianity," with its rejection of Calvinist doctrines of human depravity and its liberating emphasis on human potential for moral growth;[22] and the
election of Andrew Jackson in 1828, which would soon transform
Emerson's understanding of American politics. Emerson's journal list does reveal, however, his early awareness of the emergence
of sometimes antagonistic kinds of individualism that, ironically,
would later create confusion and argument over whose values
Emerson himself endorsed. Boston's population boomed in the
1820s, although a painful recession loomed in 1828. Emerson
rarely quarreled with the market economy per se, instead target-
ing the broader issue of materialism, and he counted successful
businessmen among his early parishioners and friends; George
Sampson, he thought, exemplified the possibility of virtue in the
marketplace. Although he saw the dawning importance of laissez-
faire capitalism in American life, it would be decades before the
appearance of terms such as "rugged individualism" and "self-
made man," labels initially worn as badges of honor by successful
entrepreneurs but tainted later in the century by association with
the avarice of economic Darwinism and the "robber barons." Nor
could Emerson yet see the full implications of the young nation's
expansionist impulse that would popularly be called "Manifest
Destiny," a slogan that would lose its original connotation of idealistic mission to spread democracy when it was invoked in the
1840s to rationalize war with Mexico, lingering as an ugly signifier
of American foreign policy.

The elements that Emerson labels "Transcendentalism," however, are a good starting point to understand the intellectual
sources of his concept of individual identity that would become
"self-reliance." Emerson's essays are sprinkled with evidence of a
rich foreground, and as he would later write in "Intellect," he
knew that even that most personal matter of inspiration is no
simple gift to the lazy: "[I]n a moment, and unannounced, the
truth appears. . . . But the oracle comes, because we had previously laid siege to the shrine" (*CW*, 2:197). All his life Emerson

laid siege to the shrine by constant reading and conversation. Phyllis Cole recently has revealed, moreover, what—given our simplistic preconceptions about "Emersonian individualism"— can only be called a stunning irony: the fact that Emerson's very sense of self-reliance was arrived at *collaboratively* with his brilliant and independent Aunt Mary Moody Emerson, who introduced him to an eclectic range of classical and new philosophy and literature, encouraged him to articulate his ideas, and even provided key concepts and terms that we now consider "Emersonian."[23] Emerson's generation was awash with both traditional and radical movements proclaiming the moral centeredness and innate sanctity of the individual, but he assimilated these ideas and gave them fresh expression.[24]

"Metaphysics & ethics look inwards." Or, as Emerson explained in 1841, the age had come to reject the dominant metaphysics of John Locke, which held that the mind perceives truth from external facts and experiences mediated by the senses: The "Idealism" of the day came to be called Transcendental, Emerson claimed, from the German philosopher Immanuel Kant's use of the term to refer to ideas that are "intuitions of the mind itself" (*CW*, 1:207). Emerson was oversimplifying things. Locke was no leaden materialist; the American Transcendentalists' use of Kant was somewhat freewheeling; and Emerson himself knew better than to confuse every fleeting whim or mood with genuine intuition. Nevertheless, Emerson became the leading American spokesman for a new metaphysics coming from Europe, largely via such British commentators as Thomas Carlyle and Samuel Taylor Coleridge, that announced the inner reserves of each person to know truth. Emerson's generation had been prepared for such new ideas by the Scottish Common Sense philosophy that dominated the Harvard curriculum in the early nineteenth century. Thinkers such as Thomas Reid and Dugald Stewart, writing in large part to answer the skepticism of David Hume, were concerned to establish a basis for ethics by showing empirically how the mind works to apprehend truth. Each person, they believed, possesses a timeless and universal moral sense that can be cultivated. Implicit in their teaching was introspection, which, combined with the idealist teachings of German philosophers and theologians, reached a young American audience anxious to find a moral basis to challenge what they perceived to be stagnant institutions and corrosive social problems.

Emerson's classical training—especially Plutarch's *Lives* and *Morals*—afforded examples of ethical conduct and heroism, and Plato, with his Doctrine of Forms declaring the reality of the Ideal, held lifelong fascination. Emerson was deeply grounded in the Stoics, who demonstrated the divinity of the Creation; the importance of ascetic, virtuous living; and, perhaps most important for Emerson, the perpetual change, flux, and transition that pervades the laws of nature. The Swedish mystic Emanuel Swedenborg was a more modern advocate of the "correspondences" the mind perceives between the natural and spiritual realms, and Emerson was drawn enthusiastically to the contemporary American Swedenborgian Sampson Reed, whose "Oration on Genius" (1821) and *Observations on the Growth of the Mind* (1826) proclaimed the divinity of Nature and "the powers of the mind." Young Americans theologically trained to examine the state of the soul also eagerly received new concepts of human nature, the imagination, and artistic expression emanating from British and European Romanticism. Emerson responded warmly to Byron's restless depiction of the soul and, more lastingly, to Wordsworth's elevation of the common man as a topic of literature, his concept of the poet as seer, his exploration of solitude as both occasion for and subject of contemplation, and his celebration of the soul's mystical connection with nature. From the German Goethe, whom Emerson encountered in translation as early as 1827 and regarded as a heroic modern figure, he learned to appreciate natural *processes* and, accordingly, to understand an organic aesthetics of fluid form.[25] Emerson's radical faith in the divinity of each person also closely resembles the Quaker concept of the Inner Light, or indwelling of Christ's spirit in each human breast; Emerson turned to Quaker writings during crises in his own life and often declared his affinity with that sect's commitment to truth and reform.

Cumulatively, these components of Emerson's education and experience point toward the dignity of the individual, indeed, the divinity of each soul. And together they suggest why the term

Transcendentalist is something of a misnomer in the New England context: Theologically, *transcendent* refers to a God who is above or apart from the world; Emerson's God, or Over-Soul, is detectable by the mind as pervading the entire Creation, including the soul, and is therefore an *immanent* divinity, perception of whom energizes the individual. By training and inclination Emerson posed basic questions related to identity: Who am I? Where am I? Why am I here? What *ought* I to do as a moral being?[26] We must discard, then, stereotypes of Emerson as a self-created Romantic visionary who merely rejected the past, of a hermetically sealed prophet of easy inspiration. His doctrine of intuition, moreover, is no less radical for being the product (as his journals and manuscripts further testify) not of lightning flashes of insight but of extensive reading, years of reflection, and careful revision. Emerson's self-reliance is not merely the sum total of influences or abstract ideas but rather the most striking expression by an American of a historic international shift in the very structure of sentiment and feeling.

Emerson's challenge as a minister, lecturer, and essayist was to find fresh ways of naming and describing the age's new sense of personal power without relying on the institutional language of churches, schools, and politics. Several of his most striking terms and phrases have come to seem familiar and stale over a century and a half, while others have been metamorphosed beyond anything he would have recognized or approved. Long a charged term in American life, *individualism* still bedevils literary and cultural critics and readers of Emerson. But in Emerson's young adulthood the term scarcely existed. In Noah Webster's *American Dictionary of the English Language*, published in 1828, the year before twenty-five-year-old supply preacher Waldo Emerson would be ordained by Second Church in Boston, the term *individualism* was not to be found.[27] *Individual* was defined straightforwardly as "[a] single person or human being," and even *individuality* was matter-of-factly given as "[s]eparate or distinct existence; a state of oneness." Just as tellingly, Webster offered no definition of *self-culture* or *self-reliance*, terms that were central to the emerging culture of liberal Unitarianism and, soon thereafter, Emersonian Transcendentalism. Webster conceived even of *self* as primarily a component of pronouns; his "Use 3" only hinted at Romantic connotations of the term: "*Self* is sometimes used as a noun, noting the individual subject to his own contemplation or action, or noting identity of person. Consciousness makes every one to be what he calls *self.*"

As a young minister at the Second Church in Boston (1829–1832), Emerson was already wrestling with the implications of the "Self"—an unfashionable term in the late twentieth century, when literary theorists have treated "self-construction," according to Daniel Walker Howe, "as essentially pathological."[28] But to Emerson, immersed in intersecting traditions that valued habits leading to moral growth, nurturing the self was life's great project. A theological liberal, he encouraged his parishioners to cultivate God's gifts, reason and feeling, in the unending growth of the soul to approach the "likeness to God" preached by his hero William Ellery Channing in his acclaimed 1828 ordination sermon for the Reverend F. A. Farley in Providence, Rhode Island. The doctrine of *likeness* would always be for Emerson not license to boast Godlike power but rather a standard against which to measure character. Although Emerson retained a strong New England Puritan sense of the snares to which human nature is vulnerable, he eventually went beyond Channing in drawing out the implications of the potential divinity in each person, insisting on the literalness of his favorite Scripture verse, "[B]ehold, the kingdom of God is within you" (Luke 17:21).[29] But he remained concerned with the "twofold nature in every individual," the "strange dualism" that is humanity's burden as well as glory (*CS*, 4:219). And so, like Benjamin Franklin in his concern with "practical considerations," he urged self-improvement not as self-promotion but as "duty" (4:72). The nineteenth century, he knew, enjoyed "freedom of choice of pursuit," which is to be preferred over old constraints of heredity; but he went on in a Puritan vein to caution that with this blessing more is asked of us. Are we "better" (4:73)? Scriptures declare us "a law to ourselves" (Romans 2:14 [*CS*, 4:74]), but the habits we develop fit or unfit us, he thought, for the afterlife (4:75).

Emerson's more Transcendental notion of self-reliance begins to appear even in earlier sermons but always with qualifications.

Despite our partial perception of truth, for example, Emerson believed in the unity of "[m]oral excellence," as exemplified in the aphorisms of the ancients (2:41). Although he believes in the instinctual "perception of right in the soul," his focus is not on freedom and self-assertion but on "self-command" (2:42). Individual accountability is of paramount concern for the modern Christian because all history is marked by the "struggle" of reason with pride (2:44). Emerson was faced, then, with the paradox of our "free agency" and our "dependence on God" (2:71). Even our "social life" is at odds with "independence of character." How, then, do we distinguish among persons and judge behavior? "The merit of all action," Emerson stresses, "is measured by the principle" (2:73); and he defines immortality itself as the "transferring of the whole being from self to God" (2:74).

In a Fast Day sermon given first in April 1830, moreover, Emerson emphasized the importance to the individual of "civil relations." The government, he thought, should be "out of sight" (2:162), leaving its citizens "in entire freedom"; he praises the government for intruding only in matters of taxes and the jury system, and finds it a positive force in actually redressing problems. But as he surveys the social scene, he finds cause for worry. He sees "a licentious press" serving "party purposes," and "selfishness" plaguing the "common usages of trade." Pervading all affairs is the problem of "Self interest," which fosters "disunion." All have a stake in civic matters, and politics is essentially a measure of "private virtue" (2:163–64). And since this is so, what is needed above all is the salutary influence of "a solitary individual" (2:165). Here again the Emersonian paradox comes full circle: the virtuous individual is not self-seeking but self*less*, acting according to principle. The purpose of life, he says in another sermon, is "conducting life well," an "unceasing effort at self culture." This process, always accompanied by laws of "retribution" and "compensation," demands constant watchfulness (2:246–48).

When Emerson begins in his sermons to use "self-reliance" by name, then, his listeners were fully aware that he refers not to one's lower, materialistic, egotistical "self" but to one's higher, principled, moral Self. In this sense he can declare that we must not "distrust" ourselves but instead must "value our own souls"

(2:263). Great men, he explains, exhibit "individuality" of character but similarity of "purposes." Society exhibits superficial
"tame resemblance of one man's thoughts and conversation to
another's" (2:264). We must not, however, "*imitate* any being"
(2:265) but rather cultivate that "self-reliance which grows out of
the Scripture doctrine of the value of the soul" (2:266). Though
no worshiper of the past, Emerson had great respect for the
lessons of history, and he had long been interested in biography
as moral exempla modeled by heroes. Never a "hero worshiper"
in the manner his friend Carlyle came to advocate, Emerson
regarded biography as one more piece of ballast to stabilize the
self against the risks of mere self-regard. As he would state in
"Uses of Great Men" in *Representative Men* (1850), "Other men are
lenses through which we read our own minds" (*CW*, 4:4). And in
his sermons dawned a more Romantic, or Transcendental,
theory of biography whereby the individual does not copy but
rather *is* the measure of the virtues and flaws of "great men."[30]
Self-trust, he insists in one sermon, solves the problem of "rote"
religion. "The only way for a man to become religious is to be so
by himself." To "trust in self" is a God-given imperative, so long
as you remember the "*origin of self*," which is God (3:202).

All this concern with self-examination, effort, and humility—
all this dedication to what Emerson calls "social duties," "noble"
as opposed to "selfish passions," and charity based on "love of
God" (3:84, 87)—may sound to the modern ear like priggish
moralism; the inspiring, provocative, even radical Emerson of the
great essays may seem to have gone into eclipse. Emerson, however, calls this selfless moral life "sublime" (3:87, 90), and his lifelong commitment to moral purpose is the key to understanding
what he means by *self-reliance*.

Even as a teenager Emerson associated the moral philosophy
of the ancients with contemporary behavior (*JMN*, 1:341), and
the moral sentiment provided an alternative to Calvinistic determinism as he reflected on free will (*JMN*, 2:146–47). He came to
regard the "immortality of moral truth" not as a merely reflective, intellectual process but as an activity (*JMN*, 3:21); and in the
summer following the death of Ellen, he was associating the
"*moral sublime*" with "hear[ing] of a person of noble feelings," an

emotion that can be provoked by reading (he cites the verse of Edward Young as well as Shakespeare and Bacon [*JMN*, 3:274]). By 1836 the "moral sublime" has become more fully defined, embracing not simply moral standards, conscience, behavior, and beauty but feeling as well. Over the course of his life, Emerson's thought and writing evolved from the exhortations of his Unitarian sermons, to the Romantic exuberance of his great Transcendentalist lectures and essays, to more pragmatic considerations of human limitations. The constant factor in his intellectual life, however, is a conviction that all personal growth and expression exists in a moral context, an ethical imperative that does not stifle the individual but, to the contrary, gives our lives vital, even heroic, purpose.[31] In his early lectures and essays, Emerson was now ready to give expression in a distinctly American setting to the spirit of a new age that he had encountered in the 1820s.

By 2 March 1837, when Emerson rose at the Masonic Temple to deliver his lecture "The Individual," he was articulating ideas that he had been contemplating for years and that decades of earlier writers had also rehearsed. But he was on uncharted ground. The Revolution had declared all men politically equal; the Common Sense philosophers had declared the moral sense innate in all people; and the Romantics had exalted imagination and creation as a divine liberation. What this meant for life in a competitive free-market democracy, however, was far from clear. As the editors of this lecture observe, Emerson actually titled the lecture "The Individual," the term *individualism* not then being "in common usage" (*EL*, 2:173). Indeed, as Koenraad W. Swart explained in a pioneering essay, the term from its beginnings in Europe had a "perplexing variety of meanings": "first, the idealistic doctrine with equalitarian implications of the rights of man, or what may be called political liberalism; secondly, the anti-statist, largely utilitarian doctrine of *laissez faire*, or economic liberalism; thirdly, the aristocratic cult of individuality, or Romantic individualism."[32] Emerson at various times seems to endorse each of these often mutually canceling ideologies, which has compounded the difficulty of locating the "tradition" of individualism to which he belongs: (1) He believed that all people partake of the "Universal Mind" and therefore innately possess the dig-

nity and responsibility of self-reliance, a conviction that led him
inexorably to speak out on matters of social injustice, especially
slavery; (2) although he lamented the materialism of the age, he
could declare "[t]he Marine Railway, the U.S. Bank, the Bunker
Hill monument [among the] perfectly genuine works of the
times" (*JMN*, 5:150), and he had faith that, properly employed,
money is, "in its effects and laws, as beautiful as roses" (*CW*, 3:136
[a statement that F. O. Matthiessen found "staggeringly innocent"]); and, of course, (3) he continually declared the virtual divinity of the private individual, which, we have seen, derives
from several traditions.[33] In the lecture that preceded "The Individual," Emerson had described "The Present Age" as "The Age
of Trade," a politically liberating force but one that risked intellectual "bribery" with the unleashing of "large masses," popular
opinion, and superficiality (*EL*, 2:160, 161). It was "an age of facts
and not of principles"; and for all the dynamic forces unleashed
in such a time, "we pay a great price for this freedom" (166, 169).
"The Individual" draws on Emerson's classical, Christian, and
Romantic ideals to awaken his audience to reserves of character
still dormant in this "era of the increased political and moral
power of individuals" (*EL*, 2:173). What he calls "society" divides
the individual, who fails to perceive that the "improvements of
our day are mechanical and do not exalt man" (175). The new individual, potentially as great as the heroes of antiquity, "finds
again like them new perils to virtue." Emerson is convinced that
"[a]ll men are of one essence" (178), a stance that deters arrogance, injustice, and selfishness even as it affords a moral base for
truth by positing the "identity" of truth "from the first to the last
seer" (180). Indeed, arriving at principles "imposes a new duty
upon the cultivated mind of our time" (181). The fully realized individual has achieved not prosperity but a kind of stoic wisdom
"that his place is as good as any place; his fortunes as good as
any" (185). Such an individual has experienced truth personally,
but the experience affirms a sense of cosmic place—"the eternity
of man; the identity of the soul in every age" (187).

By 1842, however, Emerson was noting that many of his
reform-minded contemporaries "think that the vice of the age is

to exaggerate individualism, & they adopt the word *l'humanité*" (*JMN*, 8:249). In France especially, at least until the revolution of 1848, *individualism* was a pejorative term implying either the social disruptions of capitalism or Romantic tendencies to "eccentricity" or "isolation."[34] "'Democratic individualism,'" Lawrence Buell has observed, is "something of an oxymoron."[35] And already in the mid-1830s, of course, the French social critic Alexis de Tocqueville was shrewdly observing a pattern of tensions, ironies, and awkward paradoxes in American life. He saw a culture proclaiming the ascendancy of the individual, where introspection was rarely found; a society boasting its foundation on religious principles, where religious tenets and institutions seldom informed public life; a democracy of equality and freedom, where conformity and the "tyranny of the majority" often suppressed minority opinions. Tocqueville noted, "'Individualism' is a word recently coined to express a new idea. Our fathers only knew about egoism." The new idea might *seem* less insidious: "Egoism springs from a blind instinct; individualism is based on misguided judgment rather than depraved feeling." But by whatever name, the result was withdrawal from a sense of history and from community. Moreover, Tocqueville observed that "[i]ndividualism is of democratic origin and threatens to grow as conditions get more equal."[36] Emerson would read *Democracy in America* in April 1841 and meet Tocqueville in Paris in May 1848. But in much the same spirit he had already been forming his own opinions about the paradoxes of American democracy. "When I spoke or speak of the democratic element," he wrote in his journal in September 1836, "I do not mean that ill thing vain & loud which writes lying newspapers, spouts at caucuses, & sells its lies for gold, but that spirit of love for the General good whose name this assumes. There is nothing of the true democratic element in what is called Democracy; it must fall, being wholly commercial" (*JMN*, 5:203).[37]

This helps to explain why Emerson's important little book *Nature* (1836), published six months before he presented the lecture "The Individual," declares the priority of the individual even as it resists the American doctrine of self-assertion. In a famous pas-

sage Emerson evokes the moment of mystical awareness not as a
moment of "mean egotism" or of Romantic defiance but of oneness, of self*less*ness:

> In the woods, we return to reason and faith. There I feel that
> nothing can befal me in life,—no disgrace, no calamity, (leav-
> ing me my eyes,) which nature cannot repair. Standing on the
> bare ground,—my head bathed by the blithe air, and uplifted
> into infinite space,—all mean egotism vanishes. I become a
> transparent eye-ball. I am nothing. I see all. The currents of
> the Universal Being circulate through me; I am part or particle
> of God. (*CW*, 1:10)

A sense of genuine well-being consisted in an awareness of one's
microcosmic place in a changing universe of fixed law, a stance
that enacted both the Gospel declaration that in order to find
one's life one "shall lose it" (Matt. 10:39) and the cosmic acceptance Emerson was discovering in Eastern philosophy; indeed,
true self-discovery meant an *abandonment* of what is usually
meant by *self*. A platonist and spiritualist, Emerson saw the corruption of political and economic aggression as well as the failure of conventional models of spirituality. Like his European
contemporaries, he thus had trouble with the concept of sepa-
rateness, and available terminology failed him. "Who shall define
to me an Individual?" he wrote in May 1837. "I behold with awe
& delight many illustrations of the One Universal Mind. I see my
being imbedded in it. As a plant in the earth so I grow in God.
. . . Hard as it is to describe God, it is harder to describe the Individual" (*JMN*, 5:336–37). "Self-reliance," which we have seen
Emerson already using by 1830 in his sermons, is perhaps a term
closer to the idea of individual identity that Emerson was trying
to describe.[38] But even in his great essay "Self-Reliance" he wor-
ries that the very term *self-reliance* is inadequate to describe the
openness to and influx of truth, which is, after all, the *purpose* of
solitude, reflection, and integrity:

> Life only avails, not the having lived. Power ceases in the in-
> stant of repose; it resides in the moment of transition from a

past to a new state, in the shooting of the gulf, in the darting
to an aim. This one fact the world hates, that the soul *becomes;*
. . . Why then do we prate of self-reliance? Inasmuch as the
soul is present, there will be power not confident but agent.
To talk of reliance, is a poor external way of speaking. Speak
rather of that which relies, because it works and is. (*CW,* 2:40)

Emerson emphasizes organic process over final accomplishment,
and as in his more conventional sermons, he still implies a source
of inspiration and vitality that is greater than, but pervades and
animates, the individual. As Merton M. Sealts, Jr., demonstrates,
moreover, Emerson's concept of the "American Scholar" is not
confined to the inner life of the individual but implies a public
mission "to awaken the intellect in others."[39]

Emerson's ongoing critique of America's materialism and crisis of spirit is not a solitary, Byronic lament but, in the vein of
Carlyle's "Signs of the Times" (1829) or "Characteristics" (1831), a
moral critique of the age. And for Emerson the problem was
partly, in today's jargon, a generation gap. *Nature* begins with the
well-known complaint that "[o]ur age is retrospective. It builds
the sepulchres of the fathers. It writes biographies, histories, and
criticism. The foregoing generations beheld God and nature face
to face; we, through their eyes. Why should not we also enjoy an
original relation to the universe?" (*CW,* 1:7). Emerson frequently
gives voice to his generation's desire to make its own mark. *Nature's* scheme of spiraling ascent of human uses of the phenome-
nal world, from material "commodity" to "spirit" and "prospects," suggests an impulse both to harness and to surmount the
materialism of the age. (The panic of 1837 would only confirm
the folly of placing undue faith in the things of the world.)[40]
Emerson's essays and lectures, although surely not social or economic treatises, are more than abstract philosophical meditations; they are spiked with rather specific complaints about
American values.

Even as Emerson targets economic and political excesses of
the age, he refuses to offer as an alternative a retreat into some
idealized, uncontaminated solitude. An unassuming man himself, Emerson does not invite his reader to smugness or arro-

gance. For all the aspirations encouraged in *Nature*, for example, he reminds us that at present, in actuality, "[a] man is a god in ruins" (*CW*, 1:42). And for all the confidence Americans exhibit, he observed ennui and self-doubt. In "The Individual" he declares, "The age is infected with the malady of Hamlet" (*EL*, 2:180). We are no longer afflicted by the Puritans' "fear of Sin," he notes in his "Introductory Lecture on the Times," but "our torment is Unbelief, the Uncertainty as to what we ought to do" (*CW*, 1:179). His lecture and essay "The Transcendentalist" (*CW*, 1:201–16), carefully couched in the third-person voice, is a portrait not only of idealism but also of a generation's alienation from American life and failure, at present, to find an alternative course. Inspiration itself, so central to the Transcendentalist, could not be sustained continually. Even in his late lecture "The Preacher," he still finds himself "in a moment of transition" with a crisis of belief and authority. "We are born too late for the old," he laments, "and too early for the new faith" (*W*, 10:217). Not the beaming optimist of stereotype, Emerson knew ambivalence and displacement.

Emerson thus critically examined his age's celebration of individualism, but he did not stand at some Olympian distance to sniff and scoff. He shared, and gave expression to, the expansive spirit of the 1830s without becoming its dupe, as exemplified by his selectively enthusiastic appropriation of the heroic and mythic Davy Crockett. The epigraph of the colorful frontiersman and politician's self-promotional autobiography became the defining slogan of Emerson's assertive, even cocky, generation: "Be always sure you're right—THEN GO AHEAD!"[41] Quickly shortened to "Go ahead" (minus the original ethical qualification) in *Davy Crockett's Almanacks* and in the popular mind, the slogan immediately caught on even in Emerson's Yankee Boston. The *Daily Evening Transcript* reprinted several anecdotes that turned on the phrase for purposes ranging from broad humor to proud boosterism. One tells of a "fellow," always spouting the phrase, who habitually falls asleep in church. At one service the "clergyman had pronounced the words 'in conclusion,' when up jumped the fellow and exclaimed, 'Well, then, go ahead!'" (11 June 1834, p. 2). A very different anecdote boasts of two locomotives being built in Lowell, "where the union of the best Yankee and foreign mechanical skill produces the highest perfection in machinery. One is to be called the *'Double Speeder,'* and the other, *'David Crockett,'* and when they *'go ahead'* it will be in earnest" (25 July 1834, p. 2). Humor underlies this anecdote too—but it turns on a pun that appeals to the self-satisfied spirit of an entrepreneurial city outwardly confident of where it is going, and how it is getting there.

Emerson's stance toward Crockett is especially revealing because Emerson's own relation to the West, or the frontier, is often cited as an index of *his* distinctly "American" qualities. "The cardinal points of his teaching—optimism, melioration, democracy, individualism, self-reliance—derive their chief sanction and meaning," wrote Ernest Marchand in 1931, "from the psychology bred by the American frontier."[42] The classic theorist of the shaping influence of the American West, Frederick Jackson Turner, already had declared in 1920 that "the most important effect of the frontier has been in the promotion of democracy . . . [and] individualism." But Turner had observed a dark side to the frontier experience. Akin to "selfishness," "[i]ndividualism in America has allowed a laxity in regard to governmental affairs which has rendered possible the spoils system and all the manifest evils that follow from the lack of a highly developed civic spirit."[43] Ever since William Bradford described the Pilgrims' impression of Cape Cod in 1620 as "a hideous and desolate wilderness," the menace of the frontier has been a strain in American thought. When Crèvecoeur posed the question "What is an American?" during the American Revolution, he observed ambivalently that the frontier promotes not only independence and vitality but also degeneracy, lawlessness, drunkenness, and violence.[44]

In assessing Emersonian individualism and its relation to nature and the frontier, we confront both history and myth. Was the American West a field of egalitarian opportunity or an arena (in Albert J. von Frank's phrase) of "predatory individualism"?[45] The fact is, Harvard-educated sometime minister Emerson was fascinated by Crockett, whose autobiography he encountered in the months when *Nature* was taking shape in his journals. Published in 1836, the year Crockett was killed at the Alamo, *Nature* famously asserts, among other key Transcendentalist tenets, the "radical correspondence between visible things and human thoughts" (*CW*, 1:19). "This immediate dependence of language upon nature, this conversion of an outward phenomenon into a type of somewhat in human life," he goes on, "never loses its power to affect us. It is this which gives that piquancy to the conversation of a strong-natured farmer or back-woodsman, which all men relish" (20), a passage previously used in the 1834 lecture "The Naturalist" (*EL*, 1:71) and the 1835 lecture "English Literature: Introductory" (*EL*, 1:222). Emerson's correspondential theory of language is indebted, it is well known, to Platonic and Swedenborgian philosophy. But behind *Nature*'s statement that the generic backwoodsman is an originator of language is, quite specifically, Davy Crockett.[46] In the 1835 lecture, the sentence about the "piquancy" of the backwoodsman's "conversation" is followed by reference to a colorful phrase Emerson himself relished: "I showed him the back of my hand." This phrase, too, is attributed simply to "a backwoodsman"; but an 1835 journal entry indicates that Emerson considered it to be Crockett's (*JMN*, 5:64; see also *JMN*, 6:168; *TN*, 2:324; and *W*, 8:14, where, however, he attributes the phrase to "our Kentuckian orator"). And another 1835 journal entry praises Crockett and a handful of others for using the "language of Nature" (*JMN*, 5:78). The fall of the Alamo provided the nation with a motive and a rallying cry for the war with Mexico (1846–1848), which Emerson and many New Englanders vehemently protested as a veiled means of expanding the slave territory. Crockett, however, remained in Emerson's imagination not a jingo but a figure of democratic integrity, a man with a gift for transforming experience into forceful metaphor (*TN*, 1:56). He had also become an American martyr. Decades later Emerson *would* welcome armed conflict in a just cause, supporting the Civil War as a war of liberation, the only means of eradicating the abomination of slavery. But the carnage put his ideals to the test. In his Journal WAR (1862) he copied Crockett's motto as a reaffirmation of principle: "Be sure you are right, then go ahead" (*JMN*, 15:183). In selectively using Crockett as man of nature, man of true words, and man of action, Emerson, in representatively "American" fashion, had both absorbed and had a hand in shaping our frontier myth.

In Emerson's "Power," from *The Conduct of Life* (1860), the essay that so disturbed Giamatti, Crockett is implicit in the figure of the Western politician, "half orator, half assassin," who epitomizes American energy, dependent as it is upon "natural forces," an energy that, for all its untidiness, is preferable to the stultified refinement of English culture. Certainly no *self*-portrait is Emerson's appreciative sketch of the "savage" man of nature:

> Men of this surcharge of arterial blood cannot live on nuts, herb-tea, and elegies; cannot read novels and play whist; cannot satisfy all their wants at the Thursday Lecture or the Boston Athenaeum. They pine for adventure, and must go to Pike's Peak; had rather die by the hatchet of a Pawnee than sit all day and every day at a counting-room desk. They are made for war, for the sea, for mining, hunting and clearing; for hair-breadth adventures, huge risks and the joy of eventful living. (*W*, 6:68)

These robust qualities are at odds not only with the urban, sophisticated, mercantile life of midcentury Boston but also with the somewhat anemic religious, philosophical, educational, and reform (note the allusion to vegetarianism) elements that Emerson often criticized in Transcendentalism itself.

But if Emerson valued Crockett for his "natural" grasp of language, and the frontiersman as an antidote to the decadence of civilization, he did not blindly romanticize the "savage" aspects of American life, and nowhere is this more evident than in his critique of American politics. "The backwoodsman," wrote Frederick Jackson Turner, "was intolerant of men who split hairs, or scrupled over the method of reaching the right," fostering "the unchecked development of the individual" and a political climate that, in the 1828 election, had found a representative hero in Andrew Jackson. Emerson was no more an advocate of what Turner called "elaborate governmental institutions" than the Jacksonians (nor, for that matter, of elaborate theological, artistic, or intellectual institutions).[47] But he despised Jackson for releasing the very "unchecked" individualism that Turner would later diagnose. It was one thing for the artist to use "savage," "natural forces" as emblems of "human life," but quite another to embody—ironically, indeed, to institutionalize—these traits in a political movement, whereby the power of creative energy would be perverted into the crudeness and corruptions of merely political power. Jackson, whose presidency (1829–1837) spanned the crucial years from Emerson's ordination at Second Church to the publication of *Nature* and the preparation of the lecture "The Individual," represented all that Emerson abhorred in cultural and political life. Surveying history for the essential "Man" in late 1836, Emerson was appalled at the present spectacle: "[W]hen I look for the soul, shall I find a Jackson Caucus?" (*JMN*, 5:265). Jacksonian democracy shares certain key tenets with Transcendentalism. Both exalted the common man, criticized the gross materialism of new wealth, and favored limited government. But Jackson cultivated the spoils system in politics; opposed the national bank; introduced a leveling in American political life that failed, for the most part, to extend to disenfranchised minorities; promoted expansionism at the expense of Native Americans; and actively opposed abolitionism. Emerson saw the hypocrisies of Jacksonian democracy, resented the mediocrity it fostered in American life, and insisted that *his* vision gave due credit to the dignity and decency of the common man: "Do not charge me with egotism & presumption. I see with awe the attributes of the farmers & villagers whom you despise" (*JMN*, 5:493).

The essay "Power"—Giamatti's proof text and the source of Emerson's celebration of the frontiersman—must be placed in the context, moreover, of other essays in *The Conduct of Life*. Emerson's essays, like his sentences and paragraphs, play against each other and are cited separately at risk of great distortion of his vision. Briefly, the essay "Culture" also values Power but cautions against "a narrower selfism" and the "goitre of egotism" (*W*, 6:133, 134). The essay "Worship" notes that "[w]e live in a *transition period*" where genuine worship seems lost (207); but this plays against his assertion in "Power" that "[e]verything good in nature and the world is in that *moment of transition*" (emphases added [71])—indeed, since "Self-Reliance," *transition* for

Emerson had meant fluid moments of possibility, circumstances from which heroic and virtuous action may emerge. "Worship" refuses to base the sublime moral sense on any anemic religiosity. To the contrary, Emerson allows that "[e]ven the fury of material activity has some results friendly to moral health. The energetic action of the times develops individualism, and the religious appear isolated. I esteem this a step in the right direction." He goes on to suggest that "[t]he cure for false theology is mother-wit. Forget your books and traditions, and obey your moral perceptions at this hour" (214). Each of these essays in its own way reasserts the buoyant idealism of his great essays of the 1830s; read in the mutual oscillation that these essays demand, each affirms the dignity of both material and spiritual activity when they are charged with power and character founded on a person's "central solitude" (241).

Any lingering suspicion that Emerson's notion of power is a call for a Superman in the economic, political, or military arena must be dispelled by his masterful portrait of Napoleon in *Representative Men*. Napoleon, although he had died in exile in 1821, still captured the world's imagination, even in the United States. Emerson's sketch, first presented as a lecture in January 1846 and for years a popular favorite from his lyceum repertoire, evokes Napoleon's charisma even as it demolishes his monstrous, destructive egotism. Napoleon was "the incarnate Democrat," the "representative" of the middle class, "thoroughly modern" in his "delight in the use of means," a "strong and ready actor, who took Occasion by the beard, and showed us how much may be accomplished by the mere force of such virtues as all men possess in less degrees" (*CW*, 4:130, 133, 141). In one sense "Napoleon is France . . . Napoleon is Europe" (129). But in outlining his magnetic appeal, Emerson is shrewdly aware that, in his embodiment of restless marketplace values, Napoleon is also the United States: "Paris and London and New York, the spirit of commerce, of money, and material power, were . . . to have their prophet, and Bonaparte was qualified and sent" (130). In a stunning shift of focus, Emerson declares that, in Napoleon's releasing of pent-up forces, "feudal France, was changed into a young Ohio or New York," a shift that implicates the American audience in Napoleon's vices (139). For Emerson proceeds to pull the rug from under Napoleon's dazzling charm and achievements: "Bonaparte was singularly destitute of generous sentiments"; he was "egotistic, and monopolizing," "a boundless liar," "intensely selfish," and "without conscience" (145, 146, 147). His admirers "found that his absorbing egotism was deadly to all other men" (147). In the end, Napoleon's amoral materialism is symptomatic of the great modern sickness: "As long as our civilization is essentially one of property, of fences, of exclusiveness, it will be mocked by delusions. . . . Only that good profits, which we can taste with all doors open, and which serves all men" (148).[48]

The aggressive and predatory qualities of the "self-made" man in politics and commerce, then, were always central concerns in Emerson's commentary. He sought to capture instead a sense of a more enduring individualism founded on reflection, principle, and ethical action. With other American writers, he also detected a polar opposite—and in some ways darker—threat lurking within nineteenth-century individualism: the psychological and social (and hence moral) isolation of self-reliance. Emerson's worry on this score was both personal and social. It was personal because, having resigned his pulpit in 1832, he felt compelled to define, in a competitive, career-driven society, a "vocation" for himself as "thinker," lecturer, and writer. As Henry Nash Smith observed decades ago, this vocational crisis underlies Emerson's attempt in "The American Scholar" to wed thinking and action—indeed, to define thinking itself as dynamic action.[49] And Emerson's worry was social because he observed that the young adults of his own generation seemed unmoored by the relentless competition and materialism of the age. One strain in Emerson criticism considers *self-reliance* an elitist product of the Federalist Boston in which he had been raised, a kind of snooty protective shell against the unsavory hurly-burly of the rising democracy. David Leverenz has argued that the market economy created great anxiety among young men and that the literary stance of "self-reliance" really reflects a "fear of humiliation," that it is a defense mechanism carrying a "heavy interior price."[50] Emerson, too, was acutely aware that the most idealistic were, for all their passion and principles, without direction, and he ascribes this flaw most bluntly to those young people popularly called Transcendentalists, a stance showing extraordinary self-awareness given his widespread identification as the leader of that "party."[51]

Generations of college students have been taught that American literature is founded on a great rift between the irrepressible, self-reliant optimism of Emerson and the brooding, haunted, neo-Calvinist meditations of Hawthorne and Melville on the impenetrability of nature and the inevitable corruption of the human psyche. We tend to forget that their fictional "quarrel" with Emerson is grounded in large part on their respect for his integrity. Hawthorne gently satirized the devotees who flocked to be near Emerson, stating that he himself "sought nothing from him as a philosopher," but he admitted the personal appeal of one "so quiet, so simple, so without pretension." And Melville, Merton Sealts reminds us, once thought Emerson "a great man."[52] Emerson, moreover, was no fool who could not conceive of evil. True, he characteristically sees evil as limitation or as social injustice rather than as a literal cosmic fact. But Emerson, too, was above all a keen observer of character who, as often as he celebrated our potential, chronicled our failures and self-deceptions. In what amounts to countercultural analyses of the dangers of the isolated Self, Hawthorne and Melville dissected the progressivist, optimistic ideals of their age, anticipating by well over a century Bellah's critique of the "socially unsituated self." In *The Blithedale Romance* (1852), Zenobia, who has been deluded by her unrequited love for Hollingsworth, has a kind of epiphany, albeit mingled with anger and self-pity. She suddenly sees that his treatment of the other Blithedale utopians and his single-minded pursuit of prison reform are not altruistic, and she charges him with being "[a] cold, heartless, self-beginning and self-ending piece of mechanism! . . . It is all self! . . . Self, self, self! . . . You are a better masquerader than the witches and gypsies yonder; for your disguise is a self-deception."[53] Melville's Ahab, despite the grandeur of his titanic defiance of the universe, is American literature's most tragic isolated Self, his obsession with an idea paralleled by his withdrawal from the human community. But Hawthorne and Melville were anticipated by a decade by Emerson's essay "Intellect," with its own classic analysis of monomania:

> Truth is our element of life, yet if a man fasten his attention on a single aspect of truth, and apply himself to that alone for a long time, the truth becomes distorted and not itself, but falsehood. . . . How wearisome the grammarian, the phrenologist, the political or religious fanatic, or indeed any possessed mortal, whose balance is lost by the exaggeration of a single topic. It is incipient insanity. Every thought is a prison also. (*CW*, 2:200–201)

A central strain of American thought since the earliest years has worried about the excesses of individualism, from John Cotton's concern that "liberty" not destroy the Massachusetts Bay Colony's fragile ecclesiastical and political fabric, to James Madison's worry that "absolute democracy" meant strife and "faction." This additional irony of democracy informed Emerson's disgust with Jacksonian politics. But his more fundamental concern was with the threat of isolated individualism, an awareness felt all the more keenly because he had often been charged himself, since the "Divinity School Address" (1838), with infidelity and antinomianism. Antinomianism, an old heresy that asserted that God's "Elect" are immune from moral law, had implied since the 1630s in New England the fear of spiritual, ecclesiastical, and social anarchy. Because of their anti-Lockean emphasis on intuition and their criticism of institutional authority in the name of the "higher law," Transcendentalists like Emerson were subject to charges of being the new antinomians—a charge Emerson notes in both "The Transcendentalist" (*CW*, 1:204) and "Self-Reliance."[54] Emerson took pains to show that true self-reliance, being reliance on a higher power, is cause not for arrogance but for humility. Like all great moralists, he was convinced that we are free, but free only to do right. As he wrote in "Self-Reliance," "If any one imagines that this law [self-reliance] is lax, let him keep its commandment one day" (*CW*, 2:42). In this light, his critiques of monomania, corrupt power, and antinomianism constitute not a blind assertion of the autonomous self's prerogatives but a major phase in America's long-standing wariness of the un-moored self.

For Emerson, then, genuine individualism was not narcissism, monomania, or isolation. Indeed, it was the *answer* to these diseases of the self as well as the remedy for the "existing evils" of institutional and social life. As he affirmed in "New England Reformers" in 1844, for all the reformist turmoil of the 1830s and 1840s, "in each of these movements emerged a good result, a tendency to the adoption of simpler methods, and an assertion of the sufficiency of the private man." Group reform, in turn, had its limits, for however "excellent" a protest might have been "when it was done the first time, . . . of course, [it] loses all value when it is copied." He was encouraged, however, that New England had witnessed "a steady tendency of the thoughtful and virtuous to a deeper belief and reliance on spiritual facts" (*CW*, 3:150–51).

One final great irony of Emersonian individualism needs to be mentioned. Even as Emerson is still often invoked to endorse national mission or personal aggrandizement, late-twentieth-century psychology and literary theory have announced the *disappearance* of the self as a meaningful, knowable entity. The nineteenth century's faculty psychology, we are now told, was naive in positing a stable center of knowledge, insight, and growth. The Romantic (and Transcendentalist) Self is now seen as simply another version of the now discredited Judeo-Christian Soul. Personality is diagnosed as a bundle of volatile moods and emotions endlessly stirred in a soup of conflicting perceptions, experiences, and impulses. The notion even of authorship has been questioned. Only the text matters, we have been told; the "author" is a mere fiction, the product of accumulated cultural forces, a mere game of words.

Now Emersonian self-reliance is, in a sense, to blame for this development. The nightmare image that opens the essay "Experience"—of waking on a "stair" whose base and destination are obscured—is calculated to disorient. "Sleep lingers all our lifetime about our eyes. . . . All things swim and glimmer" (*CW*, 3:27). Emerson's more buoyant declaration in "Circles" is also invoked as evidence of his modernism: "I unsettle all things.

No facts are to me sacred; none are profane; I simply experiment, an endless seeker, with no Past at my back" (*CW*, 2:188). Even in these skeptical, unsettling essays, however, Emerson celebrates small victories and provisional insights. "Experience" insists on no transcendence *above* the world of phenomenon and perception: "We live amid surfaces, and the true art of life is to skate well on them" (*CW*, 3:35); and "If I have described life as a flux of moods, I must now add, that there is that in us which changes not, and which ranks all sensations and states of mind" (42). Even as Emerson expressed the flawed, fragmentary nature of perception that thwarts permanent insight and knowledge, he held to his belief in the abiding centrality of character and the reality of self. In "Circles," even as the "flying Perfect" evades final codification, final meaning, the quest is inherently valuable: "[T]his incessant movement and progression, which all things partake, could never become sensible to us, but by contrast to some principle of fixture or stability in the soul" (*CW*, 2:179, 188).

And so Emerson's vision of individualism unsettles even his unsettlers. He was challenged, sometimes discouraged, by the "lords of life" that threatened to derail the "self" by baffling understanding, perception, consciousness itself. His "optimism" was a hard-earned faith forged against the backdrop of early illness, personal loss, and doubt. Indeed, these stubborn facts are often the starting point of his essays, whose charged prose requires the reader, too, to *earn* hope and genuine self-reliance.[55] He did not succumb to the nihilism and sophism that marks so much late-twentieth-century criticism. He remained a product of a democratic, classical, Judeo-Christian tradition who honed his views of character on mysticism, Stoicism, and moral philosophy. He accepted the challenge of flux implicit in each of these traditions, confronting head-on the psychic and social destabilization that were intensified by the gross materialism of his age and the disruptive insights of modern science. But he remained an advocate of human dignity founded on the centrality of character. His enduring appeal is not that he endorsed certain ideologies but that he never lost faith in the potential of the individual, the potential not to achieve final truths or successes—and surely not to dominate others—but to grow continually. Emerson explores the many moods, states, and dimensions of self: the glories of unfettered horizons, the despair of loneliness, the terror of alienation and disorientation, the obligation of ethical treatment of others, the existential imperative to create meaning, the need for continual self-culture. He accepts, even requires, a large measure of equivocalness, of flawed vision, of paradox—a stance that balks those who want either to vilify or to worship him. Not bland self-confidence or arrogant self-assertion but openness and courage are the hallmarks of Emersonian individualism. And these are the qualities that for generations have made Emerson a representative, modern American and the great teacher of self-reliance.

NOTES

1. THE WRITINGS OF HENRY D. THOREAU, *Journal Volume 2: 1842–1848*, ed. Robert Sattelmeyer (Princeton, N.J.: Princeton University Press, 1984), p. 224.

2. Edgar Lee Masters, *The Living Thoughts of Emerson* (London: Cassell and Company, 1947), p. 2. On Emerson's creative "provocation" of others, see Merton M. Sealts, Jr., "Emerson as Teacher," in *Emerson Centenary Essays*, ed. Joel Myerson (Carbondale: Southern Illinois University Press, 1982), pp. 180–90; reprinted in Sealts, *Beyond the Classroom: Essays on American Authors* (Columbia: University of Missouri Press, 1996), pp. 3–14.

3. Interview, 13 August 1990, Concord, Mass. See my "Don Henley, Walden Woods, and Emerson," *Emerson Society Papers* 1 (Fall 1990): 4.

4. Lance Morrow, "The Bishop of Our Possibilities," *Time*, 10 May 1982, p. 124. Christopher Newfield has recently made the case that Emersonian individualism is based on deep "contradictions" that mark "a very significant shift in the history of U.S. liberalism from a democratic toward a corporate kind of liberalism. It does so by introducing submission at the center of an extravagant American freedom"; see *The Emerson Effect: Individualism and Submission in America* (Chicago: University of Chicago Press, 1996), pp. 6, 10.

5. F. O. Matthiessen, *American Renaissance: Art and Expression in the Age of Emerson and Whitman* (New York: Oxford University Press, 1941), p. 368. On John D. Rockefeller's appropriation of self-

reliance in the industrial arena, see Howard Horwitz, "Transcendent Agency: Emerson, the Standard Trust, and the Virtues of Decorporation," in *By the Law of Nature: Form and Value in Nineteenth-Century America* (New York: Oxford University Press, 1991), pp. 171–91.

6. Henry B. Parkes, "Emerson" (1941); reprinted in *Emerson: A Collection of Critical Essays,* ed. Milton R. Konvitz and Stephen E. Whicher (Englewood Cliffs, N.J.: Prentice-Hall, 1962), p. 128.

7. Allen Tate, *Reactionary Essays on Poetry and Ideas* (New York: Scribner's, 1936), p. 7.

8. Clarence Gohdes observed this with respect to Europe in "An American Author as Democrat," in *Literary Romanticism in America,* ed. William L. Andrews (Baton Rouge: Louisiana State University Press, 1981), p. 11.

9. John Lydenberg, review of *Ralph Waldo Emerson: Portrait of a Balanced Soul,* by Edward Wagenknecht, and *The Power and Form of Emerson's Thought,* by Jeffrey L. Duncan, *American Literature* 47 (March 1975): 122.

10. See also *EL,* 3:187. In his 1841 lecture "The Conservative," Emerson observed that from the point of view of the "reformer," one who seeks "comfort . . . take[s] sides with the establishment" (*CW,* 1:195). Karl Keller's take on Emerson as a resister of the state is found in "Emerson and the Anti-imperialist Self," *American Transcendental Quarterly,* no. 18 (Spring 1973): 23–29.

11. See H. L. Kleinfield, "The Structure of Emerson's Death," *Bulletin of the New York Public Library* 65 (January 1961): 47–64; reprinted in *Ralph Waldo Emerson: A Profile,* ed. Carl Bode (New York: Hill and Wang, 1969), pp. 175–99.

12. Len Gougeon, *Virtue's Hero: Emerson, Antislavery, and Reform* (Athens: University of Georgia Press, 1990), p. 342.

13. Jerome Lawrence and Robert E. Lee, *The Night Thoreau Spent in Jail* (New York: Hill and Wang, 1970), p. 67. For a more plausible version of this dramatic rendition, see Walter Harding, *The Days of Henry Thoreau* (New York: Knopf, 1970), pp. 205–6.

14. See F. DeWolfe Miller, *Christopher Pearse Cranch and His Caricatures of New England Transcendentalism* (Cambridge: Harvard University Press, 1951), plate 3 following p. 36.

15. B. L. Packer describes Emerson's style: "The ambiguities, lacunae, paradoxes, and understatements with which Emerson is so generous turn the sentences of his essays into charged terminals

that the reader must take the risk of connecting" (*Emerson's Fall: A New Interpretation of the Major Essays* [New York: Continuum, 1982], p. 6).

16. Oliver Wendell Holmes, "The New Portfolio," in *A Mortal Antipathy*, vol. 7 of *The Writings of Oliver Wendell Holmes*, 14 vols. (Boston: Houghton, Mifflin, 1900), p. 18. Martin Bickman nicely states what we miss when we merely paraphrase Emerson or settle for generalizations about his lively prose: "A central paradox is that we cannot simply render or present an Emerson of process as a substitution for an Emerson of wisdom and statement. We must show him—or catch him—engaged in his dynamic constructions of meaning through our own active and dynamic constructions, in our making of it happen" ("'The Turn of His Sentences': The Open Form of Emerson's *Essays: First Series*," *ESQ: A Journal of the American Renaissance* 34 (1st and 2nd Quarter 1988): 73.

17. A. Bartlett Giamatti, *The University and the Public Interest* (New York: Atheneum, 1981), pp. 172, 174, 176.

18. Wilson Carey McWilliams, *The Idea of Fraternity in America* (Berkeley: University of California Press, 1973), pp. 285, 286. A classic essay on Emerson and friendship is Carl F. Strauch, "Hatred's Swift Repulsions: Emerson, Margaret Fuller, and Others," *Studies in Romanticism* 7 (Winter 1968): 65–103.

19. Quentin Anderson, *The Imperial Self: An Essay in American Literary and Cultural History* (New York: Knopf, 1971), p. 54. Keller's article ("Emerson and the Anti-imperialist Self") is in large part a rebuttal of Anderson. Anderson extends his treatment of the "isolation" he finds embodied in Emerson in *Making Americans: An Essay on Individualism and Money* (New York: Harcourt Brace Jovanovich, 1992), p. 154.

20. Robert N. Bellah et al., *Habits of the Heart: Individualism and Commitment in American Life* (New York: Harper and Row, 1985), pp. 55, 65.

21. Robert D. Richardson, Jr., *Emerson: The Mind on Fire* (Berkeley: University of California Press, 1995), p. 45.

22. On Emerson and Unitarianism, see David M. Robinson's *Apostle of Culture: Emerson as Preacher and Lecturer* (Philadelphia: University of Pennsylvania Press, 1982), and his "Introductory Historical Essay," *CS*, 1:1–32, as well as his essay in this volume.

23. Phyllis Cole, *Mary Moody Emerson and the Origins of Transcen-*

dentalism: A Family History (New York: Oxford University Press, 1998). Cole expanded on this collaboration in "Emersonian Individualism as a Two-Person Project" (paper presented at the Emerson Society panel "Emerson: Influences and Resonances," Thoreau Society Annual Gathering, Concord, Mass., 10 July 1998). We should read the essay "Self-Reliance," she concluded, "as an internal conversation rather than a flat pronouncement."

24. Richardson's *The Mind on Fire* is a model of clarity in presenting the often obscure and complex reading and ideas that ignited Emerson's imagination. For concise definitions and explanations of the sources, nature, and influences of American Transcendentalism, see also *Biographical Dictionary of Transcendentalism*, ed. Wesley T. Mott (Westport, Conn.: Greenwood Press, 1996); and *Encyclopedia of Transcendentalism*, ed. Wesley T. Mott (Westport, Conn.: Greenwood Press, 1996).

25. See Gustaaf Van Cromphout's fine monograph *Emerson's Modernity and the Example of Goethe* (Columbia: University of Missouri Press, 1990).

26. David Robinson has movingly shown how Thoreau's famous encounter with Mount Ktaadn in *The Maine Woods* takes up and extends the question Emerson asks at the beginning of the essay "Experience": "Where do we find ourselves?" (*CW*, 3:27); see "Thoreau's 'Ktaadn' and the Quest for Experience," in *Emersonian Circles: Essays in Honor of Joel Myerson*, ed. Wesley T. Mott and Robert E. Burkholder (Rochester, N.Y.: University of Rochester Press, 1997), pp. 207–23.

27. *An American Dictionary of the English Language*, ed. Noah Webster, 2 vols. (New York: S. Converse, 1828).

28. Daniel Walker Howe, *Making the American Self: Jonathan Edwards to Abraham Lincoln* (Cambridge: Harvard University Press, 1997), p. 5. Howe's important study rehabilitates the often discredited tradition of faculty psychology, defining *individualism* as "the belief that ordinary men and women have a dignity and value in their own right, and that they are sufficiently trustworthy to be allowed a measure of autonomy in their lives" (p. 9).

29. On Emerson's concept of the God within, see Wesley T. Mott, *"The Strains of Eloquence": Emerson and His Sermons* (University Park: Pennsylvania State University Press, 1989), pp. 53–78.

30. Van Cromphout discusses Emerson's shift from a Plutarchan

to a Goethean approach to biography in *Emerson's Modernity and the Example of Goethe*, pp. 98–115. On Emerson and biography see also Merton M. Sealts, Jr., *Emerson on the Scholar* (Columbia: University of Missouri Press, 1992), esp. pp. 46–59, 155–72; and Ronald A. Bosco, "The 'Somewhat Spheral and Infinite' in Every Man: Emerson's Theory of Biography," *Emersonian Circles*, pp. 67–103. In his biographical lectures of the 1830s and in *Representative Men*, Emerson came to place "great men" in historical and cultural context and to judge their "representative" failures as well as achievements.

31. Jonathan Bishop observed that "[t]he entire Soul-Nature relation can only become *emotionally* interesting when Soul seems to mean Self and Self means Me. We cannot take the impersonality of spirit seriously until it becomes a personal event"; Emerson, he suggested, is "fully aware of this paradox, not to say pleased with it" (*Emerson on the Soul* [Cambridge: Harvard University Press, 1964], p. 93).

32. Koenraad W. Swart, "'Individualism' in the Mid-nineteenth Century (1826–1860)," *Journal of the History of Ideas* 23 (January–March 1962): 77–90; quotation on p. 77.

33. Matthiessen, *American Renaissance*, p. 4. Important discussions of Emersonian individualism include Yehoshua Arieli, *Individualism and Nationalism in American Ideology* (Cambridge: Harvard University Press, 1964); Harold Bloom, "Emerson: Power at the Crossing," in *Ralph Waldo Emerson: A Collection of Critical Essays*, ed. Lawrence Buell (Englewood Cliffs, N.J.: Prentice Hall, 1993), pp. 148–58; also in Buell's collection, Sacvan Bercovitch, "Emerson, Individualism, and the Ambiguities of Dissent," pp. 101–29; and Charles E. Mitchell, *Individualism and Its Discontents: Appropriations of Emerson, 1880–1950* (Amherst: University of Massachusetts Press, 1997).

34. Swart, "'Individualism,'" pp. 78–81, 83.

35. Lawrence Buell, *Literary Transcendentalism: Style and Vision in the American Renaissance* (Ithaca, N.Y.: Cornell University Press, 1973), p. 272.

36. Alexis de Tocqueville, *Democracy in America*, ed. J. P. Mayer and Max Lerner, trans. George Lawrence (1835, 1840; New York: Harper and Row, 1966), p. 477. For useful commentaries, see Abraham S. Eisenstadt, ed., *Reconsidering Tocqueville's* Democracy in America (New Brunswick, N.J.: Rutgers University Press, 1988), esp. Seymour Drescher, "More Than America: Comparison and Synthe-

sis in *Democracy in America*," pp. 77–93, and Arthur Schlesinger, Jr., "Individualism and Apathy in Tocqueville's *Democracy*," pp. 94–109.

37. John Dewey remains the greatest critic of the paradoxes and ironies of American life—the frequent discrepancies between our myths of individualism and its realities—who at the same time champions Emerson for his perceptive and dynamic contribution to the national character. See especially *Individualism Old and New* (New York: Minton, Balch and Company, 1930) and *Philosophy and Civilization* (New York: Minton, Balch and Company, 1931). In a similar vein, Harold Bloom insists, "Individualism, whatever damages its American ruggedness continues to inflict on our politics and social economy, is more than ever the only hope for our imaginative lives" ("Emerson: Power at the Crossing," p. 157).

38. The first use of the term *self-reliance* noted by the *Oxford English Dictionary* is in Harriet Martineau's *Society in America* (1837). Swart notes that Emerson used the term *individualism* favorably in his 1846 journal as the Brook Farm community was collapsing (p. 86). But see also his 1842 Journal N (*JMN*, 8:251) and the 1844 lecture "New England Reformers" (*CW*, 3:157).

39. Sealts, *Emerson on the Scholar*, p. 244. David Lyttle offers two helpful discussions of Emerson's sense of the individual and subjectivity: "Emerson's Transcendental Individualism," *Concord Saunterer*, n.s., 3 (Fall 1995): 89–103; and "'The World Is a Divine Dream': Emerson's Subjective Idealism," *Concord Saunterer*, n.s., 5 (Fall 1997): 93–110.

40. See William Charvat, "American Romanticism and the Depression of 1837," *Science and Society* 2 (Winter 1937): 67–82; reprinted in *The Profession of Authorship in America, 1800–1870*, ed. Matthew J. Bruccoli (Columbus: Ohio State University Press, 1968), pp. 49–67. Packer suggests that Emerson's "American Scholar" is actually creatively liberated by the "squalor" of the business world (*Emerson's Fall*, p. 95).

41. *A Narrative of the Life of David Crockett, of the State of Tennessee, Written by Himself* (Boston: Allen and Ticknor, 1834; Philadelphia: E. L. Carey and A. Hart, 1834).

42. Ernest Marchand, "Emerson and the Frontier," *American Literature* 3 (May 1931): 174.

43. Frederick Jackson Turner, *The Frontier in American History*, foreword by Ray Allen Billington (1920; New York: Holt, Rinehart and Winston, 1962), pp. 30, 32.

44. William Bradford, *Of Plymouth Plantation, 1620–1647*, ed. Samuel Eliot Morison (New York: Modern Library, 1952), p. 62; J. Hector St. John de Crèvecoeur, *Letters from an American Farmer* (London: Davies and Davis, 1782).

45. Albert J. von Frank, "'Build Therefore Your Own World': Emerson's Constructions of the 'Intimate Sphere,'" *Emersonian Circles*, p. 9.

46. On Emerson's fondness for broad language and humor and his attraction to Crockett, see also V. L. O. Chittick, "Emerson's 'Frolic Health,'" *New England Quarterly* 30 (June 1957): 209–34, and David S. Reynolds, *Beneath the American Renaissance: The Subversive Imagination in the Age of Emerson and Melville* (New York: Knopf, 1988), pp. 448–54, 487–97.

47. Turner, *The Frontier in American History*, p. 254.

48. In "Nominalist and Realist," Emerson offers a slightly more playful but no less cogent critique of hero worship: "All our poets, heroes, and saints, fail utterly in some one or in many parts to satisfy our idea. . . . there are no such men as we fable; no Jesus, nor Pericles, nor Caesar, nor Angelo, nor Washington, such as we have made. We consecrate a great deal of nonsense, because it was allowed by great men. There is none without his foible. Must I believe that if an angel should come to chaunt the chorus of the moral law, he would eat too much gingerbread, or take liberties with private letters, or do some precious atrocity? It is bad enough, that our geniuses cannot do anything useful, but it is worse that no man is fit for society, who has fine traits. . . . [each] want[s] either love or self-reliance" (*CW*, 3:134).

49. See Henry Nash Smith's seminal essay "Emerson's Problem of Vocation: A Note on 'The American Scholar,'" *New England Quarterly* 12 (March 1939): 52–67; and Sealts's definitive *Emerson on the Scholar*.

50. David Leverenz, *Manhood and the American Renaissance* (Ithaca, N.Y.: Cornell University Press, 1989), pp. 72, 74. Leverenz considers Emerson a victim of the American cult of manhood.

51. See "The Transcendentalist." Packer argues that even "[t]he term 'self-reliance' implies dualism, disunion, a poor frightened individual attempting to rely *on* that Aboriginal Self presumed to be within. . . . When the soul is really present, Emerson insists, all *sense* of dualism ceases" (*Emerson's Fall*, p. 145).

52. Nathaniel Hawthorne, "The Old Manse," in *Mosses from an Old Manse*, vol. 10 of *The Centenary Edition of the Works of Nathaniel Hawthorne* (Columbus: Ohio State University Press, 1974), p. 31; Merton M. Sealts, Jr., *Pursuing Melville, 1940–1980* (Madison: University of Wisconsin Press, 1982), p. 251.

53. Nathaniel Hawthorne, *The Blithedale Romance*, vol. 3 of *The Centenary Edition of the Works of Nathaniel Hawthorne* (Columbus: Ohio State University Press, 1964), p. 218.

54. See Wesley T. Mott, "Emerson and Antinomianism: The Legacy of the Sermons," chap. 6 in *"The Strains of Eloquence."* For a broader treatment of antinomianism in American culture, see Amy Schrager Lang, *Prophetic Woman: Anne Hutchinson and the Problem of Dissent in the Literature of New England* (Berkeley: University of California Press, 1987).

55. See Gertrude Reif Hughes, *Emerson's Demanding Optimism* (Baton Rouge: Louisiana State University Press, 1984).

Emerson, Nature, and Natural Science

William Rossi

> What mischief is in this art of Writing.
> . . . We sit down with intent to write
> truly & end with making a book that
> contains no thought of ours but
> merely the tune of the time.
>
> *(JMN*, 4:314–15, 19 August 1834)

Ralph Waldo Emerson lived through a time when the physical environment was extraordinarily transformed, no less than the broadly cultural forms through which his contemporaries conceived and experienced nature. The emergence of agricultural and industrial capitalism, and the rapid population growth they stimulated, dramatically changed both urban Boston and, eventually, rural Concord landscapes.[1] While these transformations are registered only obliquely in Emerson's writing about nature, their effect, if only in affording him a measure of physical comfort and reflective detachment, can hardly be overestimated. Indeed, the stance of detachment and the apparently abstract level on which Emerson engages nature have led recent commentators to devalue his writing, especially in comparison with the more empiricist rendering of nature perfected by his onetime

protégé, Henry Thoreau.[2] But, as for many of his contemporaries, for Emerson the physical presence of nature mattered less
than its putative meaning or the "higher" presence mediated
through the physical.

If this partly explains why Emerson *had* more of a nineteenth-
century audience than Thoreau did, including a substantial
British one, it also suggests both the necessity and something of
the difficulty of situating Emerson's "nature" historically. Perhaps no single term in Emerson's lexicon is more important for
understanding his multivalent achievement. Yet the sheer profusion and protean significance of "nature" for Emerson presents
the first obstacle to a critical yet sympathetic historical analysis of
it. This profusion is itself a measure of how deeply Emerson's
conception of nature informs his writing. As Eduardo Cadava
observes, "Like the weather, whose cyclical and repetitive character is joined always to its unpredictability and constant alteration,
his language works to trace the permanency of the infinite vari-
ability that makes nature nature."[3]

Second, for a self-consciously American writer such as Emerson, nature is by definition ahistorical: to move alone into nature is
to move outside of history and culture. Discounting to the point
of invisibility the presence of centuries-old native cultures
granted free play to a pastoral ideology in which American nature
appeared uncultivated in comparison with European, and thus
was made more readily the scene of individual encounters with
transhistorical truth and new visions of human possibility.[4]
"Here," as he puts it in *Essays: Second Series*, "no history, or church,
or state, is interpolated on the divine sky and the immortal year"
(*CW*, 3:100). But, as Cadava demonstrates, "Emerson's engagement with history and politics" is evident in the way nineteenth-
century political and social history is inscribed even in the meteo-
rological language he uses and, more important, in the way "his
words and sentences" also "work to engage already-changing historical and political relations," relations which Cadava explores by
measuring how "Emerson's language [of nature] works to revise
the [political] language he inherits."[5]

To situate Emerson's nature in history, this essay will take a
different but complementary approach. As Emerson was well

aware, in an era when post-Enlightenment science was rapidly becoming the principal interpretive authority of nature, a solitary experiential encounter with nature's "truth" also carried overtones of scientific discovery. Emerson's long-standing enthusiasm for science is well established; and, as Michael Branch has observed, his "enduring fascination with natural history, natural philosophy, or natural science" is evident enough in the titles of many of his works, from the early lecture "The Uses of Natural History" (1833) and his first book, *Nature*, to his unfinished major work, *The Natural History of Intellect* (1870s).[6] But while an abiding interest in contemporary science deeply informed Emerson's stance and vision, like the representations and explanations it produces, science, too, is necessarily embedded in history and culture. Consequently, just as the disciplinary definitions of natural knowledge changed from "natural history" to "natural science" in accord with the increasing professionalization and sophistication of science, so the meaning of "nature" as mediated by science also changed dramatically in the five decades of Emerson's career. Given the key role science played in the secularization of nature and of nineteenth-century society generally, then, tracing Emerson's nature(s) in relation to the shifting cultural status and definitions of natural knowledge as well as to the changing conceptions of nature stimulated by science will help us see more precisely how, despite Emerson's claims to the contrary, "history" is, after all, "interpolated on the divine sky and the immortal year" in the nature of his writing.

A Common Discourse of Nature

Emerson could represent himself as discovering and disseminating a knowledge of nature that complemented that of natural philosophers, or natural "scientists" (as they were first called in 1833), because he shared with them and with other Anglo-American contemporaries the broad cultural discourse of natural theology, a language of nature he had inherited (to borrow Cadava's terms) and through which he wrote contemporary relations to nature. Formally and narrowly defined, natural theology or "natural religion" seeks to establish a knowledge of God accessible to all rational human beings without recourse to supernatural revelation. As promoted in the modern era by seventeenth-century deists, a theology based on nature could ground the existence of God through evidence of the lawlike regularity of the natural world (the argument from design), thereby rendering belief both rational and universal and thus avoiding sectarian dispute. But if rationalists wished to dispense with revelation, orthodox divines in the later seventeenth and eighteenth centuries, most influentially Joseph Butler in *The Analogy of Religion, Natural and Revealed, to the Constitution and Course of Nature* (1736), used natural theology to complement revelation and thus deflect the threat of scientific materialism.

The single most popular and often-cited example of nineteenth-century natural theology is William Paley's *Natural Theology* (1802). Written in response to critiques of natural theology by Immanuel Kant and David Hume, Paley's book brought the teleological argument from design to bear on the minute consideration of apparently purposeful structural adaptations of organisms to their environments, such as the adaptive organization of the eye to the reception of light. To appeal to a growing urban audience and to supplement Butler's now traditional argument based on the analogy between moral laws and natural laws, Paley relied heavily on mechanical and industrial metaphors, drawing examples from contemporary natural history to argue that just as examining the carefully planned mechanisms of a watch leads one to infer a designer of that watch, so empirically studying intricate natural "mechanisms" leads one to infer a designer of nature. Moreover, judging from the "vast plurality of instances" in which "the design of the contrivance is *beneficial*" and even pleasurable to the animal or human being possessing it, Paley also inferred that the designer is benevolent, concluding, "It is a happy world after all."[7]

Paley's book has often been characterized as the sole, imperial instance of an unchanging genre, one given scientific credibility by the eight Bridgewater Treatises published in the 1830s, most of them written by prominent Oxbridge scientists commissioned explicitly to demonstrate the "Power, Wisdom, and Goodness of God, as manifested in the Creation."[8] Defined this way, nineteenth-century natural theology has been represented as an impediment to a scientific understanding of nature and, at the same time, as a stumbling block to vibrant belief, reducing the inward power of spiritual experience to a logical operation, "as if a philosophical truth like God, or freewill . . . were something deposited at the foot of an induction," in the words of one of its most trenchant nineteenth-century critics.[9] Until very recently, historians have thus tended uncritically to sympathize, on the one hand, with Darwin, who, in the process of turning Paley's conception of adaptation on its head, noted sharply that "[i]t is so easy to hide our ignorance under such expressions as the 'plan of creation,' 'unity of design,' &c., and to think that we give an explanation when we only restate a fact."[10] And, on the other hand, they have tended to agree equally with Coleridge, who expressed his disdain for "the *rational* Christian" and at the same time his "fear" of "the prevailing taste for Books of Natural Theology, Physico-theology, Demonstrations of God from Nature, Evidences of Christianity, &c. &c.," exclaiming, "*Evidences* of Christianity! I am weary of the Word. Make a man feel the *want* of it; rouse him, if you can, to the self-knowledge of his *need* for it; and you may safely trust it to its own Evidence."[11]

But if by 1851, when Emerson's friend Frederic Henry Hedge delivered the Dudleian Lecture on Natural Religion at Harvard, natural religion had become "irrelevant" and "empty" in American liberal Christianity, in large part because of Transcendentalists like Hedge and Emerson who had dissolved the distinction between natural and spiritual "evidence," outside the lecture hall—from orthodox pulpits, in periodicals and other print media, on the lyceum circuit, and in debates between scientific writers on such topics as the plurality of worlds—the "rage for design" had hardly "peaked."[12] Nor was the situation much different in Britain, where, as in America, the discourse of natural theology, "as an aspect of scientific culture, was particularly prominent and persistent." Even after the triumph of scientific naturalism led by Darwin, this discourse persisted on both sides of the Atlantic in the work of "middle-class popularizers of science," whose "audiences remained enthralled by the traditional, moral, aesthetic, teleological, and divine qualities of the natural world."[13]

As a cultural discourse of nature, natural theology was integral to the wider issue of what was called "man's place in nature." In the context of this debate, Paley's book "defined a way of looking at the world that was probably shared by the majority of his contemporaries," certainly the Protestant Christians among them, whose doctrinal differences could readily be accommodated within the ambiguity of this discourse. During the 1830s, when Emerson was redefining his vocation from that of Unitarian minister to lecturer and writer, preoccupation with the question of "man's place in nature," as evidenced in the widespread production of natural theology literature, amounted to "a major cultural event," according to one historian. Moreover, at a time when many naturalists were themselves clerics and the instability of science as an enterprise made public and ecclesiastical support for science crucial, natural theology provided a malleable discursive means "for connections between scientific and religious discourses to be made and remade rather than severed."[14] In maintaining these connections, the figure of Francis Bacon proved especially useful. Putting his own spin on the ancient book of nature topos, Bacon laid down the dictum in *The Advancement of Learning* (1605) that no "man can search too far, or be too well studied in the book of God's word, or the book of God's works, divinity or [natural] philosophy; but rather let men endeavour an endless progress, or proficience in both." Simultaneously separating and relating science and theology, Bacon's advice was quoted and alluded to endlessly by nineteenth-century writers and naturalists—as Darwin did in an epigraph to *On the Origin of Species* and as Emerson would—in support of interpretations of nature's text that ranged from literalist biblical geology to naturalistic evolutionary biology, from evangelical Christianity to pantheism.[15]

A good instance of the malleability of the discourse of natural theology was the shift away from the functionalist type of teleological explanation exemplified by Paley and some of the Bridgewater writers toward explaining biological phenomena in terms of a harmonious system of "secondary" (that is, natural) laws analogous to those discovered in the physical sciences. This was a significant transformation in the discourse both for nineteenth-century natural science and for understanding Emerson's writing of nature. In the late 1830s, naturalists began to describe themselves as "philosophical naturalists" to signify their interest "in discovering the *laws* of the living world" rather than being content "with the mere description of individual beings." And it was "precisely this search for laws or generalizations that, in the course of the nineteenth century, transformed the study of natural history into the science of biology." Yet despite their hostility to explicitly teleological explanation, "the laws, of whatever sort, that [naturalists] substituted for particular explanations in terms of purpose were themselves thought to be purposeful. Each law was supposed to play its part in carrying out the creator's grand design."[16] Thus, while the introduction of "natural law" has often been portrayed as a kind of bugle call to the final battle between the forces of science and religion in this period, that warfare model for understanding those relations is now seen as having concealed much more than it has revealed.[17] In fact, the discourse of this "new" natural theology accompanied the professionalization of biology and in many ways sustained scientific inquiry into the natural world in both epistemological and rhetorical terms.

This is not to deny the vigorous efforts during this period to employ science on behalf of "revelation," particularly in antebellum America, where biblical geology was especially strong, nor to overlook the presence of naturalists and radical intellectuals, already in the first half of the century, who conceived natural law in strictly material terms, an interpretation that very much concerned Emerson and that became more prevalent following the notorious publication of an early evolutionary tract, *Vestiges of the Natural History of Creation* in 1844.[18] It is rather to point up the importance, especially for a figure like Emerson, of the "common intellectual context" provided by the discourse of natural theology and the complex interpenetration of cultural interests it helped support. As a rhetorical resource employed for multiple audiences and multiple purposes—social, philosophical, aesthetic, ethical, political and religious—this discourse, though "common," was far from homogeneous. Nor was it without internal problematics. Especially following the publication of *Vestiges,* in the later 1840s and 1850s, the common context was fragmented both within religious culture, by denominational differences, and more broadly by the heavy burden that "religious apologists . . . placed on the sciences, which they were eventually unable to carry."[19] Again, although this discourse nourished relations between professional science and a generally educated public, from the beginning those relations were strained by the widening gap between an increasingly specialized science and its public.[20]

Moreover, at the heart of natural theology lay an ontological and epistemological problem that was only exacerbated by the increasing specialization and consequent fragmentation of natural knowledge, a problem that would become central to Emerson's philosophical and literary project, indeed to his vocation: articulating the relationship between what, in broad nineteenth-century terms, was called the "moral" and the physical spheres of creation. For "if design could only be perceived in the physical world, it would be difficult to maintain that the Creator of nature was also responsible for man's intellectual and spiritual character." The primary task of natural theology, then, was to demonstrate the unity of these two spheres, a difficult task given the way "Christian religious and moral values were invested in [a] Cartesian dualism of mind and matter" that assumed the superiority of the human mind (as the locus of free will and moral responsibility) over inert matter.[21] Ultimately this dichotomy was not resolved so much as abandoned, only to be reinscribed in the "fundamentally altered" structure of relations between science and the public in the 1870s and 1880s, once the secularization of nature was complete and the "radical distinction" enforced between experts "professionally concerned with the explication of secular nature and the general public with their moral concerns."[22] Even in this state of affairs, however, the discourse of natural theology proved its rhetorical resilience, and not only in the middle-class popularization of science. Reformulated in an "agnostic worship of nature," natural theology inspired the late-century promotion and practice of "the religion of science" by such well-established and visible professional naturalists as

Thomas Henry Huxley and John Tyndall. Ironically, a key source of their inspiration, mediating the transition from a religious to a scientific culture, was the natural supernaturalism of Thomas Carlyle and Ralph Waldo Emerson.[23]

From "Moral Science" to *Nature*

Referring to Emerson's reading of William Paley and others, Robert D. Richardson, Jr., observes that the design argument was "not what mattered most" to Emerson in this literature; he was "much more interested in the relationship between the natural world and the human mind than . . . in the natural world as proof of a designing deity."[24] But while this interest is certainly "a distinguishing mark of both American and German transcendentalism," it was also shared by many of Emerson's less radical Anglo-American contemporaries who likewise assumed that the two spheres of moral and physical creation were somehow closely related. Although it must seem paradoxical now, because of this assumption Emerson's initial approach to this problematic relationship, and the first step toward his radical formulation of "nature," began as an inquiry into moral philosophy. As in most antebellum liberal arts institutions, at Harvard College, from which he graduated in 1821, moral philosophy provided "the integrative, synthesizing" element in the curriculum. Within that curriculum the subject of natural theology played an essential role, complementing revelation as matter did spirit and thus helping to sustain the ontological and epistemological dualism on which Unitarian theology was based. But design was evident not only in "external" nature but also in the structure of mind itself. Indeed, as Daniel Walker Howe notes, Harvard moralists were actually more satisfied by "the argument for the existence of God from the design of the human mind" because, as Francis Bowen wrote, the evidence of consciousness was "even more direct, logical, and convincing" than the evidence of the material universe.[25]

As a student of moral philosophy at Harvard, Emerson had a keen interest in this dimension of the subject, what he described in his 1821 Bowdoin Prize Dissertation as efforts "to institute and methodize the science of morality."[26] And as a young minister six years later, he confessed "anxious to do more than doubt" the "rec[eive]d maxim that there are no discoveries in morals." "I desire to assert distinctly," he wrote, not only that there *are* "discoveries in morals" but also that the "science of morals does advance" (*JMN*, 3:60–61). The importance Emerson attaches to "discoveries" makes it clear that, like Bowen, he was guided by the belief that he was articulating universal elements of the mind's constitution. This notion of "moral science" was derived from the Scottish Common Sense realism that underpinned the Harvard curriculum in moral philosophy. But it has also been traced to the cultural and intellectual instability of "science," both the term and the enterprise, during this period. Part of the cultural work of professionalizing bodies like the British Association for the Advancement of Science (founded 1831) was to "make 'science' mean natural knowledge," when the word was still used and understood in the broad sense of *scientia*.[27] And while the cultural work of nascent institutions like the British Association was going forward, "the aims, method, and cultural implications of science" were the subjects of extensive public debate in the quarterlies and other periodicals on both sides of the Atlantic.[28] Thus, in the mid-1830s, Emerson could admire Coleridge as an "acute psychologist" and practitioner of "our profoundest Science" for his penetrating observations of mental activity construed as manifestations of the psyche or soul (*JMN*, 5:85–86). Indeed, Emerson sounds like an odd combination of clinical psychologist and moral philosopher when reflecting in his journal on dreams as one of the "keys by which we are to find out the secrets of our own nature." They are like "comparative anatomy" or "test objects"; "that must be a good theory of the Universe, that will explain these phenomena" (*JMN*, 3:321–22).

Before this time, however, Emerson had begun moving toward much stronger claims for revelation, resulting in a "shift in [his] concept of the very grounds of religious belief" and a dissatisfaction with the argument of Paley, who, for other Unitarians besides Emerson, "was deficient in enthusiasm."[29] This tendency was further fed by his reading in 1830 of Coleridge's *The*

Friend and *Aids to Reflection*, where, as we saw, Coleridge spurned the Paleyan mechanical model of design and accompanying "rational" evidence in favor of intuitive spiritual experience that would be "its own Evidence."[30] But Emerson's religious enthusiasm and piety also had sources closer to home, having long been nurtured by his aunt Mary Moody Emerson, whose own sensitivity to the beauty of nature and partiality to Joseph Butler's analogical argument for "the compatibility of moral and physical laws in the universe" stimulated Waldo's.[31] At bottom, he felt that while "arguments from design could prove the existence of God," they could not account for "God's providence," a limitation noted as well by other natural theologians and naturalists.[32] Yet even after Emerson's inquiry took him deeper into consciousness, intuitive experience, and ultimately philosophical idealism, he continued to refer to it in terms of "science."[33] Thus, as Wesley Mott suggests, in terms of the design argument, Emerson's conviction that "consciousness [provides] better evid[ence] than proof" ought not be construed as "rejecting science or denying the importance of reason" but rather as widening their domains.[34]

One of the last sermons Emerson preached before resigning his pulpit illustrates more precisely his mode of making the design argument at this time while also pointing toward his subsequent radical revision of it. While noting the popular association of science with skepticism, he argues instead that astronomy illustrates beautifully "the irresistible effect" of science "in modifying and enlarging the doctrines of theology" (*CS*, 4:156). Although nominally preaching on a text from *Acts*, the real text of this sermon is nature, to which he immediately draws the congregation's attention by enumerating a series of "useful reflextions" on the "remarkable spectacle" of a recent solar eclipse, the grandeur and beauty of which "makes a kindred impression upon all men." The first of these, the "feeling of joy" and "pride" in "the powers of the human intellect" that predicted the eclipse, is quickly subordinated to "a better reflexion": that "[t]his human mind is but a derived light from the source of wisdom as yonder sun is but a spark of his enkindling." Translating this metaphorical "reflection" explicitly into the problematic of natural theology, he concludes, "It is only the knowledge of God that unites this bright outward Creation of brute matter to the brighter inward Creation of intelligent mind," since "the God of nature and the God of the Bible are . . . the same."[35] As a Unitarian minister reading the book of nature, Emerson does not go as far as he would in a few years, when in *Nature* he indistinguishably "blends scientific objectivity and religious enthusiasm" through the natural symbol of light, "treating the 'inner light' of the radical Protestant tradition as though it behaved according to Newton's laws."[36] Here he is careful not to identify the human mind simultaneously with the "spark" of the sun and the "Infinite Mind." But within this liberal orthodoxy, the figure of the human knowledge of God as "a spark of his enkindling" shoots ahead not only to the symbolism of light in *Nature* but also farther to the opening paragraphs of "The Poet," suggesting how Emerson's philosophical and literary imagination is captivated by the act of knowing, which here is associated with "God's government," and prompts the conclusion that because "this enlargement of our religious views . . . comes to our minds inevitably by the progress of science, . . . it cannot be doubted that it was designed" (*CS*, 4:158).

Emerson's view of the capacity of science to enlarge the doctrines of theology in this sermon bears the distinct influence of John Herschel's *Preliminary Discourse on the Study of Natural Philosophy*, which he had read the preceding winter and which "quickened his already lively interest in science."[37] His excitement owed in large part to the way Herschel (son of the famous astronomer for whom Uranus was originally named) supported Emerson's own expanding conception of the mind's relationship to nature. Under the aegis of Bacon, an engraving of whose bust embellished the title page above the legend "Minister and Interpreter of Nature," Herschel explicated and updated Baconian induction for a popular audience, as "the process of considering a class of phenomena, or two associated classes of phenomena, as represented by a general *law*, or single [unifying] conception of the mind."[38] While he lays out particular methodological prescriptions, Herschel nonetheless presents science as the achievement of "man," a heroic, virtuous, and autonomous exploration of the laws of nature, an exploration both unified in all its "departments" and accessible to "any person of good ordinary understanding."[39] As Richardson notes, "Herschel's enthusiasm for science rivals and takes over the language of religious enthusiasm."[40] More specifically, Herschel emphasizes that "constituted [as] a speculative being," "man" does not contemplate "the objects around him . . . with a passive, indifferent gaze" but is actively drawn to explore "a system disposed with order and design," through which "he is led to the conception of a Power and an Intelligence superior to his own." Nor does this inquiry disclose only external "phenomena and relations." But "[a] world within him is thus opened to his intellectual view," affording an "insight" into "boundless realms beyond," an insight which "is in reality the source of all his power, the very fountain of his predominance over nature."[41]

Emerson was thus well primed to undertake a more intensive study of nature almost a year before he sailed for Europe and made his momentous visit to the Museum d'Histoire Naturelle in Paris, the center of French natural history, botany, and zoology. As we have seen, and as Herschel's "insight" exemplifies yet again, the beliefs (in the words of a critic Emerson quotes in his journal) that a "subtle and mysterious analogy . . . exists between the physical and moral world" was virtually a cliché in the intellectual culture of this period, a popular refrain, to borrow Emerson's metaphor from this chapter's epigraph, in "the tune of the time."[42] Herschel's *Discourse* not only echoed but also helped focus Emerson's inquiry, enlarging his sense of the unifying power of the mind to discern general "laws." That generalizing power was evident to Emerson in the Paris Museum, where it was reflected in the natural systems of classification used to order nature. More than this, though, as David Robinson notes, Emerson was impressed by "the physical evidence" of the "unity and dynamism of nature."[43] Standing in "the collection of comparative anatomy" before the arrangement of "a perfect series from the skeleton of the balaena [whale] . . . to the upright form and highly developed skull of the Caucasian race of man," amid the "bewildering variety of animated forms" and "the upheaving principle of life every where incipient," he felt that "there is an occult relation between the very worm, the crawling scorpions, and man." "I am moved by strange sympathies," he reported in his journal and a subsequent lecture: "I say continually 'I will be a naturalist'" (*JMN*, 4:199–200; *EL* 1:10).

How seriously Emerson entertained the vocation of professional naturalist is unclear. It did not take him long to realize he lacked the temperament for "counting stamens or filaments or teeth," craving instead the unifying insight that would "integrate the particulars," as extolled by Herschel (*JMN*, 4:287–291). The facts of "natural history [have] no value," he protested; "it is like a single sex. But marry [natural history] to human history & it is poetry" (*JMN*, 4:311). Emerson's impatience with the tedium of taxonomy should not obscure the fact that the "marriage" of the moral and physical spheres he wished to celebrate had been implicit in his inquiry from the beginning. Moreover, because of the way that "science" and "poetry" have so often been opposed to one another (and were seen by other Romantics to be opposed), Emerson's rejection of natural history as a vocation, and his desire to produce "poetry" from the marriage of natural history and human experience can conceal the extent to which his pursuit of "science" in the broad sense continued rather than abated.[44]

Part of the "mischief" in the "art" of Emerson's writing has in fact been to conceal the immediate cultural resources and resonances that enabled his project and thus unintentionally to obscure its scope and Emerson's own ambition. We get a glimpse of that ambition, and of how Emerson conceived the union of "moral science" and physical science, in a journal passage written in early November 1833, on the eve of his first natural history lecture and two months after he had begun to plan "my book about nature" on the ship back home from Europe (*JMN*, 4:237):

> Bacon said man is the minister & interpreter of nature: he is so in more respects than one. He is not only to explain the sense of each passage but the scope & argument of the whole book. He is to explain the attractiveness of all. . . . There is not a passion in the human soul[,] perhaps not a shade of thought but has its emblem in nature. And this does not become fainter this undersong, this concurrent text, with more

intimate knowledge of nature's laws[,] but the analogy is felt
to be deeper & more universal for every law that is revealed.

Let a man under the influence of strong passion go into
the field & see how readily every thought clothes itself with a
material garment. . . . Now I say is it not time something
was done to explain this attractiveness which the face of nature has for us renewed this 2d day of November? . . .

I wish to learn the language [of nature] not that I may
know a new set of nouns & verbs but that I may read the
great book which is written in that tongue. . . .

To an instructed eye the universe is transparent. The light
of higher laws than its own shines through it. (*JMN* 4:95–96)

As he had begun his inquiry ten years earlier, so here, in this
preview of *Nature,* Emerson begins from the standpoint of
"moral science": the assumption that the "attractiveness" of nature as experienced "in the fields" and "under the influence of a
strong passion" is a universal element of "man's" mental constitution. Especially notable is his repeated desire not only to read
nature but also "to explain . . . the scope & argument of the
whole book," and to do so from its total effect on the perceiver.
As Albert J. von Frank observes of the natural history lectures,
"Emerson does not deploy" the argument from design "as
Bishop Paley had done, to confirm the existence of God" as the
creator of nature, "but instead to draw attention to the effect" of
nature "itself, showing how nature is to be understood as a
medium for self-regarding human consciousness."[45] But what is
perhaps most striking about this passage is the role played by the
figure of Bacon. As noted earlier, Bacon's dictum regarding the
"book of God's word" and the "book of God's works" was often
invoked by naturalists and natural theologians. So Emerson invokes him here, not casually but to enable his own project. Ultimately, that is, Emerson here casts *himself* as "the [secular] minister and interpreter of nature."

Two years later, well into the composition of *Nature,* Emerson
had so completely absorbed Bacon's dictum into his own project
of uniting the two spheres that there was no need to invoke the
figure himself: "Man stands on the point betwixt the inward spirit

& the outward matter. He sees that the one explains, translates the other: that the world is the mirror of the soul. He is the priest and interpreter of nature thereby" (*JMN*, 5:103). By this time, he had also developed the rhetorical means or "method" of articulating that "point betwixt the inward spirit & the outward matter": the doctrine that matter and spirit "correspond" to, or "translate," each other.

Emerson is usually thought to have developed the rhetorical means of marrying mind and nature by appropriating the doctrine of correspondence from the eighteenth-century mystic and naturalist Emanuel Swedenborg, although, as Lawrence Buell notes, the idea was "in the air."[46] Indeed, a less mystical version of this doctrine formed the theoretical climate of Anglo-American natural science in which Emerson immersed himself upon his return from Europe. The key explanatory principle in this science was derived from the functional comparative anatomy of George Cuvier, one of the architects of the exhibition of organic life that so enraptured Emerson at the Paris Museum. In his anatomy and in the natural system of classification based on it, Cuvier used the Aristotelian "final cause" or purpose as a synonym for his fundamental principle of "the conditions of existence." According to this principle, "since no animal could exist without the condition which rendered its existence possible, the parts of an animal were necessarily correlated to assume internal harmony as well as harmony with its environment."[47] While overt natural theology was virtually nonexistent in post-Enlightenment, Catholic France, and although Cuvier (who was Protestant) deliberately avoided referring to God or Providence in his work, his "conditions of existence" easily served the metaphysical and intellectual requirements of Anglo-American natural theology, where it was translated into the doctrine of "perfect adaptation." Most obviously in the popular Bridgewater Treatises (though hardly confined to them), perfect adaptation "served as a complete explanation of organic phenomena," one in which the "condition" of a being's "existence" was thus conceived as given by a benevolent deity or incomprehensible final cause itself inscribed in that condition.[48]

This theory lies behind what strikes modern readers as the

oddly passive and static conception of adaptation in pre-Darwinian nature writing. Because the adaptation of organisms is conceived as preordained or designed, the environments are always said to be adapted to *them* rather than vice versa. Thus, for example, in his second natural history lecture, Emerson cites the "history of navigation" as affording instances "of the accurate adjustment of the powers [of the sea] to the wants of man" (*EL*, 1:38). As a "complete explanation," then, perfect adaptation implied the correspondence or "ray of relation" between the moral and physical worlds, observer and observed, that Emerson sought, a relation he was able to perform in *Nature* precisely because he participated so deeply and imaginatively in the cultural project of natural theology as it informed contemporary natural science.

Fully as much as his philosophical idealism, then, the assumption of perfect adaptation and the larger "design" it mirrors underpin both the cosmic optimism of *Nature* and what seems a rather abstracted narrative perspective. "We must trust the perfection of the creation so far," Emerson's speaker says in the second paragraph of the book,

> as to believe that whatever curiosity the order of things has awakened in our minds, the order of things can satisfy. Every man's condition is a solution in hieroglyphic to those inquires he would put. He acts it as life, before he apprehends it as truth. In like manner, nature is already, in its forms and tendencies, describing its own design. Let us interrogate the great apparition that shines so peacefully around us. Let us inquire, to what end is nature? (*CW*, 1:7)

Like the design nature is already describing, "every man's condition" is conceived here as identical to the "end" or final cause waiting to be read as a "hieroglyphic," and soon to be previewed in the notorious transparent eyeball passage that follows in the first chapter. In the next four chapters, Emerson then follows up the purpose of nature and the true condition of "every man" in a stepwise, loosely inductive manner, demonstrating the increasingly unifying "uses" nature serves, from "commodity" up to "discipline." While this logical structure derives from the ser-

monic form out of which Emerson's lecture and essay style developed, the procedure of "enumerating the values of nature
and casting up their sum" is also followed by the Bridgewater authors, several of whom emphasize as well the "discipline" that
nature serves for humanity.[49]

But while the Bridgewater authors typically draw the inference of design from innumerable evidences of perfect adaptation, Emerson aims poetically to represent this "condition" from
within design, as theophany. At the same time, his theoretic
ambition is fulfilled by intimating the "solution" to this "hieroglyphic" intuitively, rather than inferentially—in Coleridgean
terms, as an intuitive truth of Reason rather than a logical conclusion of Understanding.[50] Because "the one aim of all science,"
Emerson asserts, is "to find a theory of nature," and a "true
theory" is one that is "its own evidence," this mutually reinforcing double emphasis on theoretical explanation and poetic revelation addresses what Emerson felt were the moral and spiritual
deficiencies of the conventional design argument, of which Coleridge also had complained. Finally, the social and political implications of *Nature,* no less than Emerson's poetic style and epistemological stance, ran directly counter to the conservatism of
many treatises of natural theology, which tended to emphasize
human dependency on the standing order. Radically protestant
in its religious enthusiasm, *Nature* was also potentially radical in
other ways. Because "'Nature is not fixed but fluid,'" Emerson
looked for "a correspondent revolution in things" as the spirit of
nature was realized (*CW,* 1:44, 45).

Emerson and Evolution

Emerson was able to consider becoming "a naturalist" in the
early 1830s and to pursue his inquiry through scientific theory
not only because of the common context provided by natural
theology but also because the process of professionalization was
only then getting under way in England and the United States.
Even while he was devising and performing the bold, unifying
trope of correspondence, the social forces of scientific profes-

sionalization were undermining the unified perspective of "all science" that Emerson wished to claim.[51] Thus, the palpable tension between "the poet" and "the theorist" in *Nature* resonates from cultural as well as personal sources.[52] Indeed, despite plentiful descriptions of "the unity of science," like Herschel's, even within the developing scientific community the specialization of knowledge was threatening to disintegrate what William Whewell called "the empire or commonwealth of science." At virtually the same moment when Emerson stood in the Paris Museum, as "part of a strategy to prevent disintegration" Whewell had coined the term "scientist" to "highlight the common enterprise in which astronomers, chemists, geologists, and botanists were engaged."[53]

But if the theoretical stance Emerson tried to establish in *Nature* was being undercut by the increasing authority and specialization of professional science, in the aftermath of its publication Emerson was already focusing more on the problem of intellectual and social fragmentation, envisioning the American scholar, for example, as a "university of knowledges," and one who apprises us of the "commonwealth of mind" (*CW*, 1:69; *JMN*, 5:232).[54] Explicitly decrying the "moral" effects of scientific specialization in the lecture "Humanity of Science" delivered in December 1836, Emerson claimed, "Whilst the laws of the world coexist in each particle [of nature], they cannot be learned by the exclusive study of one creature. A man shall not say, I will dedicate my life to the study of this moss, and through that I will achieve nature. Nature hates cripples and mono-maniacs" (*EL*, 2:26).

As scientific literacy had been crucial to the Unitarian minister for "enlarging the doctrines of theology," so to the secular "minister and interpreter of nature" it remained essential now for sustaining the unity of the two spheres he had articulated in *Nature*. As Emerson saw it, the chief "benefit" of "the popularization of science [will be] to keep the eye of scientific men on that human side of nature wherein lie grandest truths" (*EL*, 2:38). Bearing in mind that his contemporaries regarded scientific knowledge as cutting-edge versions of the "grandest" human truths is especially important for understanding how Emerson's representations of nature develop in relation to emergent evolutionary ideas. Because of the broad discourse within which evolutionary issues were publically debated, evolution "did not just mean species, but everything from nebulae to the human mind."[55] Consequently, Emerson's self-appointed role as mediator between the scientific and "human side of nature" also positioned him at the forefront of the "human side" of evolutionary theorizing.

While his vision of physical nature changed dramatically over the course of his long life, there is reason to doubt that Emerson ever really abandoned teleology. In this respect Emerson's advancing knowledge of science continued to enlarge, rather than to undermine, his theology. Yet in this he did not differ a great deal from many contemporaries who came to accept evolutionary views. Contrary to neo-Darwinian historical accounts, rather than effecting an immediate "revolution," Darwin's theory was widely received and accommodated to an "essentially non-Darwinian conceptual framework" that stressed "the orderly, goal-directed, and usually progressive character of evolution." Accordingly, to assess Emerson's relation to evolutionary theory more precisely as it emerged in the first half of the nineteenth century, we will do better to distinguish between progressionism and transmutationism.[56]

Although these two theories were often conflated as "development," especially after 1844, Emerson's contemporaries were quite sensitive to the essential difference between them, for it involved nothing less than naturalizing the widely sought "connection" between the moral and physical spheres of creation. Where transmutationists interpreted the history of life, evident in the fossil sequence, as a history of genealogical descent down to humanity, progressionists argued that the increasing complexity of those organisms reveals a goal-directed progress toward humanity and the unfolding of a divine plan. At best progressionism was "evolution without physical continuity. The continuity exists only in the mind of God, who has created a succession of new and higher life forms after the extinction of all of their predecessors through a series of divinely invoked universal catastrophes."[57]

Early in his career Emerson held the view that, as he put it in his natural history lecture "The Relation of Man to the Globe," "from times incalculably remote there has been a progressive preparation for [man] . . . preparing [the world] to be habitable by him. He was not made sooner, because his house was not ready" (*EL*, 1:29). This view implied neither transmutation nor any continuity between mammals and other orders, contrary to the impression Emerson seems to give in extolling "the upheaving principle of life every where incipient" in the Paris Museum exhibitions.[58] As might be expected from the spiritualization of matter effected in *Nature*, in the 1830s Emerson could be downright repulsed by the materialist implications of transmutation, not only because of an inclination, deep in the spiritual traditions that formed him, to privilege spirit over matter, but also because of the specter of determinism that such theories raised. In response to the grim picture of natural law given by Thomas Malthus, who argued that as a result of unrestrained sexual passion human population increase led naturally to vice, starvation, and death, Emerson wrote: "Malthus revolts us by looking at a man as an animal. So do those views of genius semi-medical which I spit at" (*JMN*, 5:227).[59] Presumably, this is why, although Emerson celebrates Lamarck's attempt at a unifying vision of nature, he finds his "system . . . imperfect" (*JMN*, 5:220). At the same time, as Evelleen Richards has shown, the path Darwin took to evolution, "along the route that led to natural selection," was not the only one. Rather, "there were a number of paths that ran along side and sometimes intersected with Darwinism."[60] Much to the consternation and horror of many progressionists, progressionism, brought down to earth by the anonymous author of *Vestiges*, would turn out to be one of them.

Before considering Emerson's complex relation to that "beastly book," as one prominent geologist called it, we should note the effects of two developments in Anglo-American science and its popularization on Emerson's representations of nature following the publication of his first book in 1836.[61] The first of these has already been mentioned: the development of a more comprehensive and encompassing conception of natural "law," in the context

of a new natural theology. Although in *Nature* "the perfection of
the creation" is assumed to be sustained by the "permanence of
laws," attention to them is subordinated to the disclosure of the
"end" or final cause of nature. Perhaps Emerson was wary of the
common association of mechanistic natural law with French scientific materialism, an association that even threatened the early
nineteenth-century reputation of Newton.[62] In any case, while
references to natural law certainly do occur in Emerson's earlier
writings, beginning with his lecture series on "The Philosophy of
History," delivered in winter 1836–1837, the concept assumes a new
prominence, with subtle but significant effects on his representation of human relations to nature.

On one level, in addresses during the late 1830s and in *Essays:
First Series* (1841), Emerson still maintains that "in the divine order,
intellect is first, nature secondary" (*CW*, 1:123). As in "The American Scholar" address (1837), where "vanquish[ing] and plant[ing]"
"the wilderness" is a metaphor for "extend[ing] by being, my dominion," so in *Essays* the same impulse to "reduce [nature] under
the dominion of man" makes itself felt (*CW*, 1:59, 2:20). Now, however, the new emphasis on the all-embracing present "law" places
humanity within a comprehensive "natural" unity much more
than previously, an effect that correspondingly reduces the power
attributed to human will as the agency of "dominion." In this respect, "Spiritual Laws" focuses a theme that runs through the *Essays*: "[W]e are begirt with laws which execute themselves. . . .
Place yourself in the middle of the stream of power and wisdom
which animates all whom it floats" (*CW*, 2:79, 81). "Power and wisdom" are, of course, two attributes of God that the Bridgewater
and other writers of natural theology purport to establish. But
where these authors infer such attributes from "natural facts,"
inviting their readers to step back and behold the evidence and the
logical conclusion, Emerson places his readers "in the middle of
the [experiential] stream" that, as it "animates all whom it floats,"
further elides the traditional distinctions between "the soul,"
"God," and "nature," leading a conservative writer and reader of
the discourse such as Bowen to protest "the grave error of representing the Divine Being as a mere abstraction . . . without
consciousness, personality, or intelligence."[63] Again, in tracing

"the natural history of the soul" in an address on "The Method of Nature," Emerson identifies "ecstacy" as "the law and cause of nature" and, simultaneously, as the divine state through which "the best in any [human] work" is performed. "Draw[ing] from nature the lesson of an intimate divinity," he effectively renders that divinity more intimate, as a "Supreme Presence" in nature, than any personality above or apart from it (*CW*, 1:130).

Related to this is a discernible shift in the way Emerson represents "final causes" in nature. Where his first book followed the "end" or final cause of nature up to "Spirit," and where the American Scholar and the Divinity School addresses inculcated the sublimity of rising intellectually and morally to that vision, Emerson now claims that "Nature knows" no "single end." Indeed, "if man himself be considered as the end, and it be assumed that the final cause of the world is to make holy or wise or beautiful men, we see that it has not succeeded." Rather,

> All is nascent, infant. . . . We can point nowhere to anything final; but tendency appears on all hands: planet, system, constellation, total nature is growing like a field of maize in July; is becoming somewhat else; is in rapid metamorphosis. The embryo does not more strive to be man than yonder burr of light we call a nebula tends to be a ring, a comet, a globe, and parent of new stars. (*CW*, 1:125, 126)

This image of growth unfolding lawfully throughout nature and the universe, while of course a Romantic commonplace, can nonetheless be tied more directly to a second development in Anglo-American science and its popularization that carried Emerson's progressionism farther in the direction of a genuinely evolutionary vision. In its popularization by the Scottish political economist and astronomer John Pringle Nichol, the nebular hypothesis Emerson sketches here became a standard "natural fact" in support of a progressionist cosmology, one that Nichol used to support a broad social reformist program.[64] As its secret author, Robert Chambers, would do three years later in *Vestiges*, Emerson here conflates the growth of nebulas with that of embryos as manifestations of the same "tendency" in "total nature." Like

Chambers, too, he was inspired by Continental theories concerning a morphological "unity of type" or, as Darwin referred to it in comments cited earlier, "unity of plan."

Initially, Emerson's exposure to morphology came through Goethe, who coined the term to designate a general *Urtype* underlying both both plant and animal anatomy.[65] Working from the belief that nature constituted a harmonious whole, in his classic *Metamorphosis of Plants* Goethe argued that plant organs are all metamorphosed variations of a primal leaf "type"; and the like assumption facilitated his discovery of the intermaxillary bone in the human skull, a bone hitherto found only in "lower" vertebrates. Although the search for a vertebrate archetype was carried out by Carl Gustav Carus, and fully elaborated in the 1840s by British comparative anatomist Richard Owen, Goethe was widely regarded as the founder not only of "the leading idea of modern botany," as Emerson wrote in *Representative Men* (1850), but also of the entire research program known as "transcendental morphology."[66] While for Goethe "the archetype may have had only an ideal not an actual existence," it was emphatically "not a Platonic idea." Indeed, "the vertebrate archetype provided a direct stepping-stone to the notion of evolutionary ancestors," leading Ernst Haeckel in 1866 to identify Goethe as "a principal founder of evolutionary theory."[67] The archetype acquired this evolutionary dimension through its apparent embodiment in the phenomenon of embryonic repetition, in which the whole history of nature appeared to be telescoped in the embryonic development of higher vertebrates, the so-called law, made famous by Haeckel, that "ontogeny recapitulates phylogeny."[68]

In pre-Darwinian biology and in science writings, this law was more often expressed as a powerful metaphor, "the gestation of nature," in which "the history of nature [was] construed as one long gestation analogous to a normal human pregnancy." According to Evelleen Richards, it was precisely the ambiguity of this metaphor, "encapsulat[ing] the organicism, the uncompromising developmentalism, anthropocentrism, and insistence on the fundamental unity of all nature," that "gave the metaphor of gestation its explanatory power and led to its wide deployment in nineteenth-century biology."[69] Just as Cuvier's functionalist adaptation had been made to serve Anglo-American natural theology in the 1830s, so the metamorphic development of a unitary "type" such as the vertebrate—"striving" through the history of nature like "the embryo" does "to be man," in Emerson's image—confirmed the operation of general "laws" of nature in the new natural theology.

In progressionist terms, "unity of type" at once placed "man" within a larger natural whole and privileged him as her highest production or "end." Properly sanitized of transmutationist taint, "unity of type" could even be promoted in a Bridgewater Treatise as proof of a larger "unity of design." This interpretation no doubt contributed to Emerson's appreciation of Peter Mark Roget's treatise, *Animal and Vegetable Physiology*, "the only good one I believe in the series except [Charles] Bell['s]," he confided to Margaret Fuller while reading the volume in October 1838 (*L*, 2:169).[70] A Fellow of the Royal College of Physicians and Fullerian Professor of Physiology at the Royal Institution, Roget (of *Thesaurus* fame) provided in this dense, two-volume work abundant and authoritative testimony concerning the "laws of Analogy" by which "the manifold structures and diversified phenomena of living beings . . . are extensively, and perhaps universally connected." In his conclusion, Roget summarized the latest Continental researches in support of the hypothesis that, through "innumerable modifications," "Nature" keeps "a certain definite type or ideal standard" to which "she always shows a decided tendency to conform."[71] But the most startling evidence of the "progressive metamorphoses" through the vertebrate type came from embryology. As Roget summarized the law: the physical characteristics "which distinguish the higher animal, on its attaining its ultimate and permanent form" are "those which it had received in its last stage of embryonic evolution." Nor was "the human embryo exempt from the same metamorphoses." For in its own "progressive development," the embryo traversed the entire vertebrate series, from fish through "reptile" and "quadruped" to its present form.[72] Roget took pains to disclaim the radical materialist implications of his hypothesis, in effect attempting to confine his readers' interpretation of "evolution" to the progressionist sense of an "unfolding" metaphysical design. Yet the very urgency of his denunciation, not to mention the length and exuberance of his summary (placed at the elevating end of the book), indicates Roget's ambivalence as well as the ambiguity noted by Richards: the uneasy coexistence of idealist and materialist interpretations in the same "natural fact."

Thus when Emerson figures "[a]n individual man [as] a fruit which it cost all the foregoing ages to form and ripen," and one "with whom so long the universe travailed in labor," he invokes a process of "gestation" that could be read as simultaneously ideal and actual, spiritual and physical (*CW*, 1:127–128, 129). At the same time, in his writings during this period, unity of type becomes the symbol of a central unity and teleology evident in nature and in every aspect of human life: "Every thing is made of one hidden stuff; as the naturalist sees one type under every metamorphosis. . . . Each new form repeats not only the main character of the type, but part for part all the details, all the aims, furtherances, hindrances, energies, and whole system of every other" (*CW*, 2:59). Whether Emerson was willing or able at this moment to go the whole hog, as Huck Finn would say, is ultimately less important than how these new figural resources and his own bold theorizing in tune with transcendental morphology enriched his representations of nature and humanity's relation to it.

For one thing, it enabled the expression of a sympathetic, even filial, identification with nature only partially registered earlier, as when Emerson pauses briefly during the upward spiral of his argument in *Nature* to protest: "I have no hostility to nature, but a child's love to it. . . . I do not wish to fling stones at my beautiful mother, nor soil my gentle nest" (*CW*, 1:35–36). Second, while remaining uncompromising in his progressionism, refiguring nature in this way complicated his previously single-minded emphasis on linear ascent by opening it out, conceptually as well as aesthetically, into nonlinear forms, such as in the "law of undulation" in "Intellect" (*CW*, 2:197). Even in "The Over-Soul," one of the more otherworldly essays in *Essays: First Series*, the "flowing robe" in which the soul is "clothed" materializes and develops through the imagery of biological metamorphosis:

After its own law and not by arithmetic is the rate of its progress to be computed. The soul's advances are not made by gradation, such as can be represented by motion in a straight line; but rather by ascension of state, such as can be represented by metamorphosis,—from the egg to the worm, from the worm to the fly. (*CW*, 2:163)

Perhaps the most complex and memorable instance of this development is the essay "Circles." A paean to nonlinearity, "Circles" traces "the same law of eternal procession" through the "incessant movement and progression which all things partake," and in a multitude of forms and directions: as eternally and unexpected, as "always another dawn risen on mid-noon, and under every deep a lower deep opens"; "tend[ing] outward . . . to immense and innumerable expansion"; vertically "scal[ing] this mysterious ladder" (*CW*, 2:186, 188, 181, 179). Unrestricted by either the theological or the scientific orthodoxy that constrained Roget, deeply sympathetic with transcendental biology, and positioned to interpret for a general audience that "side of nature wherein lie grandest truths," Emerson was prepared for *Vestiges* as well as anyone could have been.

Vestiges was so popular and so widely perceived as dangerous in large part because in it Robert Chambers rewrote the familiar progressionist narrative as a transmutationist one. He understood that the "reception of novelties in science" is "regulated very much by the amount of kindred or relative phenomena which the public mind already possesses and acknowledges, to which the new can be assimilated."[73] Consequently, the model of progressive development he presented in *Vestiges* was just as teleological and linear as those of the progressionists. And initially it seemed just as innocuous. Beginning with the "birth" of the universe according to the nebular hypothesis, the veiled author argued that life had developed from a simple monad (or "globule") "up" to the complexity of higher mammals, including humanity, a process that might yet result in an even "higher" human state, given the right social and political conditions, making "room," as Emerson put it in his journal, "for a better species of the genus Homo" (*JMN*, 9:232).

But where Roget, in considering the same body of Continental research that Chambers drew upon, had resisted the "seductive speculations" of the "transcendental school," insisting that "there still exist specific differences, establishing between them an impassable barrier of separation, and effectively preventing any conversion of one species into another," Chambers explicated a host of hints or "vestiges" culled from recent research in various mainstream and marginal scientific disciplines, in favor of what, in his defense, he pointedly called "the *actual* progression of species."[74] Having begun on earth by electrical means (here Chambers cited controversial experiments by Andrew Crosse, who claimed to have generated mites through electricity), the progressive development or "natural history of creation" was effected by an ordinary, natural, even domestic "law." Citing the experimental research of Geoffroy Saint-Hilaire on malformations as instances of aborted or "arrested development," Chambers argued that if conditions disrupting the normal process of gestation could result in underdeveloped organisms that resembled earlier evolutionary "types," then past conditions protracting the normal length of gestation might well have produced more "advanced" species. Thus, the mechanism of transmutation, "the production of new forms, as shewn in the page of the geological record, has never been anything more than a new stage of progress in gestation, an event as simply natural, and attended as little by any circumstance of a wonderful or startling [i.e., miraculous] kind, as the silent advance of an ordinary mother from one week to another of her pregnancy."[75] By making gestation the mechanism of the development process, Chambers literalized the metaphor that had long carried such "transcendental" speculations. In the process, as James Secord has noted, he domesticated transmutation itself, "infus[ing] with all the domestic virtues" a subject that had been "associated in the public mind with radical revolutionaries and dissolute foreigners."[76]

In "attempting to weave a great generalization out of the truths already established" in specialist disciplines, Chambers unwittingly challenged scientific authority, making it necessary for scientific reviewers to publicly "clarify the meaning of science and scientific practice."[77] What especially troubled and, in some cases, infuriated many professional scientists was that Chambers's vision of a universe under "law" was in perfect accord with the new natural theology many of them shared. As he recurred to this vital point in his conclusion:

> Thus the whole is complete on one principle. The masses of space are formed by law; law makes them in due time theatres of existence for plants and animals; sensation, disposition, intellect, are all in like manner developed and sustained in action by law. It is most interesting to observe into how small a field the whole of the mysteries of nature thus ultimately resolve themselves. The inorganic has been thought to have one final comprehensive law, GRAVITATION. The organic, the other great department of mundane things, rests in like manner on one law, and that is, DEVELOPMENT. Nor may even these be after all twain, but only branches of one still more comprehensive law, the expression of a unity flowing immediately from the One who is First and Last.[78]

Although panned as an atheistic and materialistic tract by many orthodox reviewers, especially in the United States, on the whole the book was generally well received among certain groups of liberal Christians, rationalists, and radicals.[79] Indeed, while vigorously attacked by Francis Bowen in the *North American Review*, the Unitarian *Christian Examiner* followed the English liberal Unitarian *Prospective Review*, the *Westminister Review*, and others in Britain that saw "nothing atheistic, nothing irreligious, in the attempt to conceive creation, as well as reproduction carried on by universal laws."[80] In the context of the liberal reception of Chambers's book and the discourse in which he presented natural law, Emerson's enthusiasm for *Vestiges*, as "a good approximation to that book we have wanted so long & which so many attempts have been made to write," whose author, he thought, had "come as near to succeeding as a man [who was] not a poet could," is not surprising (*L*, 3:283; 8:23). His interest in Chambers's theory was ardent enough, apparently, that, in Britain three years later, he not only met twice with Chambers but sought out Andrew Crosse as well.[81]

But where orthodox commentators interpreted Chambers's natural theology as a vicious masquerade, for Emerson, who was committed to a similarly sweeping vision of natural law, Chambers's "theology" did not go far enough: "What is so ungodly as these polite bows to God in English books?" he wrote in his journal. "Everything in this Vestiges of Creation is good except the theology, which is civil, timid, & dull" (*JMN*, 9:211). If we link this criticism with his qualified praise of Chambers as "good" for one "not a poet," we can understand how far Emerson's metamorphic vision of nature had taken him, without imagining that he somehow mystically "anticipated" evolution. In Emerson's reading, what is "ungodly" and "timid" in Chambers's "theology" is his failure to recognize and to represent the identity of self, God, and the metamorphic power of nature. As he had put it in "The Method of Nature": "[A]s the power or genius of nature is ecstatic, so must its science or the description of it be. The poet must be a rhapsodist: his inspiration a sort of bright casualty: his will in it only the surrender of will to the Universal Power, which will not be seen face to face, but must be received and sympathetically known" (*CW*, 1:132). Bearing in mind Emerson's ecstatic elaboration of metamorphosis and law in this and other post-*Nature* writings, and looking ahead to his Vestigian representations of natural process in subsequent years, we need not wonder what "poet," in Emerson's mind, might better have represented "everything good" in *Vestiges*.

Freedom, Force, and Fate

We can now understand how, looking back in the early 1860s, Emerson might well have characterized his vision of nature a decade earlier as "my Darwinism" (*TN*, 1:49). While not evolutionary in either the naturalistic or the purely technical sense in which Darwin's theory is now understood, the evolutionary progressionism Emerson began to envision in the 1840s was nonetheless in tune with the "transcendental" evolutionary theorizing summed up and further stimulated by *Vestiges*. The genuinely evolutionary (rather than merely progressionist) way Emerson imagines human-nature relations at this point is evident in their decidedly more material representation.

Thus, in the opening lecture of *Representative Men*, we readily recognize his Baconian figure of the minister and interpreter of nature of fifteen years earlier when he asserts that "the possibility of interpret[ing nature] lies in the identity of the observer and the observed," because "[e]ach material thing has its celestial side, . . . its translation through humanity into the spiritual and necessary sphere." But now the corollary is that humanity is "not only representative but participant" in the material body of nature and thereby also in the "ends" to which "all things continually ascend." "The reason why [the observer] knows" the physical qualities and organisms of nature is that, in the immense scheme of evolutionary time that now informs Emerson's vision more precisely, "he is of them: he has just come out of nature, or from being a part of that thing. Animated chlorine knows of chlorine, and incarnate zinc of zinc. Their quality makes his career, and he can variously publish their virtues, because they compose him" (*CW*, 4:7).

As significant as this evolutionary transformation in Emerson's representation of nature was, however, the publication of *Essays: Second Series* (1844) indicated that, in the "moral" domain, an arguably more profound change had already taken place in Emerson's conception of humanity as "participant" in nature. The opening chapter, "The Poet," seems not just to reaffirm the high idealism of the late 1830s and early 1840s but to soar higher still. With his "better perception," the poet beholds and articulates the Goethean archetype incarnate, familiar from *Essays: First Series*: "that within the form of every creature is a force impelling it to ascend into a higher form" (*CW*, 3:12). As the theorist and poet of *Nature* had followed the "end of nature" up to "spirit," so, in beholding "the flowing or metamorphosis," this ideal poet embodies scientific as well as literary "genius." He knows not only the "facts" of "astronomy, chemistry, vegetation, and animation." But "[h]e knows why," and thus posesses "true science," much as Emerson had imagined his own vocation ten years earlier (*CW*, 3:19).

In comparison to "The Poet," the cosmology, epistemology, and poetics of *Nature* appear almost static. But reading "The Poet" in relation to the next essay, "Experience," reveals the dark underside of its almost manic optimism. Poets are "liberating gods," it turns out, because they represent the few who can open "new passages . . . for us into nature," making "the metamorphosis . . . possible" (*CW*, 3:18, 16). Having "set [his] heart on honesty" in "Experience," Emerson acknowledges in "The Poet" as well that most of us most of the time "lack the affirmative principle, and . . . have no superfluity of spirit for new creation." So rare is inspiration and the perception of "unity" that perhaps "there is no power of expansion in men" (*CW*, 3:40, 27, 33).

True, earlier essays do occasionally look on "our experience" skeptically. "Compensation," for example, attempts to give due weight to the perception that "[t]here is a crack in every thing God has made. It would seem, there is always this vindictive circumstance stealing in at unawares, even into the wild poesy in which the human fancy attempted to make bold holiday, and to shake itself free of the old laws, . . . certifying that the law is fatal." But typically (as the phase "it would seem" betrays here), the voice of the speaker in these essays occupies a stable perspective and position apart from the *appearance* of "vindictive circumstance." In "Compensation" that perspective opens onto the "deeper fact" that, finally, "the soul" lies "[u]nder all this running sea of circumstance" and is identical with "real Being." Similarly, the "incessant movement and progression" in "Circles" comes to rest in the "principle of fixture or stability in the soul," a "central life" that is "somewhat superior to creation, superior to knowledge and thought, and contains all its circles" (*CW*, 2:63, 70, 188). "Experience," reflecting the ordinary and often "unhandsome" condition the essay explores, offers no such position and secures no ultimate affirmation (*CW*, 3:29). Rather than affirming progressionist ascent thematically or structurally, the essay traces a labyrinthine path in which "one section of the essay yields to the next, as one mode of experience grows out of another," with every affirmation Emerson wrests from his struggle revealing a "hidden negation," and "each step toward resolution . . . generat[ing] a further complication."[82]

As Robinson has shown, the ongoing dialogue with skepticism, initiated in "Experience" and growing out of Emerson's personal sense of the limitations of Transcendentalist vision, develops directly into the ethical and pragmatistic orientation of his later work. At the same time, *Essays: Second Series* also suggests that Emerson experienced skepticism as part of a broader cultural and intellectual tendency: the growing naturalistic movement to define natural law in purely material terms. The real threat posed by *Vestiges,* as many reviews and books written against it show, was Chambers's extension of natural law into the "moral" domain of mind. Once human as well as animal behavior is "proved to be under [the domain of] law," Chambers wrote triumphantly, the "old metaphysical character [of mind] vanishes in a moment, and the distinction usually taken between physical and moral is annulled."[83] As the expositor of Transcendentalist vision, Emerson had been implicated in the failure of that vision to realize its social promise. As secular minister and interpreter of nature, he was equally implicated now that "natural law" had turned into a double-edged tool. Such a redefinition not only threatened individual moral agency but also, for Emerson and others, rendered the universe morally bankrupt, evacuated of "beneficent purpose" (*CW,* 3:112).

His later enthusiasm for *Vestiges* notwithstanding, in "Experience" Emerson diagnosed this threat clearly enough in the tendency among "physicians" to reduce human behavior to "temperament," an explanation in which "[s]pirit is matter reduced to an extreme thinness: O *so* thin!" and that "puts all divinity to rout" (*CW,* 3:31). Emerson's most visible target here is the popular science of phrenology, upon which in fact Chambers had drawn heavily for the annulment he announced.[84] But his critique encompasses the wider trend he disparages as "this trap of the so-called sciences" that allows no "escape . . . from the links of the chain of physical necessity" (*CW,* 3:32). On the same grounds, in *Representative Men* and in "Fate" he would reckon with the "rule," formulated by "the new science of Statistics," (which Chambers also cited), "that the most casual and extraordinary events, if the basis of population is broad enough, become matter of fixed calculations," a rule that would reduce

Emerson's representative men of genius to blips on the screen of history.[85]

The magnitude of this threat, and the consequent importance of maintaining a faith that "the results of life are uncalculated and uncalculable," helps account for Emerson's peculiar animus against "generalizing" in these essays (*CW*, 3:40). Even early in his career, his ambivalence toward this act of mind is implicit in his persistent characterization of it as "tyrannical." But so long as the power of generalization was understood as creating an "order & classification in the mind" that discloses "the correspondent Order actually subsisting in Nature," it could be celebrated as a means of disclosing unity and design, as with the schoolboy in "The American Scholar," who, "tyrannized over by [his] own unifying instinct," comes to see "that he and [nature] proceed from one root" (*JMN*, 5:168; *CW*, 1:54–55). But in *Essays: Second Series*, Emerson is more apt to valorize the capacity of nature to escape knowing. Now, nature "resents generalizing and insults the [natural] philosopher every moment with a million fresh particulars." Any reductive effort to "get rid of the parts by denying them" only reveals that the philosopher is himself "the more partial" (*CW*, 3:139). Significantly, Emerson's primary strategy for fashioning a "new philosophy" to circumvent these contemporary threats and to recuperate a moral universe is thus to "take them in," rather than simply deny their validity. For in a meaningful universe not even "skepticisms are . . . gratuitous or lawless." Rather, they are parts of a larger whole that, "[t]o the intelligent, . . . converts itself into a vast promise and will not be explained" (*CW*, 3:33, 112).

The problem posed by materialist deployments of natural law, severely limiting the ethical and metaphysical possibilities Emerson had long explored, only loomed larger in the years after *Essays: Second Series*. By 1850 a host of such limitations had arranged themselves in his mind under the category of "Fate," a "fact" he identified with nature as early as 1845.[86] Lecturing on the subject often during the 1850s, he made "Fate" the most formidable essay of his last major book, *The Conduct of Life* (1860). More relentlessly than in "Experience," Emerson "honestly state[s] the facts," building up through the first half of the essay the overpowering presence of "this mountain of Fate," "this cropping out in our planted gardens of the core of the world," into every sphere of contemporary life: "in matter, mind, and morals; in race, in retardations of strata, and in thought and character as well" (*W*, 6:5, 12, 19, 21). As his geological metaphors suggest, "Nature" is a symbol for all of these manifestations, representing the rule of material law in moral as well as physical domains. And the challenge to the project of natural theology is made explicit by Emerson's grim substitution of Bacon's dictum: The book of nature is not the book of God; "The book of Nature is the book of Fate" (*W*, 6:15).

Emerson's moral pragmatism is abundantly evident in his determination to address the pressing contemporary issues brought together under "fate" not in general terms but through the "practical question of the conduct of life."[87] Yet the physical metaphors that animate "Fate" and its companion essay, "Power," also indicate how Emerson's sense of the problem of "conduct[ing]" "life" and "power" still resonates as much as ever with the contemporary question of "man's place in nature." In connection with the pressure exerted by reductionism, beginning in the mid-1840s, Emerson begins to rely increasingly on metaphors drawn from physics and chemistry, the better to suggest an elemental essence (*CW*, 3:42). Thus, in the key essay "Nature," in *Essays: Second Series*, he revives from Coleridge the distinction between *natura naturata* (nature as object) and *natura naturans* (nature as vital process); and he then breaks the latter term into two interpenetrating and quasi-physical properties, "Motion, or change" and "Rest, or identity" (*CW*, 3:105–6). Likewise, in "Experience," while abjuring the capacity of any generalization to convey the "ineffable cause," which "refuses to be named," he elects a phrase by Mencius, "vast-flowing vigor," as closer than most. And generally in later writings, he more frequently employs metaphors of "force" and "energy."[88]

The fulcrum for moving the mountain of Fate in Emerson's essay is a complex figure of polar force: "man" as "a stupendous antagonism, a dragging together of the poles of the Universe" (*W*, 6:22). Like a reprise, "Fate" exhibits several of the theoretical concepts Emerson had appropriated from science through the discourse of natural theology—the perfect adaptation or "mu-

tual fitness" between organisms and *"habitat"*; the teleological
and progressionist "ascending effort . . . of the Universe"; the
"Unity in things" revealed through "the omnipresence of law"
(*W,* 6:37, 35, 25). None, however, is more central to the essay or
better illustrates how, in this late work, Emerson fashioned a peculiarly tensive harmony of his own through that discourse than
polarity.

Emerson had long been intrigued, as were Coleridge and
Goethe, with figures of polar dynamism as useful natural symbols for reconciling opposite qualities or terms into a larger
whole. Like Coleridge, Emerson understood polarity not as simple dualism but rather as a relation between two opposing elemental forces that together constitute an underlying, tensive, and
vital unity. According to Coleridge, the effort to comprehend
polar relations will always lead to contradiction because the relationship itself is not logical but imaginative, an intuitive truth of
Reason rather than a proposition of Understanding. But Emerson's models for conceiving polarity were not only literary ones.
Due in part to the availability of newly translated writings of
German nature philosophers and naturalists (which Emerson
read at this time), in the late 1840s and 1850s polarity was widely
employed as as explanatory principle in Anglo-American science,
particularly in the idealist biology of Richard Owen and Edward
Forbes, who Emerson met in England, and in the work of Harvard scientists Asa Gray and Jefferies Wyman.[89]

Emerson's most explicit, if abstract, articulation of the paradoxical polar relation Coleridge described occurs at the end of
Essays: Second Series in the essay "Nominalist and Realist," where
it enables him to reassess the problem explored in "Experience"
that we have no access to "universality . . . in its primary
form." Yet because "Nature keeps herself whole, and her representation complete in the experience of each mind," glimpses of
that whole will come if we "see the parts wisely." Thus,

> The end and the means, the gamester and the game,—life is
> made up of the intermixture and reaction of these two amica-
> ble powers, whose marriage appears beforehand monstrous,

as each denies and tends to abolish the other. We must reconcile the contradictions as we can. . . . All the universe over, there is but one thing, this old Two-Face, creator-creature, mind-matter, right-wrong, of which any proposition may be affirmed or denied. (*CW,* 3:143–44)

In "Fate" Emerson names the opposing pole in this "old Two-Face" "Power." Like Fate, Power is a force manifested both in nature and, as the freedom of thought and will, in humanity. Because the two elements are conceived as interpenetrating one another in an irresolvable tension, in the moral terms of the essay, "fate slides into freedom and freedom into fate." At the same time, polarity obliterates the traditional dichotomy of "man" and "nature." For humanity is simultaneously constituted a part of the "elemental order" and of "the spirit which composes and decomposes nature": for "the lightning which explodes and fashions planets, maker of planets and suns, is in him" (*W,* 6:22, 36).

This cosmic force field of "the cunning co-presence of two elements which is throughout nature" is always kept in view in the essay. But through physical and chemical metaphors of "fusion" and "reaction," Emerson channels this paradigm into the more pragmatic purposes of the essay and the book: not to overcome material fate but to transform it into moral freedom and power (*W,* 6:22, 29, 20). Faced with fate and "incompetent to solve" the contradictions "of the time," Emerson writes at the beginning of the essay, "we can only obey our own polarity." Paradoxically, for many readers, following that same course leads him at the end to urge them to "build altars to the Blessed Unity," whose other face is "the Beautiful Necessity," confident (though it "passes understanding") that underlying them is "a Law which is not intelligent but intelligence."[90]

Emerson's fascination with what he called "the powers and laws of thought" was also channeled into another project in his later career. Inspired in an 1848 lecture by Richard Owen while in England, he determined to make a "masterly enumeration" of the natural laws of mind comparable to Owen's scientific enumerations, which impressed him as having "the widest application" (*W,* 12:3, 426). Although he never finished the project, three lectures related to it were collected and published posthumously by his editor, James Elliot Cabot, as *Natural History of Intellect.* While, as Richardson notes, "these lectures continue and deepen the problems raised in *Nature,*" they also lack the assurance embodied in the prophetic voice of that earlier work, Emerson's first, bold effort to articulate the unity of the moral and physical spheres of nature.[91] As in *Nature,* his deep faith in the parallelism and perpetual dialogue of mind and nature persists. But, as the title of the collection suggests, Emerson's confidence in his cultural position as interpreter of nature had significantly diminished in the face of a greater demand for rigor and "system" in studies of "morals" or mind as in those of nature. Inspired by a scientific lecturer to a parallel project, he is notably self-conscious about his lectures' absence of method, wholly lacking in "that systematic form which is reckoned essential in treating the science of the mind," and approximating closer an outdated "natural history," even "a sort of Farmer's Almanac of mental moods" (*W,* 12:11). But if these very late writings inevitably reflect, as part of the tune of their time, the increased positivism and regard for professional expertise that shaped the social and intellectual climate in which they were delivered, further separating the very domains Emerson had long sought to unify, he also had auditors for whom his harmonies still resonated.[92] Their responses to his lectures, and those of innumerable readers since then to his writings of nature, testify to Emerson's continuing power to speak to a public "nature" still accessible to all.

NOTES

I would like to acknowledge research support for this essay from the National Endowment for the Humanities and the University of Oregon Summer Research Program.

  1. For recent accounts of the transformation of Concord landscape, see Robert A. Gross, "Culture and Cultivation: Agriculture and Society in Thoreau's Concord," *Journal of American History* 69 (June 1982): 42–61; Brian Donahue, "Damned at Both Ends and Cursed in the Middle: The Flowage of the Concord River Meadows,

1798–1862," *Environmental Review* 13 (1989): 47–68; and David R. Foster, *Thoreau's Country: Journey through a Transformed Landscape* (Cambridge: Harvard University Press, 1999).

2. See, for example, Donald Worster, *Nature's Economy: A History of Ecological Ideas* (Cambridge: Cambridge University Press, 1985), pp. 103–107; Robert Kuhn McGregor, *A Wider View of the Universe: Henry Thoreau's Study of Nature* (Urbana: University of Illinois Press), pp. 34–55; Max Oehlschlaeger, *The Idea of Wilderness: From Prehistory to the Age of Ecology* (New Haven, Conn.: Yale University Press, 1991), pp. 134–36; and Laura Dassow Walls, *Seeing New Worlds: Henry David Thoreau and Nineteenth-Century Natural Science* (Madison: University of Wisconsin Press, 1995). For more balanced assessments of Emerson, see Michael P. Branch, "Ralph Waldo Emerson," in *American Nature Writers*, ed. John Elder (New York: Scribner's, 1996), 1:287–307; and David M. Robinson, "Three Moments in Emerson's *Nature*" (Paper presented at the University of Oregon, 29 October 1996).

3. Eduardo Cadava, *Emerson and the Climates of History* (Stanford, Calif.: Stanford University Press, 1997), p.2.

4. On American pastoral ideology and New World dreaming, see Lawrence Buell, *The Environmental Imagination: Thoreau, Nature Writing, and the Formation of American Culture* (Cambridge: Harvard University Press, 1995), pp. 31–82.

5. Cadava, *Emerson and the Climates of History*, p. 7.

6. Branch, "Ralph Waldo Emerson," p. 287. Important studies of Emerson and science include Harry Hayden Clark, "Emerson and Science," *Philological Quarterly* 10 (July 1931): 225–60; Gay Wilson Allen, "A New Look at Emerson and Science," in *Literature and Ideas in America: Essays in Honor of Harry Hayden Clark*, ed. Robert Falk (Athens: Ohio University Press, 1975), pp. 58–78; Carl F. Strauch, "Emerson's Sacred Science," *PMLA* 73 (June 1958): 237–50; David Robinson, "Emerson's Natural Theology and the Paris Naturalists: Toward a Theory of Animated Nature," *Journal of the History of Ideas* 41 (January–March 1980): 69–88; David Robinson, "Fields of Investigation: Emerson and Natural History," in *American Literature and Science*, ed. Robert J. Scholnick (Lexington: University of Kentucky Press, 1992), pp. 94–109; Walls, *Seeing New Worlds*, pp. 53–92; and Lee Rust Brown, *The Emerson Museum: Practical Romanticism and the Pursuit of the Whole* (Cambridge: Harvard University Press, 1997).

7. William Paley, quoted in D. L. LeMahieu, *The Mind of William*

Paley: A Philosopher and His Age (Lincoln: University of Nebraska Press, 1976), p. 82; Neal C. Gillespie, "Divine Design and the Industrial Revolution: William Paley's Abortive Reform of Natural Theology," *Isis* 81 (June 1990): 214–29.

8. For an examination of the Bridgewater Treatises as epitomizing "the essential obstacles faced by the sciences" (p. 216) in this period, see Charles Coulston Gillespie, *Genesis and Geology: A Study in the Relations of Scientific Thought, Natural Theology, and Social Opinion in Great Britain, 1790–1850* (New York: Harper, 1951), pp. 209–16. For more recent attempts to assess the role played by the treatises in contemporary culture, see John M. Robson, "The Fiat and the Finger of God: The Bridgewater Treatises," in *Victorian Faith in Crisis: Essays on Continuity and Change in Nineteenth-Century Religious Belief,* ed. Richard J. Helmstadter and Bernard Lightman (London: Macmillan, 1990), pp. 71–125; and Jonathan R. Topham, "Beyond the 'Common Context': The Production and Reading of the Bridgewater Treatises," *Isis* 89 (June 1998): 233–62.

9. Frederic Henry Hedge, "Natural Religion," reprinted in *An American Reformation: A Documentary History of Unitarian Christianity,* ed. Sydney E. Ahlstrom and Jonathan S. Carey (Middletown, Conn.: Wesleyan University Press, 1985), p. 407.

10. Charles Darwin, *On the Origin of Species* (1859; rpt., Cambridge: Harvard University Press, 1964), pp. 481–82.

11. Samuel Taylor Coleridge, *Aids to Reflection in the Formation of a Manly Character,* ed. James Marsh (Burlington, Vt.: Chauncey Goodrich, 1829), pp. 245, 248. Recent reconsiderations of nineteenth-century secularization pertinent to this essay include Frank M. Turner, *Contesting Cultural Authority: Essays in Victorian Intellectual Life* (Cambridge: Cambridge University Press, 1993), pp. 3–37; David Reynolds, *Beneath the American Renaissance: The Subversive Imagination in the Age of Emerson and Melville* (New York: Knopf, 1988), esp. pp. 13–112; and Kevin Van Anglen, "Reading Transcendentalist Text Religiously: Emerson, Thoreau, and the Myth of Secularization," in *Seeing into the Life of Things: Essays on Religion and Literature,* ed. John L. Mahoney (New York: Fordham University Press, 1998), pp. 152–70.

12. Headnote to Hedge's "Natural Religion" p. 403; James Turner, *Without God, Without Creed: The Origins of Unbelief in America* (Baltimore: Johns Hopkins University Press, 1985), p. 97; John Hedley Brooke, "Natural Theology and the Plurality of

Worlds: Observations on the Brewster-Whewell Debate," *Annals of Science* 34 (May 1977): 221–86.

13. John Hedley Brooke, *Science and Religion: Some Historical Perspectives* (Cambridge: Cambridge University Press, 1991), p. 197; Bernard Lightman, "'The Voices of Nature': Popularizing Victorian Science," in *Victorian Science in Context,* ed. Bernard Lightman (Chicago: University of Chicago Press, 1997), p. 188.

14. Brooke, *Science and Religion,* pp. 192, 198; Pietro Corsi comments on natural theology treatises in the 1830s in *Science and Religion: Baden Powell and the Anglican Debate, 1800–1860* (Cambridge: Cambridge University Press, 1988), p. 180. For the debate on "man's place in nature," see Robert M. Young, *Darwin's Metaphor: Nature's Place in Victorian Culture* (Cambridge: Cambridge University Press, 1985), esp. pp. 164–247.

15. Young, *Darwin's Metaphor,* pp. 12–13 (Bacon quoted on p. 12).

16. Philip Rehbock, *The Philosophical Naturalists: Themes in Early Nineteenth-Century British Biology* (Madison: University of Wisconsin Press, 1983), p. 4; Dov Ospovat, "Perfect Adaptation and Teleological Explanation: Approaches to the Problem of the History of Life in the Mid-Nineteenth Century," *Studies in the History of Biology* 2 (1978): 44; see also Dov Ospovat, *The Development of Darwin's Theory: Natural History, Natural Theology, and Natural Selection, 1838–1859* (Cambridge: Cambridge University Press, 1981), pp. 6–38.

17. For critiques of the military metaphor, see James R. Moore, *The Post-Darwinian Controversies: A Study of the Protestant Struggle to Come to Terms with Darwin in Great Britain and America, 1870–1900* (Cambridge: Cambridge University Press, 1979), pp. 1–122; and Ronald L. Numbers, "Science and Religion," in *Historical Writing on American Science: Perspectives and Prospects,* ed. Sally Gregory Kohlstedt and Margaret W. Rossiter (Baltimore, Md.: Johns Hopkins University Press, 1986), pp. 59–80.

18. See, respectively, Neal C. Gillespie, *Charles Darwin and the Problem of Creation* (Chicago: University of Chicago Press, 1979), esp. pp. 19–40; and Adrian Desmond, *The Politics of Evolution: Morphology, Medicine, and Reform in Radical London* (Chicago: University of Chicago Press, 1989).

19. Brooke, *Science and Religion,* p. 195; for a specific analysis of the contemporary American scene, see Turner, *Without God, Without Creed.*

20. Richard Yeo, *Defining Science: William Whewell, Natural Knowledge and Public Debate in Early Victorian Britain* (Cambridge: Cambridge University Press, 1993), pp. 28–48.

21. Richard Yeo, "William Whewell, Natural Theology, and the Philosophy of Science in Mid Nineteenth Century Britain," *Annals of Science* 36 (September 1979): 496.

22. Steven Shapin, "Science and the Public," in *Companion to the History of Modern Science*, ed. R. C. Olby, G. N. Cantor, J. R. R. Christie, and M. J. S. Hodge (New York: Routledge, 1990), p. 1005.

23. Bernard Lightman, *The Orgins of Agnosticism: Victorian Unbelief and the Limits of Knowledge* (Baltimore: Johns Hopkins University Press, 1987), pp. 147, 159, See also Turner, *Contesting Cultural Authority*, pp. 131–50; and Ruth Barton, "John Tyndall, Pantheist: A Rereading of the Belfast Address," *Osiris*, n.s., 3 (1987): 111–34.

24. Robert D. Richardson Jr., *Emerson: The Mind on Fire* (Berkeley: University of California Press, 1995), p. 142.

25. Daniel Walker Howe, *The Unitarian Conscience: Harvard Moral Philosophy, 1805–1861*, rev. ed. (Middletown, Conn.: Wesleyan University Press, 1988), p. 95. Howe traces this preference to the belief that "mind was the active and superior substance, matter the passive and subordinate substance."

26. Quoted in Clark, "Emerson and Science" p. 226 n. 9. As Clark notes, Emerson regards Bishop Butler and his *Analogy of Religion, Natural and Revealed* as the premier instance of this.

27. This instability can readily be seen in *Nature*, where the older term *natural philosophy* is used for physics and *intellectual science* is used for metaphysics (*CW*, 1:33–34) right alongside the more recent and restrictive *physical science* and *empirical science* (p. 39).

28. Yeo, *Defining Science*, pp. 33, 37.

29. Wesley T. Mott, "From Natural Religion to Transcendentalism: An Edition of Emerson's Sermon No. 43," in *Studies in the American Renaissance 1985*, ed. Joel Myerson (Charlottesville: University Press of Virginia, 1985), p. 6; Francis Bowen, *Critical Essays on a Few Subjects Connected with the History and Present Condition of Speculative Philosophy* (Boston: H. B. Williams, 1842), p. 169. As Mott points out, in 1829 Emerson complained that Paley and Newton "seemed shallow." He rejected "Paley's watchmaker God because the concept separates 'the laws of nature' from the active 'power' of God."

30. Albert J. von Frank, *An Emerson Chronology* (New York: G. K. Hall, 1994), p. 45.

31. Phyllis Cole, *Mary Moody Emerson and the Origins of Transcendentalism: A Family History* (New York: Oxford University Press, 1998), p. 111.

32. David Robinson, *Apostle of Culture: Emerson as Preacher and Lecturer* (Philadelphia: University of Pennsylvania Press, 1982), p. 129; John Gascoigne, "From Bentley to the Victorians: The Rise and Fall of British Newtonian Natural Theology," *Science in Context* 2 (Autumn 1988): 235.

33. Thus he characterized the "Spiritual Religion" that had replaced his Unitarianism, "It simply describes the laws of moral nature as the naturalist does physical laws and shows the surprizing beauties and terrors of human life"; or, thirteen months later, in February 1836, "The Idealist regards matter scientifically. The sensualist exclusively" (*JMN*, 4:364; 5:12).

34. *JMN*, 3:79; Mott, "Natural Religion," p. 6.

35. *CS*, 4:153, 154. The sermon was first preached 27 May 1832; the introductory paragraphs describing the eclipse date from 30 November 1834.

36. B. L. Packer, *Emerson's Fall: A New Interpretation of the Major Essays* (New York: Continuum, 1982), p. 78.

37. Richardson, *Emerson: The Mind on Fire*, p. 124.

38. Quoted in Richard Yeo, "Reviewing Herschel's *Discourse*," *Studies in History and Philosophy of Science* 20 (December 1989): 546.

39. John F. Herschel, *A Preliminary Discourse on the Study of Natural Philosophy* (1830; rpt., Chicago: University of Chicago Press, 1987), pp. 219, 25.

40. Richardson, *Emerson: The Mind on Fire*, p. 123.

41. Herschel, *Preliminary Discourse*, pp. 4, 6.

42. Emerson alludes to this phrase in a journal entry for 17 April 1832; it occurs in a review by Francis Jeffrey, published in the *Edinburgh Review* (*JMN*, 4:11).

43. Robinson, "Emerson's Natural Theology and the Paris Naturalists," p. 79. In *The Emerson Museum*, Lee Rust Brown argues that the unity Emerson discovered at the museum "was a version of precisely the kind of writing to which he had long aspired" (p. 61).

44. For a different interpretation, see Albert J. von Frank's penetrating study, "The Composition of *Nature*: Writing and the Self in

the Launching of a Career," in *Biographies of Books: The Compositional Histories of Notable American Writings,* ed. James Barbour and Tom Quirk (Columbia: University of Missouri Press, 1996), p. 12.

45. von Frank, "The Composition of *Nature,*" p. 22.

46. Lawrence Buell, *Literary Transcendentalism: Style and Vision in the American Renaissance* (Ithaca, N.Y.: Cornell University Press, 1973), pp. 149–50.

47. Toby A. Appel, *The Cuvier-Geoffroy Debate: French Biology in the Decades Before Darwin* (New York: Oxford University Press, 1987), p. 46; Baron Cuvier, *The Animal Kingdom, Arranged After Its Organization; Forming a Natural History of Animals, and an Introduction to Comparative Anatomy* (1828; rpt., London: Henry G. Bohn, 1863), p.2.

48. Ospovat, *The Development of Darwin's Theory,* p. 33. For most Anglo-American biological and geological theorists in the 1830s, "perfect adaptation had the status not of a postulate of natural theology, nor of an element in a particular ideology." Rather, it was "a *fact* apparent to all who took the trouble to observe organisms" (p. 36).

49. *CW,* 1:8; Robinson, *Apostle of Culture,* pp. 85–94. It should also be noted that, although not quite in the Emersonian sense of a mystic "ray of relation [that] passes from every other being to him," a cognate notion of "correspondence" is implied in the doctrine of perfect adaptation, and occasionally the term is used as well (*CW,* 1:19). How close the two conceptions of correspondence are can be seen in the passage from Charles Bell's *The Hand,* to which Emerson alludes approvingly in a December 1834 journal entry, understandably misidentified by his editors (*JMN,* 4:355).

Describing how the geological transformations that have produced the contemporary landscape "were necessary to prepare the earth for that condition which should correspond with the faculties to be given to man," Bell goes on to imagine, "If a man contemplate the common objects around him—if he observe the connection between the qualities of things external and the exercise of his senses, between the senses so excited, and the condition of his mind, he will perceive that he is in the centre of a magnificent system, . . . and that the strictest relation is established between the intellectual capacities and the material world" (*The Hand: as Evincing Design* [London: William Pickering, 1834], pp. 37–38).

50. Soon after learning Coleridge's distinction, Emerson listed in

his journal among the *"necessary"* truths, "scanned & approved by the Reason far above the understanding," the "saying" that "'Design proves a designer'" (*JMN*, 3:236). Emerson describes the value of Coleridge's distinction in a letter to his brother Edward on 13 May 1834 (*L*, 1:412–13).

51. As he admitted to himself and to the Boston Natural History Society in 1834, in his last natural history lecture, compared to that of "the Natural Philosopher," his natural knowledge was "quite superficial" (*EL*, 1:70).

52. While she uses a poststructuralist rather than a historicist model for understanding Emerson the "theorist," Julie K. Ellison illuminates the large extent to which Emerson represents his perspective as that of "culture," "thought," or "theory" in *Nature*; see her *Emerson's Romantic Style* (Princeton, N.J.: Princeton University Press, 1984), pp. 86–88.

53. Yeo, *Defining Science*, pp. 110, 111.

54. In *Splintered Worlds: Fragmentation and the Ideal of Diversity in the Work of Emerson, Melville, Whitman, and Dickinson* (Boston: Northeastern University Press, 1993), Robert M. Greenberg examines the "fragmentary self" in Emerson's writing of the late 1830s and 1840s in the cultural context of increasing fragmentation in American social and intellectual life; see pp. 23–81.

55. James A. Secord, "Introduction" to Robert Chambers, *Vestiges of the Natural History of Creation and Other Evolutionary Writings* (Chicago: University of Chicago Press, 1994), p. xiv.

56. Peter J. Bowler, *The Non-Darwinian Revolution: Reinterpreting a Historical Myth* (Baltimore: Johns Hopkins University Press, 1988), p. 5. In *The Meaning of Evolution: The Morphological Construction and Ideological Reconstruction of Darwin's Theory* (Chicago: University of Chicago Press, 1992), Robert J. Richards argues that, owing to the important role embryonic recapitulation played in Darwin's theorizing, his own theory was actually much more teleological than historians have recognized.

For an overview of evolutionary theory, see Peter J. Bowler, *Evolution: The History of an Idea*, rev. ed. (Berkeley: University of California Press, 1989); on the varieties of progressionism in nineteenth-century historiography, anthropology, and biology, see Bowler's *The Invention of Progress: The Victorians and the Past* (Oxford: Basil Blackwell, 1989).

57. Evelleen Richards, "'Metaphorical Mystifications': The Romantic Gestation of Nature," in *Romanticism and the Sciences*, ed. Andrew Cunningham and Nicholas Jardine (Cambridge: Cambridge University Press, 1990), p. 136.

58. Although the question is far from clear-cut, given the absence of any unified system of classification in the museum, which "displayed as many different classificatory systems as there were [curators'] chairs to which Cabinets were attached," the likehood of Emerson's having foreseen evolution there, as Ralph Rusk claimed, seems remote (Dorinda Outram, *Georges Cuvier: Vocation, Science, and Authority in Post-Revolutionary France* [Manchester, England: Manchester University Press, 1984], p. 178; Ralph L. Rusk, *The Life of Ralph Waldo Emerson* [New York: Scribner's, 1949], pp. 188–89).

Emerson could well have known of Lamarck's system, as Robinson argues ("Emerson's Natural Theology," pp. 76–80). However, his apparently evolutionary vision of "a perfect series from the skelton of the balaena [whale] . . . to the . . . skull of the Caucasian race of man" while standing before Cuvier's cabinet of comparative anatomy is consistent with Cuvier's theory of development *within* (rather than across) the four separate *embranchments* into which he divided animal life. To discourage any potential transmutationist interpretation, and to register his vehement opposition to Lamarck's model of continuous "ascent" of all life, Cuvier actually exhibited the four branches in the cabinet "in a descending order from the vertebrates to the molluscs, articulates, and radiates" (Philip Reid Sloan, "On the Edge of Evolution," introduction to Richard Owen, *The Hunterian Lectures in Comparative Anatomy, May–June* [Chicago: University of Chicago Press, 1992], p. 41; cf. Brown, *The Emerson Museum*, pp. 59–79).

59. On "Malthus and the Evolutionists," see Robert M. Young, *Darwin's Metaphor: Nature's Place in Victorian Culture* (Cambridge: Cambridge University Press, 1985), pp. 23–55. In a similar vein, two years earlier Emerson objected strongly to a "Loathsome lecture last eve. on precocity, & the dissection of the brain, & the distortion of the body, & genius, &c. A grim compost of blood & mud. Blessed, thought I, were those who, lost in their pursuits, never knew that they had a body or a mind" (*JMN*, 4:362).

60. Evelleen Richards, "A Question of Property Rights: Richard

Owen's Evolutionism Reassessed," *British Journal for the History of Science*, 20 (June 1987): 168.

61. Adam Sedgwick, quoted in Adrian Desmond, *Archetypes and Ancestors: Palaeontology in Victorian London, 1850–1875* (Chicago: University of Chicago Press, 1982), p. 29.

62. Gascoigne, "From Bentley to the Victorians," pp. 233–35.

63. Bowen, *Critical Essays*, pp. 214–15.

64. On the fortunes of the nebular hypothesis in America, see Ronald L. Numbers, *Creation by Natural Law: LaPlace's Nebular Hypothesis in American Thought* (Seattle: University of Washington Press, 1977); Pringle's use of it is examined in Simon Schaffer, "The Nebular Hypothesis and the Science of Progress," in *History, Humanity and Evolution: Essays for John C. Greene*, ed. James R. Moore (Cambridge: Cambridge University Press, 1989), pp. 131–64. For Emerson's reading of Nichol and its role in his changing conception of nature during this period, see David Robinson, "*The Method of Nature* and Emerson's Period of Crisis," in *Emerson Centenary Essays*, ed. Joel Myerson (Carbondale: Southern Illinous University Press, 1982), pp. 80–82.

65. On the pervasive importance of Goethe to Emerson, see *CW*, 4:151–66, and Gustaaf van Cromphout, *Emerson's Modernity and the Example of Goethe* (Columbia: University of Missouri Press, 1990); for the impact of Emerson's early reading of Goethe, see Richardson, *Emerson: The Mind on Fire*, pp. 170–74, and Robinson, "Emerson's Natural Theology," pp. 86–87.

66. *CW*, 4:158; R. Richards, *The Meaning of Evolution*, pp. 34–39. See also Rehbock, *The Philosophical Naturalists*, pp. 19–20, 24–99; Nicholas Rupke, "Richard Owen's Vertebrate Archetype," *Isis* 84 (June 1993): 238–44; and Appel, *The Cuvier-Geoffroy Debate*, pp. 202–37.

67. Rehbock, "Transcendental Anatomy," in *Romanticism and the Sciences*, p. 146; Rupke, "Owen's Vertebrate Archetype," pp. 242, 231; R. Richards, *The Meaning of Evolution*, p. 37.

68. Stephen J. Gould provides an exhaustive history of the hypothesis of embryonic recapitulation in *Ontogeny and Phylogeny* (Cambridge: Harvard University Press, 1977); for another view and a critique of Gould's historiography, see R. Richards, *The Meaning of Evolution*.

69. E. Richards, " 'Metaphorical Mystifications,' " p. 131.

70. For Emerson's appreciation of Bell's *The Hand*, see note 49.

71. Peter Mark Roget, *Animal and Vegetable Physiology, Considered with Reference to Natural Theology*, 2 vols. (London: William Pickering, 1834), 2:625, 627.

72. Ibid., pp. 630, 631.

73. [Robert Chambers], *Vestiges of the Natural History of Creation*, 2d ed. (New York: Wiley and Putnam, 1845), p. 140. All citations are to this edition, which Emerson owned; see Walter Harding, *Emerson's Library* (Charlottesville: University Press of Virginia, 1967).

74. Roget, *Animal and Vegetable Physiology*, pp. 636, 637; [Robert Chambers], *Explanations: A Sequel*, p. 110 (emphasis added), in *Vestiges*, ed. Secord.

75. [Chambers], *Vestiges*, p. 170. Geoffroy's research and "teratological theory of evolution" is recounted in Appel, *The Cuvier-Geoffroy Debate*, pp. 125–36.

76. James A. Secord, "Behind the Veil: Robert Chambers and *Vestiges*," in *History, Humanity, and Evolution*, pp. 185–86.

77. [Chambers], *Vestiges*, p. 279; Richard Yeo, "Science and Intellectual Authority in Mid-Nineteenth-Century Britain: Robert Chambers and *Vestiges of the Natural History of Creation*," in *Energy and Entropy: Science and Culture in Victorian Britain*, ed. Patrick Brantlinger (Bloomington: Indiana University Press, 1989), p. 27.

78. [Chambers], *Vestiges*, p. 251.

79. Secord, "Introduction," pp. xxviii–xxix; see also Desmond, *Archetypes and Ancestors*, pp. 29–31.

80. William Henry Smith, reviewing *Vestiges* in *Blackwood's* (quoted in Corsi, *Science and Religion*, p. 263). For the *Christian Examiner*, Joseph Henry Allen praised the book's testimony that "the mode of [divine] action is perfectly regular, and *can be ascertained by us*. This, we conceive, is the real value of the name [law] and of natural science which interprets it." Thus "understood, the phrase laws of nature has a meaning to us, very far from being either barren or irreverent" ("Vestiges of Creation and Sequel," *Christian Examiner* 40 [May 1846]: 339).

81. *L*, 4:19; *JMN*, 10:221. Emerson identified Crosse in a letter to William Emerson by the electrically generated mites that bore his name: "(*Acarus Crossii* in the Vestiges)" (*L*, 4:71). His meetings with Chambers were arranged by Alexander Ireland, a Manchester journalist he had met on his first European visit in 1832, and who arranged his second visit. As Chambers's intermediary with his pub-

lisher and one of only a few who knew the author's identity, Ireland was the one most likely to have revealed it to Emerson. Chambers's authorship was not disclosed publicly until 1884, thirteen years after his death (*CW*, 5:xxii–xxiii; Secord, "Introduction," pp. xxiii, xxxviii–xliii).

82. David Robinson, *Emerson and the Conduct of Life: Pragmatism and Ethical Purpose in the Later Work* (Cambridge: Cambridge University Press, 1993), pp. 60, 63–64.

83. [Chambers], *Vestiges*, p. 232.

84. Secord, "Behind the Veil," pp. 172–74.

85. *W*, 6:17. And see *CW*, 4:62, on the "terrible tabulations of the French statists."

86. "Fate is found in the bill of the bird which determines tyrannically its limits" (*JMN*, 9:297). Although it is beyond the scope of this essay, it should be noted that in his antislavery writings Emerson also links "fate" with the doctrine of black racial inferiority and thus implicitly with racial science; see, for example, *AW*, pp. 36–37.

87. *W*, 6:3; see Robinson, *Emerson and the Conduct of Life*, pp. 134–58.

88. See also Michael Lopez, *Emerson and Power: Creative Antagonism in the Nineteenth Century* (DeKalb: Northern Illinois University Press, 1996).

89. Richardson, *Emerson: The Mind on Fire*, pp. 467, 518–19; Rehbock, *The Philosophical Naturalists*, pp. 18–19, 102–13; E. Richards, "A Question of Property Rights," pp. 129–71; Toby A. Appel, "Jefferies Wyman, Philosophical Anatomy, and the Scientific Reception of Darwin in America," *Journal of the History of Biology* 21 (Spring 1988): 69–94.

90. *W*, 6:3, 48, 49. For a cogent statement of the argument that "the essay's energy is dissipated" by a "facile either/orism that takes comfort in the prospect that we can neither shun the fated nor incur the non-fated," see Lawrence Buell, "Emerson's Fate," in *Emersonian Circles: Essays in Honor of Joel Myerson*, ed. Wesley T. Mott and Robert E. Burkholder (Rochester, N.Y.: University of Rochester Press, 1997), p. 24.

91. Richardson, *Emerson: The Mind on Fire*, p. 450.

92. See Ronald A. Bosco, "His Lectures Were Poetry, His Teaching the Music of the Spheres: Annie Adams Fields and Francis Greenwood Peabody on Emerson's 'Natural History of the Intel-

lect' University Lectures at Harvard in 1870," *Harvard Library Bulletin*, n.s., 8 (Summer 1997): 1–79. As Bosco shows, the tension between this late-century positivist climate and Emerson's "poetic" approach was registered even in Cabot's and Edward Emerson's editorial disposition toward these lectures.

Emerson and Religion

David M. Robinson

We distinguish the announcements of
the soul, its manifestations of its own
nature, by the term *Revelation*. These
are always attended by the emotion of
the sublime. For this communication is
an influx of the Divine mind into our
mind. It is an ebb of the individual
rivulet before the flowing surges of the
sea of life.

(*CW*, 2:166)

This belief in the presence and power of the soul is the core of
Ralph Waldo Emerson's religious thought and the vital principle of his entire intellectual achievement. His doctrine of the
soul developed in the 1820s and 1830s as he fused the Unitarian
theology of self-culture with the spiritual and idealistic doctrines
from several Neoplatonic, oriental, and European Romantic
sources, and as his interest was kindled in the new scientific discoveries of his day. His doctrine of the soul blossomed into a passionate and visionary expression of the premises of Transcendentalism in key works of the late 1830s and early 1840s. Emerson
gradually modified his religious stance during the 1840s and 1850s
to accommodate the waning of his experience of ecstatic vision

and to reflect his growing sense of the importance of moral action as the fundamental end of religious experience. He thus developed a more pragmatic and ethically centered theory of the religious life in which work and worship, morals and vision, became increasingly synonymous concepts.

Emerson's Theological Background

The roots of Emerson's religious sensibility lie deep in the soil of Puritan New England. He was the descendant of a long line of New England ministers, and son of the minister of the First Church of Boston, William Emerson. The death of his father in 1811, when Waldo was seven, left him in the care of his mother, Ruth Haskins Emerson, a deeply pious woman, and his paternal aunt, Mary Moody Emerson, a woman of powerful intellect and a profound religious sensibility who became one of his chief spiritual influences. Steeped in the older piety of Puritan New England, but an astute reader of modern philosophy and theology, Mary Moody Emerson provided her nephew with an example of a sensibility in which intellectual rigor and religious ardor were co-equal aspects of the spiritual life.[1] These family influences were augmented by a changing religious climate in New England during Emerson's intellectually formative years. New England theology had evolved dramatically in the two centuries between the Puritan settlements and Emerson's early manhood; the Calvinism of the early Puritans had been contested, modified, and in many quarters rejected entirely. Emerson's father was among the leading ministers of the anti-Calvinist liberal party who had led most of the established churches in the Boston area to a theological stance that was characterized as "Arminian," or, eventually, Unitarian. This progressive and largely optimistic faith, still struggling for its status as a legitimate and independent religious movement, was Emerson's chief religious heritage. Rooted in older patterns of piety and belief, it was nevertheless a dynamic, evolving religious philosophy.[2]

The emphasis of Calvin and other Protestant theologians on the availability of saving grace to the "elect" of God inculcated a powerful, pietistic response in many, but it also left a complex set of theological questions and psychological pressures with which later believers and theologians grappled. The place of moral action or "works" in the Christian life and in the plan of salvation was for many problematic. If salvation is entirely the work of God's grace, what role or necessity could works play in it, if any? And if the elect are chosen by God, what place was left for the active pursuit of salvation by the individual? Finally, what assurance could the believer have of the state of his or her soul? Were there any signs, internal or external, that might provide the certainty that one had undergone a saving conversion experience?[3]

Such issues became extremely important to the Puritans in the late seventeenth century, when the children and grandchildren of the first immigrants began to face questions concerning their faith, their relationship with the church, and the state of their souls. Perry Miller has described this period as one of cultural crisis, in which the Puritan leadership had become "convinced that their societies were slowly degenerating" (*Nature's Nation*, 51), and had responded in part by reemphasizing the concept of the "preparation for salvation," a view of the conversion process that reserved God's place as the final dispenser of grace but emphasized the importance of the individual's preparing the soul, through study, self-examination, prayer, and good works, for the reception of that grace. Conversion was not necessarily an abrupt or sudden change but might be a more extended process. The nature of this process of preparation for the reception of grace thus became a central concern of New England theological thought for the next century.

The modification of the strictest form of Calvinism that the concept of "preparation" represented was also accompanied by an inclination to alter the received depiction of God and of the spiritual capacities of human nature. These Arminian tendencies became increasingly influential as an alternative to Calvinism during the eighteenth century. As Conrad Wright has pointed out, the first generation of Puritan immigrants had already moderated Calvinism to some extent through a version of "Covenant" theology that in effect bound the sovereign will of God to certain contractual obligations with his chosen people (*Begin-*

nings, 14–17). Further modifications of Calvinism continued in the 1740s and 1750s when opposition arose to aspects of the preaching and doctrines in the widespread revivals led by Jonathan Edwards and George Whitefield known as the Great Awakening. Charles Chauncy, minister of the First Church in Boston, led the opponents of the emotional preaching and excessive religious enthusiasm of the Awakening, gradually turning that critique into a reformulated liberal theology that rejected the Calvinist doctrine of innate depravity and depicted God in more compassionate terms. "By the middle 1750's," Wright notes, "Arminians no longer pretended they were orthodox, but instead began to condemn Calvinism by name and attack its dangerous tendencies" (*Beginnings,* 89).

The liberals established a stronghold in Boston and by the early decades of the nineteenth century were the dominant theological party at Harvard. Controversy between the liberals and orthodox became heated in 1805, when Henry Ware was elected Hollis Professor of Divinity at Harvard, and the controversy resulted in a split of the original congregational churches in which the Unitarians, as the liberals were now known, emerged as a new denomination.[4] In "Unitarian Christianity" (1819) William Ellery Channing, the leading spokesman for the new generation of liberals, declared the separate existence of the Unitarian movement and advanced a theological program centered on the human capacity for reason and spiritual development. By the 1820s Unitarianism had a strong foundation in Boston and eastern Massachusetts, and the split of the original Puritan congregational churches was permanent.

In "Unitarian Christianity" Channing defended the human capacity to make reasoned judgments about theology, and to act as independent moral agents in meeting life's experiences, thus rejecting the darker implications of the Calvinist doctrine of innate depravity. "Say what we may, God has given us a rational nature, and will call us to account for it," he declared. "We may let it sleep, but we do so at our peril. Revelation is addressed to us as rational beings" (76). For Channing, this affirmation of human capacity was linked with a renewed sense of the justice and benevolence of God, a denial of the Calvinist idea of the predestined election to salvation of only a certain number of individuals. This avowal of both human capability and the justice and benevolence of God was the cornerstone of the Unitarian dissent to Calvinism, the basis from which they would build a theology that emphasized spiritual potential and ongoing self-culture as the basis of the religious life.

Channing added one further dimension to this version of Christianity, one that was decisive in his influence on Emerson. This is a harder quality to specify and explain, but Emerson termed it Channing's "moral imagination" and referred to Channing's 1821 Dudleian Lecture at Harvard, "The Evidences of Revealed Religion," as a performance that exemplified this quality. It was less the specifics of Channing's arguments in defense of Christianity than his capability to present a compelling witness to the reality of lived spiritual experience that constituted for Emerson the act of "moral imagination" that was so conclusive. Channing emphasized an "internal" evidence of Christianity as decisive, "an evidence to be felt rather than described, but not less real because founded on feeling." Such a conviction in the reality of religious truth "springs up and continually gains strength, in those who apply it habitually to their tempers and lives" (143).

Channing thus provided the nucleus of the two vital elements of the Unitarian outlook as it had emerged in the first decades of the nineteenth century, a theology that referred inevitably to the doctrine of the "moral sense."[5] All individuals, according to this doctrine, possessed an innate capacity for moral choice, a confirmation of the indwelling of divine or godlike attributes within the soul; and although it might be weakened or overridden by the passions, it could also serve as the basis for an ongoing spiritual and moral cultivation, in which the soul would grow, in Channing's phrase, toward an ever-increasing "Likeness to God."

Emerson's Ministry

Emerson came into intellectual maturity in the 1820s, just as Channing had emerged as the Unitarians' leading spokesman. During the 1820s, Emerson struggled with both vocational decisions and severe health problems. His brother William had chosen to enter the ministry and went to study in Germany, the center for biblical and theological studies. But after encountering the Higher Criticism of the Bible there, in which the scriptural texts were approached as historical and cultural documents and subjected to reasoned analysis, he underwent a crisis of faith and withdrew from ministerial study. Emerson, too, had felt the pull of family tradition, with his Aunt Mary's encouragement, and his education leading him toward the ministry. He struggled with the decision, however, dreading the necessary pastoral visiting and counseling involved in ministerial work because of his innate shyness, and lacking enthusiasm for the emotionless logic he associated with theological discourse. It was at this point that the example of Channing was decisive for him, providing a version of the ministry based on imaginative, highly inspirational preaching, a kind of poetry from the pulpit that fired Emerson's vision of his own potential.

In an extraordinary moment of self-analysis, Emerson set out his doubts and hopes about his vocation in his journal in 1824. Although he had made the decision to begin his studies for the ministry, it was clear that he lacked confidence that he had the skills to succeed. Confessing his indifference to the dry reasoning of theology, he admitted instead "a strong imagination & consequently a keen relish for the beauties of poetry," qualities that were "the highest species of reasoning upon divine subjects." Such thinking is "the fruit of a sort of moral imagination" such as Channing had displayed in his Dudleian Lecture (*JMN*, 2:238).

This inner conflict about the ministry would haunt Emerson even after he successfully began his career at the Second Church of Boston, one of the city's oldest and most historically significant churches. Two major crises, however, attended the beginning of his career. The first was a crisis of health. In the middle 1820s, Emerson developed symptoms of tuberculosis, affecting his breathing, stamina, and vision, slowing down the pace of his studies, and, as they increased in intensity, threatening his life. He found that rest and avoiding overwork and stress were his best responses, and at perhaps his darkest hour in this crisis, he embarked on a voyage to South Carolina and Florida in 1826.[6] The change of surroundings, the enforced leisure of the voyage, and the warmer climate helped him regain his strength, and he returned in 1827 to begin a round of supply preaching in various New England pulpits, and eventually to take the pulpit at the Second Church in Boston from the ailing Henry Ware, Jr., one of the best Unitarian preachers of his day. Although awkward and insecure as a pastor and adviser to his congregation, a role in which he felt uncomfortable, Emerson was an original and appealing preacher, pouring much intellectual energy and spiritual intensity into a wide-ranging series of sermons.[7]

During one of his engagements as a supply preacher in Concord, New Hampshire, Emerson met Ellen Tucker, whom he would marry in 1829, after he had become minister of the Second Church. Theirs was a profoundly deep and passionate bond, into which the emotionally reserved Emerson poured much ardor, and from which he received much devotion and affection. But Ellen, too, was a victim of tuberculosis, and she died in 1831. Ellen's death shook Emerson deeply, and as Robert D. Richardson, Jr., has written, it changed him permanently, emphasizing in the most painful way the impermanent quality of happiness and achievement in the world, and thus bringing him to believe "completely, implicitly, and viscerally in the reality and primacy of the spirit" (110).

Emerson's reaction to Ellen's death, combined with his continuing restlessness in the role of a minister and his increasing inclination to push at the accepted boundaries of Unitarian theology, led to his resignation from his pulpit at the Second Church in 1832. Emerson requested that the church not require him to administer the Lord's Supper, explaining that "I cannot bring myself to believe that [Jesus] looked beyond the living generation, beyond the abolition of the festival he was celebrating and the scattering of the nation, and meant to impose a memorial feast upon the whole world" (*CS*, 4:187). Although his congregation was reluctant to let him resign, they could not grant his request. Emerson resigned, using this situation to help him set a new direction in his life that began with a trip to Europe in 1832–1833. Although he continued to preach for several years after his return, he had in fact launched a new vocation with his first independent public lectures in 1833–1834, lectures that contained the seed of his first book *Nature* (1836).

The Emergence of Transcendentalism

Emerson's emergence as an original, influential thinker in the middle and late 1830s resulted from the coalescence of three strands of inquiry: his exploration of the "moral sense," his deepening commitment to the philosophy of idealism, and his new interest in science and the study of nature. As we have seen, Emerson took the moral sense doctrine from the Unitarian tradition, a belief that he increasingly identified with both the indwelling of divinity and the power of the human imagination. Emerson's deepened interest in philosophical idealism and what he called the "spiritual philosophy," the second crucial concept in his intellectual emergence, amplified both the importance and the meaning of the moral sense, helping him construct a vision of a unified, organic cosmos. His idealism was grounded in a deep reverence for Plato and the Neoplatonic tradition, and his reading in the English Romantic writers Samuel Taylor Coleridge, William Wordsworth, and Thomas Carlyle reinforced and extended this idealism, and led him for further confirmation to the work of Immanuel Kant, Friedrich Schelling, Friedrich Schleiermacher, and other German idealist philosophers.[8] "Idealism sees the world in God," he wrote in *Nature*, in a passage that exemplifies the mixture of poetic metaphor, philosophical speculation, and visionary energy that marked his early work. "It beholds the whole circle of persons and things, of actions and events, of country and religion, not as painfully accumulated, atom after atom, act after act, in an aged creeping Past, but as one vast picture, which God paints on the instant eternity, for the contemplation of the soul" (*CW*, 1:36).

The convergence of Emerson's concept of the moral sense with his growing comprehension of idealism was supplemented by a third element, his new interest in science, one that was stimulated by his trip to the Jardin des Plantes in Paris in 1833, where he saw botanical exhibits that suggested to him both the order and the evolutionary energy of the natural world. Filled with a new ambition to become "a naturalist," he returned to America and began to lecture on scientific topics, declaring that "the greatest knowledge of natural science" is "to explain man to himself" (*EL*, 1:23). For Emerson, there was not a natural form "so grotesque, so savage, or so beautiful, but is an expression of something in man the observer" (*EL*, 1:10). The study of science was therefore not only a mode of discovery, interpretation and explanation of the external world but also, as Emerson saw it, a form of self-exploration, a means of investigation that would reinforce and extend his developing conception of the interconnections between idealism and the moral sense.[9]

Emerson's *Nature* was his first attempt at a comprehensive and systematic expression of his emerging religious vision, taking as its subject the nature of the external world and the mind's relationship to it. In *Nature* Emerson set out to explain the necessary connections among the three key strands of his thought—a belief in the human access to the moral sense, a vision of all reality as "one mind," and a conviction that the study of nature could help reveal that comprehensive unity. He begins with a dramatic account of a revelatory or mystical experience in the natural world, in which he attains an enormously expansive vision, and also loses the sense of distinction between his own identity and that of the natural world. "Standing on the bare ground,—my head bathed by the blithe air, and uplifted into infinite space,—all mean egotism vanishes. I become a transparent eye-ball. I am nothing. I see all. The currents of the Universal Being circulate through me; I am part or particle of God" (*CW*, 1:10). Emerson's "transparency" indicates his merger into the surrounding landscape, while his identity as an "eye-ball" suggests his continuing expansion of vision. He links this experience to a merger of his own being with God, as the divine "currents" flow through his veins.

Emerson uses this revelatory experience, a brief but intense occurrence, as a means of framing his larger inquiry about our comprehension of nature, and about its origins and purpose. He goes on to propose an ascending series of levels of understanding, "Commodity," "Beauty," "Language," and "Discipline," each step of which increasingly emphasizes the role of nature in the process of human self-understanding. In discussing nature as "discipline," he makes it clear that nature ultimately serves as the moral manifestation of God; in understanding nature we also recognize the unity of being that underlies all moral perception. "This ethical character so penetrates the bone and marrow of nature, as to seem the end for which it was made" (*CW,* 1:26). Emerson's concluding call to the revitalization of life, "Build, therefore, your own world" (*CW,* 1:45), was an important indication that he felt his new vision was an enabling and empowering one, capable of reinforcing the self-reliance and self-confidence of his readers, and of spurring important movements of social and political reform as the means of building the world anew.[10]

While *Nature* found a loyal readership, especially among restless younger people who were searching for alternatives to religious and political convention, Emerson achieved greater prominence through two major public lectures at Harvard, "The American Scholar" (1837), an address to the Phi Beta Kappa Society, and the "Divinity School Address" (1838), a speech to graduating ministerial students at Harvard Divinity School. In "The American Scholar" Emerson described the role of the "scholar," a term that included anyone from the poet to minister to teacher who engaged in critical study of society, nature, and the mind. He termed the scholar "Man Thinking" and defined the intellectual life in terms of growth and creativity. "To create,—to create,—is the proof of a divine presence" (*CW,* 1:57). By this standard, the life of the thinker was a continual quest for the new, an ever-renewing effort to reach beyond what had been achieved and known, a building on the past to go always beyond it.[11]

This questing and experimental attitude could, however, generate intense opposition when it was applied to the subject of religion, as Emerson discovered after his "Divinity School Address."[12] "In all my lectures, I have taught one doctrine, namely, the infinitude of the private man," he commented in his journal. "This, the people accept readily enough, & even with loud commendation, as long as I call the lecture, Art; or Politics; or Literature; or the Household; but the moment I call it Religion,—they are shocked, though it be only the application of the same truth which they receive everywhere else, to a new class of facts" (*JMN*, 7:342). Emerson's address became controversial because of his lack of emphasis on the importance of the supernatural character of Jesus and the biblical miracles, and his critique of the lifeless preaching of the contemporary church. Since religion was intuitively founded on the "moral sentiment," it could not be taken "second hand" from tradition, the church, or any other external authority (*CW*, 1:77, 80). The "proof" of the biblical miracles was therefore irrelevant to real religious belief.

The exaggerated reverence for "the *person* of Jesus" also falsified religion, Emerson argued, because Jesus should not be regarded as a supernatural being but rather as the prophet who most completely realized the divinity within every individual. Emerson thus radically democratized Jesus' claim of divinity: "He said, in this jubilee of sublime emotion, 'I am divine. Through me, God acts; through me, speaks. Would you see God, see me; or, see thee, when thou also thinkest as I now think'" (*CW*, 1:81).

Emerson was inviting controversy with these remarks, but he saw himself as an awakener, taking a message of encouragement for innovation to the new ministers in his audience. But his audience also included many of the Unitarian ministers in the Boston area, who also heard Emerson's stinging critique of the state of contemporary preaching. "I think no man can go with his thoughts about him, into one of our churches, without feeling that what hold the public worship had on men, is gone or going" (*CW*, 1:88). Emerson blamed the decline on a lifeless preaching that relied on "tradition": "it comes out of the memory, and not out of the soul; . . . it aims at what is usual, and not at what is necessary and eternal" (*CW*, 1:87). The preacher must instead be a kind of poet, "a newborn bard of the Holy Ghost" (*CW*, 1:90), deriving from the intensity of experience a message that would also move others. While this was a message of awakening, it was not a call to abandon the ministry or the church, or to work toward the establishment of a new religious denomination. Emerson urged his listeners "to rekindle the smouldering, nigh quenched fire on the altar" and to breathe "new life . . . through the forms already existing" (*CW*, 1:92). Even though he was finding a new vocation in his lecturing and writing, he urged those called to the ministry to bring an infusion of new energy into the church.

The reaction to the "Divinity School Address" was one of the key elements of the "Transcendentalist controversy," one of the most significant intellectual conflicts in American religious history. Andrews Norton, an influential Unitarian theologian, attacked Emerson's "infidelity," warning against his abandonment of the centrality of the biblical miracles and the divine nature of Jesus. Other Unitarians, though not as outraged as Norton, were uncomfortable to varying degrees with Emerson's insistence on intuition as the basis of religious authority, his intensely poetic (and hazy, some felt) language, and his attack on the churches and their practices. Emerson gained support, however, from young intellectuals like Theodore Parker, George Ripley, Orestes Brownson, and James Freeman Clarke, who found in Emerson a convincing expression of their own restlessness with the prevalent Unitarian theology, and others like Margaret Fuller, Henry David Thoreau, Christopher Pearse Cranch, and John Sullivan Dwight, who saw in Emerson a literary and aesthetic example, a man who made it seem as if a life of art and letters was indeed possible in America.[13] By 1840 the Transcendentalists had decided to publish their own magazine, the *Dial*, which served as a medium for theology, literature, and social theory, giving this alternative movement a short-lived but influential voice in American culture.[14]

The Moral Law and the Development of the Soul

In addition to his two major addresses of the late 1830s, Emerson also presented annual series of lectures on such topics as "The Philosophy of History" (1836–1837), "Human Culture" (1837–1838), "Human Life" (1838–1839), and "The Present Age" (1839–1840), extending his work as a preacher into a larger national stage. These lectures increased his public following and served as the basis for his second book, *Essays* (1841).[15] In such early lectures as "Religion" (1837), "Holiness" (1838), and "Religion" (1840), Emerson continued to propound a theory of religion that stressed the apprehension of the moral sense and the continual effort to cultivate the innate potential of divinity within the self. "The moments in life when we give ourselves up to the inspirations of this sentiment, seem to be the only real life. The mind is then all light" (*EL*, 2:345). He distilled this religious vision into the essays "Compensation," "Spiritual Laws," "The Over-Soul," and "Circles" in *Essays* (1841), providing there a revitalized understanding and language for religious experience.

"Compensation," now largely overlooked in Emerson's canon, is his most effective exposition of the nature of the moral law, a demonstration of how every decision and act is "moral" because of its involvement in an inescapable web of cause and effect. Emerson explicates this process as a manifestation of the law of "polarity, or action and reaction," the phenomenon by which every fact or event in nature is answered by its opposite. "An inevitable dualism bisects nature, so that each thing is a half, and suggests another thing to make it whole; as spirit, matter; man, woman; odd, even; subjective, objective; in, out; upper, under; motion, rest; yea, nay" (*CW,* 2:57). Emerson argues that "the same dualism underlies the nature and condition of man" (*CW,* 2:58), implicating itself in the inescapable consequence of every act we take. Revising the Christian theology that stressed an eventual retribution in the afterlife for acts during life, Emerson argued instead that "every act rewards itself, or, in other words, integrates itself," moving inevitably to its sometimes unwanted or unintended completion. "Crime and punishment grow out of one stem. Punishment is a fruit that unsuspected ripens within the flower of the pleasure which concealed it" (*CW,* 2:60).

The universe is thus a self-regulated system, physically and morally, in which no single element or act can be isolated from its larger context. An act always carries with it the full consequences of its effect on reality, and those consequences inevitably entail what we know as "reward" and "punishment." "Justice is not postponed. A perfect equity adjusts its balance in all parts of life" (*CW,* 2:60). Punishment is not a judgment from some external source such as God but a manifestation of the "balance" of reality.

This self-regulating balance arises from the deeper implication of the law of polarity, the unbreakable unity of being, in which "the universe is represented in every one of its particles." Every part of nature is a microcosm of the entirety of nature, Emerson argues, and is thus in our practice inseparable from that entirety. "Every thing in nature contains all the powers of nature. Every thing is made of one hidden stuff" (*CW*, 2:59). When this law is perceived in ethical or moral terms, it means that one cannot "detach the sensual sweet, the sensual strong, the sensual bright, &c. from the moral sweet, the moral deep, the moral fair." Self-indulgence, greed, sensuality, and all other self-centered acts are self-condemning, for they violate the soul's law of unity. To violate this law through self-serving action is to cut oneself off from the necessary unity of things, an isolation that cannot be long sustained. "This dividing and detaching is steadily counteracted," Emerson explains. "The parted water re-unites behind our hand" (*CW*, 2:61). Or, translating this concept into the law of reward and punishment, "You cannot do wrong without suffering wrong" (*CW*, 2:64).

The unified moral universe that we encounter in "Compensation" is extended in "Spiritual Laws" and "The Over-Soul," both of which emphasize the necessity of recognizing the transcendent sources and ends of the natural world and of human life. In "Spiritual Laws" Emerson argues the futility of assuming that we can, through the exercise of our wills, achieve satisfactory or fulfilling ends. The better posture is one of openness and humility, based in a recognition that "there is a soul at the centre of nature, and over the will of every man, so that none of us can wrong the universe." Out of this recognition of our fundamental powerlessness, however, a new and different sense of power can emerge. "We need only obey. There is guidance for each of us, and by lowly listening we shall hear the right word" (*CW*, 2:81). While these essays indicate a striking kinship between Emerson's thinking and some of the fundamental concepts of Hinduism and other Asian religions, their roots are more in the traditions of Neoplatonism and Christian mysticism, as Arthur Versluis has shown.[16] But Emerson did have a keen interest in Asian religions, originating in the 1820s and deepening throughout his life. Although initially skeptical of what he felt were the pantheistic and "superstitious" qualities of Asian religions, he found an affinity with Hinduism's mythical representations of the indwelling of God in the individual, and the concept of the universe as the manifestation of one mind, doctrines that he had worked out on a Platonic basis, but for which he found important confirmation in Asian scripture. Using both Western and Eastern traditions, he attempted to forge a universal religion, incorporating the truths from both. Versluis notes that Emerson shared with Thoreau a "sense of contemporaneity with all ages" and attempted in his thinking to transcend "temporal and cultural boundaries" (79).

The "soul at the centre" is the subject of "The Over-Soul," Emerson's extended exposition of the immanent God of the soul and nature. "We live in succession, in division, in parts, in particles. Meantime within man is the soul of the whole; the wise silence; the universal beauty, to which every part and particle is equally related; the eternal ONE" (*CW,* 2:160). While this reformulation of the concept of God is a profound statement of affirmative faith, it also had its troubling qualities for many of Emerson's readers, for it abandoned the idea of a personal deity. The Over-Soul is better conceived as a source of energy, an enabling power, of which each individual is a particular manifestation. "The soul in man is not an organ, but animates and exercises all the organs; is not a function, like the power of memory, of calculation, of comparison, but uses these as hands and feet; is not a faculty, but a light; is not the intellect or the will, but the master of the intellect and the will; is the background of our being, in which they lie,—an immensity not possessed and that cannot be possessed" (*CW,* 2:161). Rather than possession or control, we must exercise a kind of vigilant watchfulness and openness to the disclosures of the soul, or its revelations, the "influx of the Divine mind into our mind" (*CW,* 2:166).

This stance of perpetual openness to new revelation was the focus of "Circles," in which Emerson depicted the self as a perpetually expanding circle, whose circumference represented simultaneously the fact of attainment or accomplishment and the need to continue it. "There is no virtue which is final; all are initial" (*CW,* 2:187), Emerson warned, emphasizing the danger of complacency and the always renewing need to push ahead to the next act, discovery, or goal. Emerson thus represented the spiritual life as one of process, of perpetual change and energy, in which "nothing is secure but life, transition, the energizing spirit" (*CW*, 2:189). In such a world, there was no secure identity except in movement and direction, and even that identity had elements of the unpredictable. "Life is a series of surprises. We do not guess to-day the mood, the pleasure, the power of to-morrow, when we are building up our being" (*CW*, 2:189). For Emerson, such surprises were a crucial guarantor that experience was open, and that the self could be continually renewed and refreshed. "I am only an experimenter. . . . I unsettle all things" (*CW*, 2:188), he declared, emphasizing the restless condition of the soul and its necessity to resist complacency and to push forward perpetually.

This religious vision depended on both determination and energy for its enactment. While Emerson emphasized transformation and empowerment, his doctrine could leave the individual vulnerable to spiritual exhaustion and loss of purpose or direction. In "Circles" he gave the Over-Soul a new name and a new characterization, "the moral fact of the Unattainable, the flying Perfect, around which the hands of man can never meet, at once the inspirer and condemner of every success" (*CW*, 2:179). This paradox of achievement meant that the inspiration to further accomplishment carried with it the eventual condemnation of that accomplishment, and thus created a perpetual, insatiable longing. Emerson expressed this problem through the objection of an imagined skeptical reader who accuses him of arriving at "a fine pyrrhonism, at an equivalence and indifferency of all actions" (*CW*, 2:188). His philosophy undercuts the motivation to act because each act creates the conditions of its own devaluation in our desire for the new. Such a vision threatened motivation and thus moral action itself. Emerson dismissed the objection with a reaffirmation of his faith in the value of experimentation and change, but its presence in "Circles" suggests how his Transcendental optimism was, even as he articulated it, being undermined.

A second form of doubt also emerged during the early 1840s, connected with the waning of Emerson's experience of mystical consciousness. He had based much of his faith on such intense moments of enlightenment, but he came to feel that they were unreliable and increasingly rare. Such experiences come of their own, as moments of grace, but depart just as quickly and mysteriously. They thus provide an increasingly unreliable basis for faith. As he remarked in one journal entry, "We wish to exchange this flash-of-lightning faith for continuous day-light, this fever-glow for a benign climate" (*JMN*, 8:99). Thus he was forced in the 1840s to reexamine and test the faith he had developed, and that decade marks for him a significant intellectual turn.

Emerson's Ethical Vision

Emerson's crisis of faith was deepened by the death of his five-year-old son Waldo in 1842. Emerson's poem "Threnody" is an elegy for Waldo, and there is also an important reference to his death in Emerson's greatest essay, "Experience" (1842), in which he explores his changing assumptions and records his struggle against a loss of faith and optimism.[17] "Where do we find ourselves?" (*CW*, 3:27), he begins, indicating the loss of assurance and direction that marks this new phase. "Experience" is replete with images of bewilderment, enervation, and isolation, and Emerson repeatedly depicts as fragmented and chaotic the world that he had previously shown to be an exemplum of unified purpose. "Well, souls never touch their objects," he writes. "An innavigable sea washes with silent waves between us and the things we aim at and converse with" (*CW*, 3:29).

While "Experience" is ultimately an affirmative essay, the affirmation that Emerson offers is more tempered and of a different quality from the optimistic faith of his early essays. Midway through the essay he declares that happiness is "to fill the hour" (*CW*, 3:35), seeing in concerted action a certain release from fruitless introspection and an avenue to fulfillment that philosophy may never yield. "To finish the moment, to find the journey's end in every step of the road, to live the greatest number of good hours, is wisdom" (*CW*, 3:35). While the circumstances of life are complex and unpredictable enough to prevent us from relying

completely on such pragmatic remedies, "Experience" moves toward ethical purpose and pragmatic action as the most reliable
reconstitution of spiritual experience. Even in the face of repeated loss and defeat, experience teaches us to maintain a
courageous and tenacious patience. "Never mind the ridicule,
never mind the defeat: up again, old heart!—it seems to say,—
there is victory yet for all justice; and the true romance which the
world exists to realize, will be the transformation of genius into
practical power" (*CW*, 3:49).

By endorsing the end of "practical power," Emerson was placing new emphasis on the life of morally directed action, and on
the larger goals of political transformation and the accomplishment of social justice. During the late 1840s and early 1850s, as his
reputation and public influence grew, he elevated ethical work
over mystical vision as the focus of the spiritual life and preached
a religion of action, in which the devotion to a principled task became a new route to enlightenment and a new mode of worship.[18] "I like not the man who is thinking how to be good," he
remarked in his journal, "but the man thinking how to accomplish his work" (*JMN*, 15:462).

Emerson's change in emphasis was reinforced by the climate
of social experiment and political reform in the 1840s, which
brought a number of his friends to regard political commitment
as the fundamental measure of religion. By temperament Emerson was not inclined toward political engagement, but he came
to see that in some areas, particularly slavery, it was the right and
necessary step for his moment in history. He watched with sympathy and interest while friends such as George Ripley and Bronson Alcott undertook utopian communal experiments at Brook
Farm and Fruitlands, and although he remained skeptical about
the viability of such experiments, he shared the alienation from
conventional social patterns and practices, and concurred in the
hope for a social system that shared goods and power more
justly, and was less competitive and materialistic.[19]

In later volumes *The Conduct of Life* (1860) and *Society and Solitude* (1870), Emerson criticized the materialistic and consumerist
qualities of American culture and tried to redefine the American
myth of success in terms of higher principle. He condemned the

"shallow Americanism" (*W,* 7:290) that focused entirely on the amassing of wealth by any means as the measure of success, and insisted that the performance of satisfying work or the accomplishment of worthwhile and helpful duties was a better measure of success. Wealth cannot be defined in purely economic terms, he explained in the essay by that title; it is better thought of as widened possibilities of living, and opportunities for deeper experience. Money can be useful in creating such opportunities, but it can also be obstructive. When it becomes an end in itself, it destroys the very possibilities of richer experience that it should have made available.

Emerson thus engaged American culture as a critic of its values and practices, calling his readers back to a principled life of "plain living and high thinking" (*W,* 7:116) and urging a renewed attention to the details of ordinary life and daily experience. His conscience was also engaged deeply by the continued existence of slavery in America, and he became an increasingly outspoken opponent of it during the 1840s and 1850s, seeing the antislavery movement as a great moral crusade. Len Gougeon has traced the stages by which Emerson became committed to antislavery, and this deepening political commitment paralleled and reinforced his new pragmatic emphasis.[20] Of particular note are Emerson's two addresses on the Fugitive Slave Law in 1851 and 1854, in which he emphasized the moral violation that slavery represented and fiercely attacked the public policy that condoned its continuation. The law, which required the cooperation of citizens and public officials in the North in the return of escaped slaves, was for Emerson "contrary to the primal sentiment of duty," and, therefore, "the resistance of all moral beings is secured to it" (*AW,* 58). It was for him a case in which a higher law, grounded in moral duty, must override a flawed civil enactment. "This law must be made inoperative," he declared in 1851. "It must be abrogated and wiped out of the statute-book; but whilst it stands there, it must be disobeyed" (*AW,* 71).

This call to resist and disobey the law signaled the growing seriousness of the political crisis as Emerson saw it, and although he did not welcome the building tensions and the threat of disunion and war, he saw no alternative but to face it with the conviction of a religious duty, making it clear that slavery was a grave moral challenge, and identifying its eradication with the broad sweep of historical progress. "I know that when seen near, and in detail, slavery is disheartening. But Nature is not so helpless but it can rid itself at last of every wrong" (*AW,* 85). Emerson's historical optimism was a crucial part of his message as an antislavery writer; for him, slavery was a fundamental violation of the natural order of the world, and could not be permanent. But its eradication, while perhaps inevitable, required the exertion of will and energy within the present generation. "Liberty is never cheap," he remarked, admitting that "mountains of difficulty must be surmounted" in the struggle to attain it (*AW,* 86). But as he also added, "Liberty is aggressive. Liberty is the Crusade of all brave and conscientious men" (*AW,* 88). That willful aggressiveness, the historical manifestation of the moral sense through the human will, is the element of nature that ultimately can restore the rightful moral balance to the world. The "Providence" that guides the world, he says in conclusion, "will not save us but through our own co-operation" (*AW,* 89).

Emerson's Later Religious Writings

Emerson's orientation toward moral and political action, a shift reinforced by the historical circumstances of the American political crisis, did not completely displace his continuing interest in speculative and poetic work. Although his faith in the kind of immediate mystical enlightenment represented by the "transparent eye-ball" experience waned, he increased his attention to other sources or processes of revelation, finding in the closely related categories of inspiration and symbolism important means through which the world reveals itself to us.

Emerson distilled much of his later thinking about perception and inspiration into "Poetry and Imagination" (*W,* 8:1–75), an essay that evolved through several versions from the 1840s until its presentation as a lecture in 1872.[21] Although its specific context was literary creativity, the essay is closely related to Emerson's continuing speculation on religious understanding, since for him the inspiration that made poetry possible and the inspiration that we link to religious knowledge and piety were inseparable. Both poetic and religious understanding were forms of symbolic perception, the capacity to see the connections among the separate entities of nature, and to recognize, through the perpetual expansion of such kinships, the ultimate unity of the universe. "God himself does not speak in prose" (*W*, 8:12), he wrote, referring to the poetic and symbolic quality of the world's various scriptures, and to the idea he had advanced earlier in *Nature*, that the parts of the world themselves were symbolic, always suggesting a larger truth beyond their simple factuality. "Nature itself is a vast trope, and all particular natures are tropes" (*W*, 8:15), he declared, thus making perception a constant work of associating and drawing analogies. "All thinking is analogizing," a pushing at the boundaries of the separate identities we confront to find larger categories of association. Emerson names the imagination as the "reader of these forms," the intellectual faculty driving this "endless passing of one element into new forms, the incessant metamorphosis" (*W*, 8:15).

Emerson's depiction of the power of imagination and metaphor in the perception of the ultimate nature of reality is part of a growing interest in the nature of perception that marks his later thought, a focus of one of his most ambitious projects, *The Natural History of Intellect*. Although he was never able to complete the project as fully as he had originally conceived it, he offered a provisional version in a series of lectures at Harvard in 1870.[22] Impressed with the progress that scientists had made in their understanding of the history and processes of the natural world, Emerson believed that the same kind of intellectual model could be developed to explain the nature and processes of the mind. Moreover, he felt that progress in natural science would necessarily result in an increased understanding of the realm of the mental.

Emerson's commitment to the work of modern science was less a divergence from the idealism that he had espoused in *Nature* and other early works than a way of confirming it. "I believe in the existence of the material world as the expression of the spiritual or the real," he declared, adding that "I await the insight which our advancing knowledge of material laws shall furnish" (*W*, 12:5). He regarded scientific progress as the advancing ability to explain the universe in terms of the functioning of laws, thus reducing the seemingly disparate particulars of phenomena to the expression of a unified force or system. "There is in Nature a parallel unity which corresponds to the unity in the mind and makes it available. This methodizing mind meets no resistance in its attempts" (*W*, 12:19–20).

Imagination, whether expressed in poetic metaphor or the refinement of an explanatory natural law, was the conjunction of the mind's innate push toward the perception of unity with the corresponding revelation of unity in the physical universe. The perpetual tendency of the imagination was thus to reduce multiplicity to unity, to perceive order through chaos. Unwavering in his belief in the integral unity of the world, Emerson continued to seek and find confirmations of this fundamental belief in psychology, mythology, the natural sciences, and almost every other human expression or endeavor. It was his deepest and longest held belief, the foundation of both his religious and his ethical vision.

Even though Emerson's belief in a fundamentally unified cosmos, ordered by law and permeated with spiritual energy, could yield much of religious significance and value, it left open one of the questions that pressed men and women the hardest in the nineteenth century, the immortality of the soul. Emerson's "Over-Soul," the Transcendentalist answer to the Christian concept of the deity, was explicitly impersonal, an energy or law of being that could not be reduced to human definition or analogy. While he was willing to say that "I am a better believer, and all serious souls are better believers in the immortality, than we can give grounds for" (*W*, 8:346), he was careful to distinguish between such a faith and the more commonly accepted notion of the continuing existence of the separate, individual consciousness. He lectured often on the subject, recognizing that the undermining of traditional Christian beliefs that resulted from modern science left many in a kind of anguished doubt. But as his late compilation "Immortality" (*W*, 8:321–52) suggests, he also recognized that he could offer only a limited form of assurance in calling his audience to a larger view of what immortality might mean when separated from the fate of particular individuals. Confessing that "there is a drawback to the value of all statements of the doctrine," he registered a reluctance in "writing or printing on the immortality of the soul." Readers come with a desire for confirmation and reassurance about their personal fate, something that he cannot provide: "the hungry eyes that run through it will close disappointed; the listeners say, That is not here which we desire" (*W*, 8:345).

Emerson believed that the conventional religious hope for personal immortality was a distortion of both individual identity and the nature of existence itself. His strategy therefore was to bring his readers to consider the issue from a higher perspective, one that did not so immediately involve their self-interest. Without a surrender of self-interest, one cannot understand the sense in which immortality may be affirmed. "I confess that everything connected with our personality fails. Nature never spares the individual" (*W*, 8:342–43). Instead, we must come to see immortality as a larger condition or quality of reality in which we have a part, or to which we contribute. Our concern must be shifted away from ourselves and directed toward something larger than us. "The soul stipulates for no private good. That which is private I see not to be good." It is not what we believe or experience that is the basis of immortality, but what we help to create, or enact. "We have our indemnity only in the moral and intellectual reality to which we aspire. That is immortal, and we only through that" (*W*, 8:343).

There is a form of assurance or comfort in this view of immortality, but to obtain it we must surrender our demand for an eternally enduring separate consciousness, a demand that Emerson depicts as fundamentally shallow. "Here are people who cannot dispose of a day; an hour hangs heavy on their hands; and will you offer them rolling ages without end?" (*W*, 8:348). For Emerson, it is only when "the last garment of egotism falls" that the individual is "with God," a state in which he or she "shares the will and immensity of the First Cause" (*W*, 8:348–49). Religious growth is in this sense an increasing capacity to displace private needs and desires with more selfless and universal ones.

Immortality, then, "is not length of life, but depth of life. It is not duration, but a taking of the soul out of time, as all high action of the mind does: when we are living in the sentiments we ask no questions about time" (*W,* 8:347). That intensity of experience, involving as it does a commitment to a continuing energetic creativity, constitutes the religious life for Emerson. His religious vision offers one of the most challenging and original modern approaches to the question of religious faith.

NOTES

1. For information on these early family influences, see Evelyn Barish, *Emerson: The Roots of Prophecy* (Princeton, N.J.: Princeton University Press, 1989), pp. 3–71; *The Selected Letters of Mary Moody Emerson,* ed. Nancy Craig Simmons (Athens: University of Georgia Press, 1993); Robert D. Richardson, Jr., *Emerson: The Mind on Fire* (Berkeley: University of California Press, 1995), pp. 3–59; and Phyllis Cole, *Mary Moody Emerson and the Origins of Transcendentalism* (New York: Oxford University Press, 1998).

2. On the origins and development of New England Unitarianism, see Conrad Wright, *The Beginnings of Unitarianism in America* (1955; rpt., Hamden, Conn.: Archon Books, 1976). For the influence of Unitarian ideas and culture on Emerson, see Lawrence Buell, *Literary Transcendentalism: Style and Vision in the American Renaissance* (Ithaca, N.Y.: Cornell University Press, 1973); and David M. Robinson, *Apostle of Culture: Emerson as Preacher and Lecturer* (Philadelphia: University of Pennsylvania Press, 1982).

3. On the doctrine of the preparation of the soul, see Perry Miller, "'Preparation for Salvation' in Seventeenth-Century New England," in his *Nature's Nation* (Cambridge: Harvard University Press, 1967); and Norman Pettit, *The Heart Prepared: Grace and Conversion in Puritan Spiritual Life* (New Haven, Conn.: Yale University Press, 1966).

4. On the denominational emergence of Unitarianism, see Daniel Walker Howe, *The Unitarian Conscience: Harvard Moral Philosophy, 1805–1861* (1970; rpt., Middletown, Conn.: Wesleyan University Press, 1988); Conrad Wright, ed., *A Stream of Light: A Sesquicentennial History of American Unitarianism* (Boston: Unitarian Universalist Association, 1975); David M. Robinson, *The Unitarians*

and the Universalists (Westport, Conn.: Greenwood Press, 1985), pp. 25–46; and Conrad E. Wright, ed., *American Unitarianism, 1805–1865* (Boston: Northeastern University Press in cooperation with the Massachusetts Historical Society, 1989).

5. For discussions of the concept of "moral sense" in Emerson, see Stephen E. Whicher, *Freedom and Fate: An Inner Life of Ralph Waldo Emerson* (Philadelphia: University of Pennsylvania Press, 1953), pp. 6–16; Jonathan Bishop, *Emerson on the Soul* (Cambridge: Harvard University Press, 1964), pp. 66–72; and Robinson, *Apostle of Culture*, pp. 50–55.

6. On Emerson's crisis of health, see Barish, *Emerson: The Roots of Prophecy*, pp. 145–210.

7. On Emerson's preaching career, see Robinson, *Apostle of Culture*; and "Historical Introduction" (*CS*, 1:1–32); Wesley T. Mott, *"The Strains of Eloquence": Emerson and His Sermons* (University Park: Pennsylvania State University Press, 1989); and Susan Roberson, *Emerson in His Sermons* (Columbia: University of Missouri Press, 1995).

8. There is a vast literature on Emerson's intellectual sources. The best single source for understanding how his wide reading shaped his thinking is Richardson, *Emerson: The Mind on Fire*. Other important sources include Kenneth Walter Cameron, *Emerson the Essayist*, 2 vols. (Raleigh, N.C.: Thistle Press, 1945); Sherman Paul, *Emerson's Angle of Vision: Man and Nature in American Experience* (Cambridge: Harvard University Press, 1952); Henry Pochmann, *German Culture in America* (Madison: University of Wisconsin Press, 1957); David Van Leer, *Emerson's Epistemology: The Argument of the Essays* (Cambridge: Cambridge University Press, 1986); and Leon Chai, *The Romantic Foundations of the American Renaissance* (Ithaca, N.Y.: Cornell University Press, 1987). For informative discussions of Emerson's early religious development, see, in addition to Whicher and Paul, Sheldon W. Liebman, "Emerson's Transformation in the 1820's," *American Literature* 40 (May 1968): 133–54; and Robert Milder, "Emerson's Two Conversions," *ESQ: A Journal of the American Renaissance*, 33 (1st Quarter 1987): 20–34.

9. For Emerson's views of science, see Harry Hayden Clark, "Emerson and Science," *Philological Quarterly* 10 (July 1931): 225–60; Robinson, *Apostle of Culture*, pp. 71–94; Robinson, "Fields of Investigation: Emerson and Natural History," in *American Literature and Sci-*

ence, ed. Robert Scholnick, (Lexington: University Press of Kentucky, 1992), pp. 94–109; and Lee Rust Brown, *The Emerson Museum* (Cambridge: Harvard University Press, 1997).

10. On *Nature* see B. L. Packer, *Emerson's Fall: A New Interpretation of the Major Essays* (New York: Continuum, 1992); Robinson, *Apostle of Culture,* pp. 85–94; Van Leer, *Emerson's Epistemology,* pp. 19–58; and Alan D. Hodder, *Emerson's Rhetoric of Revelation* (University Park: Pennsylvania State University Press, 1989).

11. On Emerson's development and use of the concept of the scholar, see Merton M. Sealts, Jr., *Emerson on the Scholar* (Columbia: University of Missouri Press, 1992). For a discussion of the push of the intellect for ever newer creation, see Richard Poirier, *The Renewal of Literature: Emersonian Reflections* (New York: Random House, 1987); and Poirier, *Poetry and Pragmatism* (Cambridge: Harvard University Press, 1992).

12. On the "Divinity School Address" and the ensuing controversy it provoked, see Perry Miller, *The Transcendentalists: An Anthology* (Cambridge: Harvard University Press, 1950); C. Conrad Wright, "Emerson, Barzillai Frost, and the Divinity School Address," in his *The Liberal Christians: Essays on American Unitarian History* (Boston: Beacon Press, 1970), pp. 41–61, 128–31; Packer, *Emerson's Fall,* pp. 121–37; Robinson, *Apostle of Culture,* pp. 123–37; and Robinson, "Poetry, Personality, and the Divinity School Address," *Harvard Theological Review* 82 (1989): 185–99.

13. For an informative history of the Transcendentalist movement, see Barbara Packer, "The Transcendentalists," in *The Cambridge History of American Literature,* vol. 2, ed. Sacvan Bercovitch (Cambridge: Cambridge University Press, 1995), pp. 329–604.

14. On the history of the *Dial,* see Joel Myerson, *The New England Transcendentalists and the* Dial: *A History of the Magazine and Its Contributors* (Rutherford, N.J.: Fairleigh Dickinson University Press, 1980).

15. The volume was given the title *Essays: First Series* after Emerson published a second collection of essays in 1844 as *Essays: Second Series.*

16. See Arthur Versluis, *American Transcendentalism and Asian Religions* (Oxford: Oxford University Press, 1993), pp. 54–61.

17. On the significance of "Experience," see Whicher, *Freedom and Fate,* pp. 109–22; Packer, *Emerson's Fall,* pp. 148–211; Van Leer,

Emerson's Epistemology, pp. 143–87; and David M. Robinson, *Emerson and the Conduct of Life: Pragmatism and Ethical Purpose in the Later Work* (New York: Cambridge University Press, 1993), pp. 54–70.

18. For a detailed discussion of Emerson's move toward a more pragmatic, ethically oriented outlook, see Cornel West, *The American Evasion of Philosophy: A Genealogy of Pragmatism* (Madison: University of Wisconsin Press, 1989), pp. 9–41; Robinson, *Emerson and the Conduct of Life;* James M. Albrecht, "'Living Property': Emerson's Ethics," *ESQ: A Journal of the American Renaissance* 41 (1995): 177–217; and Michael Lopez, *Emerson and Power: Creative Antagonism in the Nineteenth Century* (DeKalb: Northern Illinois University Press, 1996).

19. For an informative consideration of the utopian experiments influenced by Transcendentalist thought, see Richard Francis, *Transcendental Utopias: Individual and Community at Brook Farm, Fruitlands, and Walden* (Ithaca, N.Y.: Cornell University Press, 1997).

20. On Emerson's commitment to the antislavery cause, see Len Gougeon, *Virtue's Hero: Emerson, Antislavery, and Reform* (Athens: University of Georgia Press, 1989); *AW;* and Eduardo Cadava, *Emerson and the Climates of History* (Stanford, Calif.: Stanford University Press, 1997). For a discussion of Emerson's influence on the antislavery movement, see Albert J. von Frank, *The Trials of Anthony Burns: Freedom and Slavery in Emerson's Boston* (Cambridge, Mass.: Harvard Univeristy Press, 1998).

21. On the significance of this later work as a key statement of Emerson's poetic theory, see Ronald A. Bosco, "'Poetry for the World of Readers' and 'Poetry for Bards Proper': Theory and Textual Integrity in Emerson's *Parnassus,*" in *Studies in the American Renaissance 1989,* ed. Joel Myerson (Charlottesville: University Press of Virginia, 1989), pp. 257–312.

22. See Ronald A. Bosco, "His Lectures Were Poetry, His Teaching the Music of the Spheres: Annie Adams Fields and Francis Greenwood Peabody on Emerson's 'Natural History of the Intellect' University Lectures at Harvard in 1870," *Harvard Library Bulletin,* n.s., 8 (Summer 1997): 1–79.

Emerson and Antislavery

Gary Collison

"Emerson," said Oliver Wendell Holmes in his 1884 biography, "had never been identified with the abolitionists."[1] Many biographers and critics have argued that just the opposite is true, pointing to Emerson's numerous private and public statements against slavery. Still, for a variety of reasons, Holmes's erroneous view of Emerson has been remarkably persistent. Not the least of these reasons are Emerson's own words. "Every reformer is partial and exaggerates some one grievance," and every reformer's obsessions are "somewhat ridiculous," wrote Emerson in his 1839 lecture "The Protest" (*EL*, 91). Even as the Civil War approached and Emerson shared the platform with abolitionists on dozens of occasions, he still disdainfully kept many of them at arm's length. "They are a bitter, sterile people, whom I flee from," he wrote in his journal (*JMN*, 14:166). Similar disparaging remarks about abolitionists and other reformers punctuate Emerson's lectures, journals, and letters. This attitude, together with his oft-expressed repugnance toward involvement in the political arena and his insistent self-portraiture of himself as a poet-philosopher, has inevitably supported the view promoted by Holmes of an aloof and remote "Sage of Concord."

The trajectory of Emerson's career and interest in antislavery provides another explanation of why he has often been thought detached from the antislavery battle. The works of his early career, *Nature* (1836), *Essays: First Series* (1841), and *Essays: Second Series* (1844), give little hint that he was at all concerned with the immediate social issues of his day. These works of the first decade of Emerson's career as an essayist and lecturer were written before he had developed a more activist stance and when radical abolitionists constituted a widely despised vocal minority. Critics who have seen Emerson as essentially opposed to abolition have concentrated on this earlier period of his career and thus viewed Emerson's position as static rather than dynamic. As was also true in the case of Henry Thoreau, Emerson's views gradually evolved until the passage of the Fugitive Slave Law of 1850 provided the impetus for a far more radical stance and for much greater participation in the campaign against slavery. Emerson delivered the majority of his important lectures on the subject of slavery in the two decades following the passage of the new law, a period of his career that until recently has been given comparatively little attention. These later works expressed a far more radical position.

Trends in historiography and literary criticism have also helped to diminish appreciation of Emerson's antislavery activities. Generations of historians saw the Transcendentalists as, at best, lightweight dilettantes who had little influence in the abolitionist arena. This view was challenged by Stanley Elkin's *Slavery: A Problem in American Institutional and Intellectual Life* (1959), which took the Transcendentalists seriously. However, Elkins concluded that their impact was largely negative because their uncompromising idealism and rigid self-righteousness rendered them unable to work practically for reform. Thus, although Elkins helped bring Emerson and the Transcendentalists onto center stage, ultimately he ended up merely adding a new twist to the historians' conventional judgments. In literature departments, the reign of New Criticism from the 1940s through the 1960s also devalued Emerson's interest in antislavery and reform. New Criticism turned away from biographical and historical contexts to focus on the words, images, metaphors, and other formal elements of Emerson's writings. While this narrowing of attention to texts rather than contexts brought about a new, unprecedented appreciation of Emerson's artistry, it also consciously marginalized the religious, political, and social dimensions and contexts of his works. This negative effect was magnified by the fact that the New Critics concentrated on Emerson's earlier, most densely poetical works.

That situation has changed dramatically. Since 1960, a flood of scholarly attention to abolitionism, slavery, African-American history, Transcendentalism, and related topics has inevitably brought attention to the byways of Emerson's career and to his connections with his cultural world. The rise of social history and cultural studies greatly expanded the field of vision of both the historical and the English professions and in the process helped to break down the wall between the two disciplines. This development has made it possible to examine how Emerson's life and ideas are woven into the fabric of his times and how important Emersonian threads have been to developing patterns of idealism in antebellum culture. Studies of Emerson's involvement with antislavery and other reforms reached their climax in 1990 with the publication of Len Gougeon's *Virtue's Hero: Emerson, Antislavery, and Reform,* an exhaustive study of Emerson's relationship to and involvement in the antislavery crusade. This work was followed by Gougeon and Joel Myerson's *Emerson's Antislavery Writings* (1995), which brought together Emerson's extant major antislavery statements, including some that had not been included in Emerson's collected works. Together these two publications reveal the dynamic evolution of Emerson's views and convincingly demonstrate what many of Emerson's contemporaries and biographers already knew—that his contribution to the antislavery movement was considerable.

To be sure, the collection of Emerson's lectures and published letters on the subject edited by Myerson and Gougeon makes a slim volume. Of eighteen extant pieces written between 1838 and 1863, only a few are extended discussions of slavery. The first extended lecture was delivered to a small audience of Emerson's neighbors in Concord. Almost all of his contributions are occasional pieces arising in response to a new public conflict over slavery. But taken together with other statements by Emerson for which no manuscript or printed copy survives and with the many passages concerned with slavery in his letters and journals, they show Emerson's intense devotion to the American ideals of liberty and freedom transforming him into a passionate advocate for the abolition of slavery. They show him thinking often and deeply about slavery, participating in abolitionist rallies, and corresponding and debating with dozens of abolitionist friends and acquaintances. They show a progressive evolution of his relationship to antislavery and a progressive evolution of his thought. They reveal that when the Fugitive Slave Law energized the movement by giving it a new raison d'être, Emerson could not help but be drawn even further into the debate.[2] Later works show how, by the 1850s, Emerson had moved away from his original "moral suasionist" view—a faith in the power of reason to convert the Southerner—toward the increasingly militant, radical stance similar to that also adopted by his friend Henry Thoreau.

The work of Gougeon and Myerson, together with newer works that build on their conclusions, such as Robert D. Richardson, Jr.'s, *Emerson: The Mind on Fire* (1995) and, especially, Albert J. von Frank's *The Trials of Anthony Burns: Freedom and Slavery in Emerson's Boston* (1998), also make the important argument that Emerson's contributions add up to far more than the mere numerical sum of his public letters and speeches.[3] As von Frank has put it, "One may make a careful survey of Emerson's opinions . . . and never come close to what it was in his thought that made a difference in the struggle" (p. xvii). The reason one would "never come close" is that such an approach lacks an understanding of the way in which antebellum American culture had accorded Emerson a privileged position. Emerson's reputation as America's leading intellectual gave *any* participation enormous power and impact. By the 1840s he had become the de facto spiritual leader to whom a large group of Americans, mostly Northerners, looked for instruction, guidance, and inspiration. Emerson's unstinting defense of idealism, with its call to higher morality and its elevation of the individual conscience over the laws of society, influenced many Americans to question the governmental policies and to apply standards to American society that exceeded—and often contradicted—those set in the political, economic, social, and even religious realms. Emerson filled a void in American culture. Von Frank even argues that "the culture was such as to allow Emerson to be almost infinitely reduplicated in others, to live and act through men and women, whom he may . . . be said to have colonized" (p. xviii). Whether or not one is willing to go as far as von Frank in assigning an almost hypnotic agency to Emerson's antislavery participation, it is clear from recent work that Emerson became thoroughly engaged in the slavery debate and ended up playing a significant role in the campaign against slavery.

Emerson's Antislavery Background

Emerson's religious and social background explains a great deal of his early reluctance to participate in reform in general and the antislavery movement in particular. The son of a Unitarian clergyman and a clergyman himself, early in his career he inevitably reflected some of the fundamental assumptions and viewpoints common to the denomination and his ministerial role. "Unitarians were conservative, believers in providential arrangements of society, believers in respectability, in class distinctions," wrote second-generation Unitarian minister O. B. Frothingham.[4] Ministers tended to reflect the views of the social class that filled the best pews, the businessmen, entrepreneurs, the aristocracy of old money. If anything, the growth of free-market capitalism in the first half of the nineteenth century exacerbated this identification with money and power. The typical Unitarian minister, with his disdain for "agitating" subjects and abhorrence of strident "enthusiasm" and "fanaticism," shunned the radical abolitionists and other zealous reformers as a species of madmen who would willingly bring down the whole of society to make their point. Emerson inherited the cast of mind and the reticent personality that were endemic among Unitarians and, as a young clergyman in Boston in the early 1830s, reflected the familiar Unitarian critique of mass reform movements from his Second Church pulpit. His private opinions were even more critical. The abolitionists are an "odious set . . . the worst of bores and canters," reads one journal entry, a fairly typical sample of Emerson's early opinions (*JMN*, 9:120). Much of this inheritance, as much temperamental as intellectual, would remain with him for his entire life. He would never lose his abhorrence of partisan politics or his distrust of organizations that demanded allegiance to a standard line of thought.

But other aspects of the New England Unitarian heritage could more than cancel the inherent conservative impulses. When the original Unitarians broke away from the Congregational Church in the early decades of the nineteenth century, they did so reluctantly and were careful to disagree with gentlemanly decorum, yet they obviously exhibited a strong reform orientation from their moment of origin. Devotion to conscience, self-culture, and independence of mind provided fertile ground on which social reform causes could naturally take hold and flourish. Also, the notion of social responsibility that was inherent in the ministry and in the Brahmin cast of mind provided a powerful springboard for a reform mentality among Unitarians. Unitarian ministers and laypersons figured prominently in the peace and temperance movements, in prison reform, in poor relief, and in other humanitarian causes that emerged in the first half of the nineteenth century when growing immigration, urbanization, and industrialization created social problems of a scale and complexity that rendered the older small-scale individual and parish-led methods of social amelioration increasingly ineffective. The most prominent first-generation Unitarian leader, William Ellery Channing, went about as far as possible in the liberal reform direction without rejecting his Congregational background entirely. Beginning as early as 1831, at almost the exact moment that William Lloyd Garrison was rejecting gradualism and African colonization as fraudulent and embracing the cause of immediate abolition, Channing swallowed the repugnance he felt for the abolitionist "agitators" and began to speak out publicly against slavery. In publishing his slim volume entitled *Slavery* in 1835, Channing lent his enormous reputation as the most highly respected preacher of the era, at least in New England, to the abolitionist movement, despite serious misgivings about the tactics of the Garrisonians and other radicals.

Emerson and other Transcendentalist ministers such as Theodore Parker and George Ripley were great admirers of Channing, whom they regarded as the elder statesman of liberal religion, and with whom many retained intimate friendships until Channing's death in 1842. Henry Ware, Jr., another first-generation Unitarian whose liberalism led him cautiously but inexorably toward a public antislavery stance, was senior pastor at Boston's Second Church when Emerson began his ministry there. Most of the second-generation Unitarian ministers who became Transcendentalists, including Emerson and Theodore Parker, would imitate these mentors in being slow to take up the cause of antislavery. But as a group they would follow and then surpass their mentors in many reform arenas. The Transcendental Club, where Emerson joined many of his former ministerial colleagues, became a forum for debating how to reform both church and society. Reform impulses from within the group led to the experimental utopian community at Brook Farm (1841–1847), founded by Ripley after he resigned from the Unitarian ministry. In antislavery, the Transcendentalist circle had the examples of other ministerial colleagues such as Charles Follen and Samuel J. May, a full-blown Garrisonian. William Henry Furness, Emerson's colleague and close friend, became increasingly vigorous in his support of the abolitionist cause. Lydia Maria Child, one of the most outspoken New England abolitionists, was sister to Unitarian minister Convers Francis, sometime "moderator" of Transcendental Club meetings. Such connections could be expanded almost endlessly. Suffice it to say that an extensive, evergrowing network of reform and antislavery Unitarian ministers and laypersons tied Emerson to the antislavery movement in dozens, even hundreds, of ways.[5]

For Emerson, another set of personal connections to antislavery would result from his 1834 move to Concord, Massachusetts, shortly after he resigned from his duties as minister of the Second Church of Boston. Although distancing him from the immediate world of Boston antislavery as well as from the Boston black community (with which, however, Emerson appears to have had only very limited contact), the move brought him into a new, more intimate and more inescapable antislavery orbit.

Many of Emerson's Concord neighbors and friends of the next three decades already sympathized with the antislavery cause by the time he arrived. The Concord Female Anti-Slavery Society took the lead in local antislavery work, promoting the cause by holding meetings, distributing literature, sponsoring lectures, and supporting other activities, including taking care of fugitive slaves. The Concord Lyceum frequently invited antislavery figures to lecture, with Emerson himself sometimes penning the invitations. Concordians were regular subscribers to William Lloyd Garrison's *Liberator*. Friends and neighbors, many of whom were leading citizens of the town, took fleeing fugitive slaves into their homes and assisted them to their next destinations. John Brown would later visit Concord to solicit support for his dangerous endeavors, and F. B. Sanborn, later Emerson's biographer, joined the so-called Secret Six conspirators who helped raise funds that John Brown used for his 1859 raid on the federal arsenal at Harpers Ferry. As with Emerson's connections to Unitarian antislavery figures, his Concord connections multiplied his links to the antislavery network almost indefinitely.[6]

Emerson's own family surrounded him with an even more intimate and no less intense antislavery climate. Concord minister Ezra Ripley (d. 1841), Emerson's stepgrandfather and a principal member of the Middlesex County Anti-Slavery Society, spoke out publicly against slavery in the 1830s. Emerson's intellectual aunt, Mary Moody Emerson, was staunchly opposed to slavery, and her influence on her nephew was profound. She regularly proselytized him and even plotted a breakfast for the visiting British abolitionist George Thompson at her unsuspecting nephew's home. About the same time, Emerson's elder brother Charles gave an antislavery lecture in Concord, and both brothers defended British writer Harriet Martineau after she aroused a storm of criticism for openly espousing sympathy with the abolitionists. Emerson's second wife, Lidian, was an active and vocal member of the Concord Female Anti-Slavery Society, as were the Thoreau women and many other wives of Concord's elite.[7]

Given his liberal-Unitarian ties, his activist Concord friends and neighbors, and his family history of involvement, antislavery was an integral part of Emerson's environment. Not surprisingly, the subject of slavery appears with considerable regularity in Emerson's private as well as public writings from 1821 onward. In 1826, he mentioned "the slave's misery" in his first sermon. Like Channing, Emerson found his opposition to slavery further strengthened by a brush with the real thing on a visit to the South for his health. Emerson made certain that his Second Church congregation knew that he hated slavery and other social evils and expected them to feel the same way. "Let every man say then to himself— the cause of the Indian, it is mine; the cause of the slave, it is mine" (*CS*, 4:115), he exhorted his Fast Day audience in 1832.[8] In 1837, prompted by the murder of abolitionist editor Elijah Lovejoy in Alton, Illinois, Emerson delivered an entire address on the subject of slavery. The address does not survive, but Emerson's notes and journal entries show that its thrust was a vigorous defense of the principle of free speech.

Joining the Cause: 1837–1843

The antislavery influences in Emerson's environment did not automatically make him into an antislavery activist. His first major foray as a reformer, an 1838 letter to President Van Buren protesting the expulsion of the Cherokees from their homelands in the South, he found a disturbing, hateful task. "I fully sympathize, be sure . . . ," he wrote in his journal, adding with annoyance, "It is not my impulse to say it & therefore my genius deserts me, no muse befriends, no music of thought or of word accompanies. Bah!" (*JMN*, 5:479). But the multiple influences of family, friends, neighbors, and colleagues, together with his growing sense of his responsibilities as an American spokesman for idealism, were to lead him inexorably into the antislavery camp.

How strands of Emerson's life and thought connect with social activism in general and antislavery in particular during his early career is nowhere better explained than in his famous 1837 address "The American Scholar," which he delivered before Harvard University's Phi Beta Kappa Society. Although the speech says nothing directly about antislavery, it has much to tell us about Emerson's positioning himself in the landscape of reform and articulates the tensions that were to continue to define his lifelong ambivalent relationship with abolitionism. On one side of his equation delineating the life of the true scholar Emerson placed the role as poet-philosopher-scholar, which he saw as demanding absolute intellectual freedom as well as long periods of intense concentration away from the jangling demands of daily life. The free mind needed separation and independence to escape the suffocating influences of tradition and conformity; without this independence, the poet-scholar would shrink into the bookworm, the pedant, and the parrot. "Society everywhere is in conspiracy against the manhood of every one of its members," he would say in "Self Reliance" (*CW,* 2:29).

But while Emerson placed absolute independence of mind and an essentially art-for-art's-sake position on one side of his formula, on the other he placed the ideal of duty. The concepts of duty and work were deeply rooted in his history and psyche. In addition to the traditional duties assigned to the scholar to remember the past and study its lessons, the true scholar for Emerson was also to be part priest, part prophet, and part poet. His role, he announced toward the end of "The American Scholar," was "to cheer, to raise, and to guide men by showing them facts amidst appearances" (*CW,* 1:62). This definition of a highly social role, a role as a leader, a shaper of public opinion, has obvious roots in his ministerial background. The resulting tension between the conflicting demands of Emerson's creative genius for isolation and disengagement and the demands of his public role as guide and preceptor to his community and to humanity would continue to define and plague Emerson throughout his career.

It is no coincidence that the 1837 sermon, his first open pronouncement on antislavery, was delivered about the same time as "The American Scholar" and the even more radical "Divinity School Address" (1838). In these revolutionary years Emerson was breaking free of the conventional role he had assumed in choosing the formal role of minister, a role that he soon found stifling. But having gained his independence from the constraints of the ministerial role, Emerson was not eager to relinquish it to a cause or crusade. While he respected the work of reform because it was built on a foundation of divine principles, he was unwilling to force his energies into a narrow channel. It took another seven years before Emerson was ready to deliver another public antislavery address. The occasion was the tenth anniversary of the emancipation of the slaves in the British West Indies on 1 August 1834. The program of antislavery lectures scheduled that day in Concord was one of many such events throughout New England. Both the Fourth of July and the first of August had become annual events in the abolitionist calendar. They were natural occasions for attacking the contradictions between America's professed ideals and its actual practices.

By 1844, it was impossible for Emerson to remain aloof from the antislavery controversy any longer. He had become a leading citizen of his town and the leading intellectual of his region, if not of the nation. He had become the spokesman for American idealism. Many of his fellow citizens expected his guiding voice and opinions on subjects of importance to the community and the nation. Moreover, by 1844 Emerson had been battered by the storm of criticism that followed his "Divinity School Address," giving him firsthand experience of the intractability of conservative, reactionary elements in American society. The experience placed Emerson in a new vantage point. He was now linked with the abolitionists by the experience of being denounced and shunned by many of the same reactionary voices in American society that had been condemning abolitionism. It was no longer possible to maintain the barrier that he had mentally placed between himself and them. Additionally, by 1844 it had become impossible to be silent without appearing to condone the continuation of slavery, especially with the imminent annexation of Texas threatening an immediate expansion of slave territory. When he was asked by his fellow citizens to speak on the subject of the West Indian emancipation, he could not refuse without appearing to be insensitive to this great story of the triumph of principle.

The historical and celebratory aspects of the 1 August anniversary gave Emerson an excellent opportunity to engage the issue of slavery in ways that suited his genius. For the first half of this, his first major public address on the slavery issue, Emerson stayed close to his sources. From Thomas Clarkson's *History of the Rise and Progress, and Accomplishment of the Abolition of the African Slave Trade by the British Parliament* (1808) and James J.

Thome and J. Horace Kimball's *Emancipation in the West Indies*
. . . (1838) he got many vivid details of the sordid history of
brutality and oppression in the slave trade, as well as the tri-
umphant story of protest and eventual emancipation in the
British West Indies. These works awakened Emerson to the humanity as well as the degradation of the slave and led him to a
deep appreciation of the heroic efforts of the slave's defenders.
He echoed his sources in cataloging the various horrors of the
slave trade and slavery in the West Indies with the heartfelt repugnance of an abolitionist. The lecture also provided a capsule
history of the antislavery crusade and capsule biographies of the
hero-activists who led the successful campaign to abolish the
slave trade and slavery. His warm tribute to the English leaders
contained none of his customary animadversions regarding the
abolitionists.

The main lines of Emerson's argument against slavery in his
address were to become the foundation of all his future statements on the subject. Like Frederick Douglass and many other
abolitionists black and white, Emerson rejected what many took
as a perfectly logical approach to evaluating slavery, namely, that
its morality could be determined by observation and simple calculation. Supported by the coerced behavior and testimony of
slaves and by racist assumptions, this kind of moral arithmetic
led slavery apologists to argue that the abuses in the system were
exceptions and that slavery was not the cruel and barbarous system it had been painted to be by the abolitionists but a largely benign and even benevolent system. Slaves were generally content
and happy, as evidenced by their cheerful demeanor, joyful
singing, and loyalty to their masters. For Emerson as for other serious thinkers, the issue could not be understood by observing
slave behavior, soliciting slaves' opinion, or weighing "kind" versus "cruel" masters to see which way, and how far, the balance
tipped. The issue for Emerson as for Douglass was the basic iniq-
uity upon which the system was founded and the distortions and
fraud that perpetuated its evils. Slavery was nothing more than
the stealing of human beings for one's own advantage. Slaveown-
ers, even the kindest and most progressive, were still robbers and
thieves who were complicit in the worst brutalities. As he would

put it later, "No excess of good nature and tenderness of moral constitution [in owners] has been able to give a new character to the system, to tear down the whipping house" (*AW,* 85).

What made the evil of slavery doubly horrific for Emerson was the willingness of members of so-called civilized society to avert their eyes from evil because they loved the advantages they gained from the system of slavery. In a powerful passage of the address, Emerson defined slavery as a "convenience" to white society. "We found it very convenient to keep them at work," he reasoned acidly, "since, by the aid of a little whipping, we could get their work for nothing but their board and the cost of whips." The sarcasm dripped from his words:

> What if it cost a few unpleasant scenes on the coast of Africa? That was a great way off; and the scenes could be endured by some sturdy, unscrupulous fellows, who could go for high wages and bring us the men, and need not trouble our ears with the disagreeable particulars. If any mention was made of homicide, madness, adultery, and intolerable tortures, we would let the church-bells ring louder, the church organ swell its peal, and drown the hideous sound.

Emerson excoriated white complicity in slavery by linking his audiences' familiar everyday comforts and luxuries with the thievery, violence, and deceit with which these luxuries had ultimately been purchased. "The sugar they raised was excellent; nobody tasted blood in it. The coffee was fragrant; the tobacco was incense; the brandy made nations happy; the cotton clothed the world" (*AW,* 20).

Overall, the address rests upon a foundation of Emersonian optimism. In the West Indian emancipation Emerson saw a sign that the slope of the world's morality tended invariably upward, and that as the world became more moral and more civilized, eventually the United States would fall into line. This argument may strike the modern ear as hopelessly naive after a Civil War, two world wars, the Holocaust, and countless other tragedies of a scale scarcely comprehensible a century and a half ago. But Emerson had no crystal ball in which to foresee the cycles of human progress and folly or the terrible consequences of technological advances in warfare. Although the Mexican War loomed on the horizon, he was looking back on a time of peace in America and on many hopeful signs of the progress of the human spirit. Reason and morality had triumphed in the West Indian emancipation beyond the fondest hopes. Freed slaves did not injure their masters. No rioting and insurrection followed. The freed slaves had shown themselves not only to be worthy of citizenship but also to be representatives of the best in humanity. "I have never read anything in history more touching than the moderation of the negroes" (*AW*, 15), wrote Emerson of the behavior of the slaves after emancipation.

Emerson's 1844 address is also noteworthy for its attack upon the almost universal denigration of the Negro. In the experience of emancipation in the British West Indies, Emerson found a powerful refutation of racist view of Africans, annihilating what he called "the old indecent nonsense about the nature of the negro" (*AW*, 29). In short, the emancipation and its aftermath proved absolutely that the widespread belief in the inferiority of the Negro was false. Emerson's views of blacks, however, would later sometimes smack of the Romantic racism that Gougeon notes was "very much in the air in Emerson's circle and elsewhere" (180). In his journals and letters, particularly in the 1850s, Emerson increasingly considered negative views of blacks, identifying them in private journal passages with "brute instinct" and calling them "imitative, secondary" (*JMN*, 13:198).[9] Nevertheless, as Gougeon notes, Emerson "ultimately . . . rejected" these speculations and during the Civil War foresaw "the rapid cultural development of blacks as an inevitable consequence of emancipation that would finally redeem them from the debilitating effects of the institution of slavery" (185).

Reluctant Advocate: 1844–1850

The 1844 *Address . . . on . . . the Emancipation of the Negroes in the British West Indies* announced Emerson's approval of the abolitionist movement and his entrance onto the antislavery stage.

"We are indebted mainly to this movement [in the British West Indies] and to the continuers of it, for the popular discussion, and a reference of every question to the absolute standard" (*AW*, 28), he said. But Emerson's admiration for the movement in Britain and the West Indies was not easily transferred to the American situation. He knew the triumphal story of West Indian abolition only secondhand and retrospectively from the point of view of its leading figures. He did not know the leaders intimately. The actuality of the American situation was far more cloudy and full of contradictions. Up close, the "incidental petulances or infirmities of indiscrete defenders of the negro" (*AW*, 32) were readily visible. Their words and methods were open to criticism; they had not yet proved themselves effective advocates for humanity; and their absolutism had not the purity of motive and purpose of Clarkson's or Granville Sharp's. They supported the cause of humanity and the highest standard of human morality, but they also recklessly fanned the flames of controversy and hatred and seemed willing to precipitate insurrection and civil war. As far as anyone could determine, they had not moved the nation one whit closer to abolishing slavery. In fact, they seemed to have polarized the nation and hardened the position of the South. They argued among themselves and denounced each other. Emerson the idealist was not ready to link arms with them in the public arena, where "the alarms of liberty and the watchwords of truth are mixed up with all the rotten rabble of selfishness and tyranny" (*AW*, 32).

For the next six years following the 1844 address, Emerson continued to be sought after to speak in support of antislavery and other reforms. As much as possible he kept to the sidelines, unwilling, as he wrote in the "Ode Inscribed to William Henry Channing" (1846), to leave his "honied thought / For the priest's cant, / or statesman's rant" (*W*, 9:76). But in these years he could no longer retreat entirely into his poetry and his study. His address on the West Indian emancipation proved very popular, and he was called to repeat it several times. He attended other abolitionist gatherings. Even the Channing "Ode," despite its disclaimer, showed him fully engaged with the evil of slavery. It contained a stinging critique of the times. "Things are in the saddle, and ride mankind" (*W,* 9:78) Emerson observed darkly, and at the end he presaged the Civil War in the line "Half for freedom strike and stand" (*W,* 9:79). In 1845, the debate over the annexation of Texas (as a slave state) drew him into the public arena once again. Later in the year he turned down an invitation to speak before the New Bedford lyceum to protest the exclusion of blacks. When his friend and constant companion Henry Thoreau protested the Mexican War by refusing to pay his taxes and was thrown into jail, Emerson found himself further caught up in the issue of slavery and found his own relative reserve on the subject directly challenged.

In 1847, Emerson briefly lent his name and pen to the efforts of fellow Transcendentalist Theodore Parker's new intellectual journal, the *Massachusetts Quarterly Review* (1847–1850). Intended as a sequel to the *Dial,* the journal was too ponderous and too dominated by reform for Emerson's tastes. Nevertheless, Emerson did not discourage the project at first, and Parker even managed to wrest an "Editor's Address" for the first issue from the him. After Emerson found himself named as the senior editor despite all his protests, he steered clear of the project. The brief address, however, showed Emerson fully in sympathy with Parker's reform agenda. Emerson pointedly lamented that American "moral and intellectual effects are not on the same scale with trade and production" and promised a journal with the "courage and power sufficient to solve the problems which the great groping society around us, stupid with perplexity, is dumbly exploring" (*W,* 11:327, 331–32).

A Full-Blown Abolitionist: 1850–1865

Enactment of the new Fugitive Slave Law in September 1850 was to transform the slavery debate and both Emerson's position toward it and his role in it. The new law superseded the old, largely unenforceable statute of 1793, under which enforcement powers and responsibilities were not clearly defined. When conflicts among federal, state, and local authorities arose, as was inevitable, there was no easy way to solve them. By the 1840s, nu-

merous states, including Massachusetts, had further weakened
the federal statute by passing "Liberty Laws" that blocked the use
of state and local jails and the participation of state and local officials in fugitive slave cases. This left the federal marshal and federal courts virtually helpless. The new Fugitive Slave Law solved
these conflicts by absolving states of responsibility in fugitive
cases, by designating special federal commissioners to hear fugitive slave cases, by authorizing federal officials aided by federal
troops when necessary to return fugitives once they had properly
been identified, and by providing for penalties of up to one thousand dollars in fines (and one thousand dollars compensatory
damages to the owner for each fugitive lost) and six months in
jail for persons accused of "aiding and abetting" fugitive slaves.
The law also authorized the federal marshal to call out a "posse
comitatus" of citizens to assist in capturing a fugitive slave or to
prevent a threatened rescue. Most outrageous of all, the law denied the right of habeas corpus and jury trial, and it prohibited a
person accused of being a fugitive slave from testifying in his or
her own defense. For all practical purposes, the "summary" hearing provided for under the new law was to be held merely to determine the identification of the accused and to verify the au-
thenticity and completeness of documents presented by the
claimant attesting to ownership. Persons accused of being fugitive slaves were thus to be treated as mere property in Northern
as well as Southern federal courtrooms. While some of the special federal commissioners as well as federal judges, who could
also conduct hearings, provided time for the accused to confer
with lawyers and to have his or her case defended at length, in
other instances commissioners or judges expedited the proceed-
ings before any defense could be mounted, sometimes before
anyone knew of the arrest.[10]

Although the new Fugitive Slave Law, the final portion of the
bills collectively known as the Compromise of 1850, ostensibly
settled the conflict over slavery, it fell far short of its goal. Only
some of the particular questions about where slavery would be
permitted as the nation expanded, and where it would be forbid-
den, were settled. Even the compromises over territorial expansion provided, at best, a temporary lull in the political arena. By

the mid-1850s, the slavery issue would turn Kansas Territory into a bloody battleground. Moreover, the compromise would do nothing to soothe the inflamed feelings of Southern extremists and their Northern abolitionist opponents. The Southern extremists felt betrayed by the compromise package, believing that the new laws unfairly confined slavery and that the Fugitive Slave Law could not or would not be enforced in the North. Northern radicals felt equally betrayed by the extreme restrictiveness of a law that suspended the Bill of Rights, immediately turning any citizen accused of being a fugitive slave into a chattel, guilty until proven innocent. This attack on basic rights of citizens energized the antislavery movement. Newspaper headlines telling of fugitives seized and returned from New York City, Philadelphia, and other Northern centers fed a growing reaction against the law. Abolitionists gleefully seized on each new case for the publicity it automatically gave to their cause. Moderate and even pro-South newspapers across the North found themselves printing stories that inevitably boosted local antislavery sentiments.[11]

"This filthy enactment" (*JMN*, 11:412), Emerson would call the new law, among other hard names. Although at first his reaction was tempered by the belief that the new law, like the old, would not be obeyed in New England, the statute automatically engaged his deepest feeling. Before the law, Emerson said, he had "lived all my life without suffering any known inconvenience from American slavery" (*AW*, 74). The law, and, particularly actual attempts to arrest fugitive slaves in Boston, would rapidly intensify Emerson's evolving activism. It had been one thing when fugitives, or slaves, resided at some remote location. It was entirely another when the slave owner and the U.S. marshal came knocking on your neighbor's door. As Emerson was to articulate again and again with great clarity and force, under the new Fugitive Slave Law, a fugitive slave case in Massachusetts automatically involved every Massachusetts citizen. What Emerson could not know in September 1850 was that attempts to seize his neighbors were inevitable. Although many assumed that antislavery sentiment would prevent a fugitive slave from being arrested in Boston, and that no owner would foolishly risk the dangers or expenses involved in trying to seize a Boston fugitive, efforts to do just that were in the works from almost the day the new statute became law. Daniel Webster and the Union-Whigs eagerly hoped for success in a Boston fugitive slave case. What better proof of the effectiveness of the Compromise of 1850 than returning a fugitive slave to his or her Southern owner from Boston, the ostensible capital of abolitionism?

The first attempt on a Boston fugitive came in late October, a little over a month after the new law became operative, when agents of a Macon, Georgia, slave owner arrived in Boston and set about securing the arrest of two fugitives, William and Ellen Craft. This was to be exactly the high-profile proof Daniel Webster and the Unionists wanted. The Crafts were well known for their amazing escape by train from Georgia. The light-skinned Ellen, dressed in male attire, had pretended to be an ailing planter journeying to the North for medical treatment, with her dark-skinned husband, William, playing her trusty body servant. After being sent on to Boston for safety, William set up a carpentry shop, while Ellen worked as a seamstress. When the attempt to arrest the Crafts became known, antislavery sympathizers were aroused. Emerson followed the developments of the case as they were reported in the press with great interest, as evidenced by comments in his correspondence and journals. When the Crafts fled from Boston, Emerson noted the successful thwarting of the law in his journal, where he had begun to keep a regular "Anti-Slavery Almanac" (*JMN*, 14:429).

During the excitement over the Crafts, Emerson made no public pronouncements. The following February, a second attempt to arrest a Boston fugitive slave, a waiter named Shadrach Minkins, ended within hours when a band of black Bostonians led by Lewis Hayden rescued the fugitive from the U.S. marshal's custody and sent him on to Montreal. Again, Emerson confined his response to his journals, letters, and conversation. In March he sent a letter to the Middlesex Anti-Slavery Society expressing his regret that he would be out of town lecturing during the annual meeting in Concord in early April. That he had been deeply stirred by the fugitive slave incidents in Boston and elsewhere is clear from one sentence in his brief letter. "At this moment it seems imperative," Emerson wrote, "that every lover of human rights should, in every manner, singly or socially, in private and in public, by voice and by pen . . . enter his protest for humanity against the detestable statute of the last Congress" (*AW,* 51). It is an uncompromising statement, a pledge to put aside his reservations about public protest and join the antislavery chorus. Not surprisingly, it found its way almost immediately into Garrison's *Liberator.*

In April 1851, after a third fugitive slave, Thomas Sims, was arrested and then actually sent back to slavery from Boston, guarded by an army of local and federal troops, Emerson made good on his "in private and in public" pledge by quickly joining in the outcry over the loss of Sims. Invited by his fellow citizens of Concord to address them in the wake of Sims's rendition, he readily agreed. "The last year has forced us all into politics, and made it a paramount duty to seek what it is often a duty to shun," Emerson declared in the opening of his speech in explanation of his change of position. With remarkable candor, Emerson confessed to being shaken by the treatment of Sims. "I wake in the morning with a painful sensation, which I carry about all day," he said, the origin of which he identified as "the odious remembrance of that ignominy which has fallen on Massachusetts, which robs the landscape of beauty, and takes the sunshine out of every hour" (*AW,* 53). Letters written about the same time, as well as journal passages filled with similar confessions of anger and despair, reveal Emerson's remarks in Concord to be genuine, not mere rhetorical hyperbole.

Emerson's speech, a jeremiad decrying the fallen moral state of Massachusetts, shows a decided radical shift. It is in this speech, Emerson's version of Thoreau's "Civil Disobedience," that he first offered a full statement of the priority of "higher law" and the necessity of resisting unjust legislation such as the Fugitive Slave Law. "Laws do not make right, but are simply declaratory of a right which already existed," he said. For this reason, "an immoral law makes it a man's duty to break it, at every hazard" (*AW,* 57). The Fugitive Slave Law, which perfectly exemplified an immoral law, "must be made inoperative. It must be abrogated and wiped out of the statute book; but, whilst it stands there, it must be disobeyed" (*AW,* 71). This conclusion was the most radical political statement Emerson had ever offered. Although more familiar Emersonian optimism about "the immense power of rectitude" (*AW*, 70) tempered the extreme statements, the address still stands among Emerson's works as a unique *tour de force* of emotion barely restrained by reason. Len Gougeon rightfully calls it "by far the most strident and acerbic of his career."[12] It proved very popular, and Emerson repeated it at least nine times, apparently most often at Free Soil Party rallies supporting John Gorham Palfrey's congressional candidacy.

Emerson's willingness to be drawn into a political campaign indicates just how ready he had become to demonstrate, almost defensively, his commitment to his principles on whatever stage was offered—to "clear my own skirts," as he said in a letter to Thomas Carlyle (*CEC*, 470). When Palfrey lost the election at the end of May, however, Emerson's distaste for the experiment, together with his heavy lecture schedule, led him to retreat from the political and reform arenas. His journal entries show him privately debating and defending his course. After chiding himself "because I had not thrown myself into the deplorable questions of Slavery," he reported finding "in hours of sanity" the reassurance that he was laboring in the cause of humanity in his own way: "I have quite other slaves to free than those negroes, to wit, imprisoned spirits, imprisoned thoughts . . . which, important to the republic of Man, have not watchman, or lover, or defender, but I—" (*JMN*, 13:80). Although he turned down every invitation to speak at abolitionist rallies, he continued to follow political and legal developments with intense interest and condemned slavery and racism in letters and conversation. Finally, in the spring of 1853, he did accept an invitation to attend a dinner honoring New Hampshire's abolitionist senator, John Parker Hale, and even prepared a speech, but he may have been crowded out of the opportunity of speaking by the horde of luminaries in attendance. His one public expression on the issues appeared that spring in *Autographs for Freedom*, a fund-raising collection like the *Liberty Bell*, to which he had submitted poems in 1851. This time Emerson's contribution was a single poem, "Freedom." As in his *Liberty Bell* contributions, the poem was at least as much about Emerson's struggle to remain poetically free as it was about the larger issues of freedom and slavery.

By 1854, new national and local conflicts were challenging Emerson to enter the public spotlight once again. First came the furious debate over the Kansas-Nebraska Act, which became law later in the spring. The result of complicated political maneuvering, the new act effectively repealed the Missouri Compromise of 1820 that banned slavery from above the 36° 30' parallel. Emerson consented to give a speech in New York on 7 March 1854, a date with great resonance for the New England antislavery brigade. Exactly four years earlier, Daniel Webster had given his famous speech supporting the Fugitive Slave Law, turning many of his former admirers, including Emerson himself, against him. Emerson's speech was not one of his strongest efforts. It lacked the passion of his 1851 speech to his Concord friends and neighbors, and lacked as well the concrete imagery that usually distinguished his best writing. Much time was devoted to balancing the claims of the parties to the antislavery debate and to his own reluctance and unsuitability as an antislavery spokesman. "Gentlemen, I have a respect for conservatism," one section began (though Emerson, in typical fashion, remade the word by defining his own idea of "true" conservatism). In his analysis of Daniel Webster's virtues and defects, too much homage was paid to virtues for abolitionist listeners. Emerson himself considered his speech an unfinished and unsatisfactory attempt at a "plea for Freedom addressed to *my set*" (*L*, 8:397), and it met with the lukewarm reaction that could be expected from the militant antislavery press. Still, the speech was a remarkable attempt at a comprehensive treatment of the corrosive effect of slavery on American life and morals, and it contained many pungent remarks about the essential role of individual conscience in the cause of freedom. "Liberty is aggressive. Liberty is the Crusade of all brave and conscientious men" (*AW*, 88), Emerson proclaimed near the end of the speech.

In January 1855, Emerson once again raised his voice in public to register his opposition to slavery. Eight months earlier a second fugitive slave, Anthony Burns, had been arrested in Boston and sent back into slavery. The case had attracted enormous interest locally and nationally. Abolitionists, who were conveniently gathered in the city for a meeting, agitated with renewed energy while initiating a variety of legal maneuverings behind the scenes. A public meeting fired up the crowd, who were then released into the streets to attack the Boston Court House and rescue Burns. Poorly planned and even more poorly coordinated, the attack might yet have succeeded. At one point Thomas Wentworth Higginson and others fought their way into the building, only to retreat when the crowd did not follow them, but not before Higginson and several others received wounds and one of their number had fatally shot one of the men guarding the Court House. Then Emerson's friend Amos Bronson Alcott, who had been in attendance at the exciting meeting, gained a measure of fame by walking up the Court House steps alone and then retracing his steps.[13]

Emerson's 1855 speech crackled with the personal outrage that comes from having his home territory once again invaded by slave catchers and his fellow citizens once again corrupted by the government and its laws. The speech contained Emerson's by-now familiar themes: the conflict between the "doctrine of the independence and the inspiration of the individual" and the need for "social action" (*AW*, 103); the "sickness of the times" (*AW*, 101) that permitted such an outrage against principle by Daniel Webster and others; and the inevitable moral development of America, which would lead to a time when slavery "will yield at last, and go with cannibalism, tattooing, inquisition, dueling, [and] burking" (*AW*, 93). The essay again shows Emerson's talent for placing the contemporary subject of slavery versus freedom in the context of the moral development of humankind and civilization. Echoes of biblical language and references to the great moral and judicial leaders of history are brought to bear upon the Burns episode to place it in the framework of historical injustice. As in other speeches, Emerson measured contemporary judges and politicians against the heroes of humankind's quest for freedom and justice and found them woefully lacking.

On several more occasions before the Civil War erupted, Emerson rose to protest slavery and to support the cause of liberty and the slave. Each occasion was to be provoked by some new crisis arising out of the intensifying national conflict over slavery. The first came after Congressman Preston S. Brooks of South Carolina caught Senator Charles Sumner of Massachusetts at his desk on the floor of the Senate and flogged him with a cane so severely that Sumner's life was endangered. Provoked by Sumner's caustic personal attacks on various Southern politicians in his "Crime Against Kansas" speech a few days earlier, the outraged Brooks had committed himself to avenging the honor of his colleagues in strict accordance with the Southern code of gentlemanly behavior. By flogging Sumner, he earned the congratulations of many of his fellow Southerners in Congress and throughout the South.[14] In the North, Brooks's outrageous behavior provoked an immediate flood of denunciations and protest meetings. At a meeting of Concord's citizens, Emerson gave a brief speech that focused on the unspotted character of Sumner, with whom Emerson had been corresponding, rather than on Brooks's villainy. In the speech, Emerson announced simply, "I think we must get rid of slavery, or we must get rid of freedom" (*AW,* 107). For Emerson, the Brooks affair confirmed the impossibility of reasoning with the South; the Southerners had been so corrupted by their institution that they were no longer capable of civilized debate. Slavery had dragged civilization back into barbarity.

Later in the year Emerson attended a meeting for the relief of antislavery settlers in Kansas territory, many of whom had traveled from Massachusetts to help make a plurality for abolition and so bring Kansas into the Union as a free state. A civil war in Kansas territory had erupted over the issue, prompting the speech from Charles Sumner that resulted in his beating. Abolitionist settlers in Kansas found themselves repeatedly attacked by Missouri "border ruffians" intent on driving them out through intimidation and violence. Lawrence, Kansas, a free-soil stronghold, was plundered by a pro-slavery band. In Concord and elsewhere, protest meetings were held to raise money and supplies for the besieged settlers. Moved by the reports of the plight of the settlers, Emerson attended meetings and at one delivered an impassioned plea for all citizens to give aid generously. "We must learn to do with less, live in a smaller tenement, sell our apple-trees, our acres, our pleasant houses" (*AW,* 112), Emerson challenged his audience. In the speech he came close to calling openly for revolution. Recalling the time when Massachusetts, "in its heroic day, had no government—was an anarchy," Emerson declared himself "glad to see that the terror at disunion and anarchy is disappearing" (*AW,* 115). Clearly he had begun to accept the idea that war was becoming not only more and more inevitable but also more and more necessary. "The war existed long before the cannonade of Sumter and could not be postponed" (*AW,* 133), he would say later.

In 1859, another shocking event propelled Emerson back into the antislavery campaign. In September, John Brown attacked the federal arsenal at Harpers Ferry in a futile attempt to start a slave insurrection. Already admired by Emerson, to whom the old man had been introduced by Henry Thoreau during Brown's visit to Concord in 1857, Brown's arrest and execution for his crazy assault removed any reservations that Emerson might have entertained about the zealous Kansas freedom fighter. In Concord, both Thoreau and Emerson added their voices to the chorus of abolitionist praise showering down upon Brown's name. In several speeches, Emerson placed Brown in company with the greatest moral heroes of history. For Emerson, Brown's willingness to sacrifice his life and the lives of his sons for the lowly slave and the highest principles illustrated true courage and devotion to humankind. "Nothing can resist the sympathy which all elevated minds must feel with Brown" (*AW,* 118), Emerson proclaimed in an address before a meeting in Cambridge for the relief of John Brown's family. In another speech entitled simply "John Brown," Emerson portrayed Brown as a figure who remedied the deficiencies of ego and self-interest that tainted the character of abolitionists and other reformers. Brown was "absolutely without any vulgar trait; living to ideal ends, without any mixture of self-indulgence or compromise, such as lowers the value of benevolent and thoughtful men we know" (*AW,* 122), Emerson declared. Clearly, he recognized in Brown's muscular, militant idealism a natural counterpart to his own image of himself as the fearless, independent American scholar. Brown fulfilled the ideal of true manhood that had been Emerson's lifelong theme and preoccupation. Emerson's approving remarks about Brown's extremist statement, "Better that a whole generation of men, women and children should pass away by a violent death, than that one word of either [the Golden Rule or the Declaration of Independence] should be violated in this country" (*AW*, 118), starkly displayed Emerson's heightened militancy as well as his near idolatry of Brown.[15]

Once the Civil War had erupted, Emerson became a passionate advocate of the cause of the Union and of freedom for the slave. With many other antislavery supporters, he called for the immediate emancipation of the slaves. When Lincoln's preliminary Emancipation Proclamation (1862) finally came, too tardy and too limited in its application to please many radical opponents of slavery, Emerson defended the president vigorously. "Forget all that we thought shortcomings, every mistake, every delay," Emerson pleaded; "call these endurance, wisdom, magnanimity, illuminated, as they now are, by this dazzling success" (*AW*, 130). By the proclamation, "we have . . . planted ourselves on a law of nature" and "shall not fear henceforth to show our faces among mankind" (*AW*, 132). His speech on the proclamation, delivered in Boston and soon published in the *Atlantic Monthly*, had a wide audience and undoubtedly helped to silence the critics and cement public opinion behind Lincoln. Emerson also composed poems for abolitionist gatherings, one of which, the popular "Voluntaries," was a tribute to the black Massachusetts Fifty-fourth Regiment and its commander, Colonel Robert Gould Shaw, who had died leading their ill-fated assault on Fort Wagner, South Carolina.

In 1863, with Lincoln's reelection in doubt and with rumors about a negotiated settlement in circulation, Emerson again took a leading role in public discussions with an impassioned speech entitled "Fortune of the Republic." Delivered on numerous occasions in one of the darkest periods of the war, with the end of hostilities still distantly in the future, the speech shows Emerson attempting to buoy up the hopes of the nation. "The people have met the dreadful issues so frankly," he declared. "The youth have shown themselves heroes. The women have shown a tender patriotism, and an inexhaustible charity" (*AW*, 152). Having long since abandoned any hope in the conversion of the South, he rationalized the terrible bloodletting in a remarkable statement in which he described the war as a process of nature, "as necessary as lactation, or dentition, or puberty, to the human individual" (*AW*, 139). By 1863, he had come to believe no sacrifice was too great when the grand principle of human freedom was at stake. "[We want] a state of things which allows every man the largest liberty compatible with the liberty of other men," he declared (*AW*, 153). Noteworthy is the fact that in both speeches he finally dropped the opening apologia of most of his antislavery statements. Now he rose to defend the war and its principles vigorously, without hint of reluctance.[16]

Even after the war, when he might have retreated to his study and his books, Emerson continued to be a spokesman for national idealism. He spoke at the memorial service for Lincoln held in Concord and at the service at Harvard to memorialize the college's war dead and welcome its returning heroes. He worried over the difficulties that lay ahead in Reconstruction. He maintained a keen interest in the work of Charles Sumner and the other Radicals as they tried to counter the Johnson administration's tendency to relax federal supervision and controls imposed on the South. In several speeches, Emerson celebrated the new nation's opportunity to advance the cause of humanity now that the blighting influence of slavery had been swept away. "Was ever such coincidence of advantages in time and place as in America today?" he asked in "Progress of Culture," his second Phi Beta Kappa address, delivered at Harvard in July 1867. "The fusion of races and religions, the hungry cry for men which goes up from the wide continent; the answering facility of imagination, permitting every wanderer to choose his climate and government . . . the new claim of woman" (*W*, 8:207–8). He participated in a tribute to William Lloyd Garrison and visited the Freedman's Institute (later Howard University) in Washington, where he delivered an impromptu talk on worthwhile books. In the last decade of his life, with his abilities declining rapidly, he gave few public addresses but continued to show an interest in the developments in the South and in the possibilities unleashed by the repudiation of slavery.

Emerson's Importance

During the mid-1850s, as Emerson had come more and more to accept the role in the antislavery campaign that had been thrust upon him, Northern public opinion had been swinging more and more to the side of the abolitionists. The Sims case in 1851 had disturbed many supporters of the Fugitive Slave Law in Boston and elsewhere throughout Massachusetts who had once believed that Southern interests needed to be respected, no matter how repugnant the system of slavery was, because the Constitution recognized and protected slavery. By 1854, when a second fugitive slave was sent back into slavery from Boston, the violation of rights of persons recognized as citizens by the Commonwealth of Massachusetts began to seem too outrageous even to the men of commerce and finance that Emerson had frequently attacked for their moral obtuseness. The murder of Kansas settlers from Massachusetts, the violent assault on Charles Sumner, and renewed fugitive slave cases throughout the North accelerated this trend. So, too, did the publication of Harriet Beecher Stowe's *Uncle Tom's Cabin* in 1852. An instant best-seller, the novel found its way into the hands of many people who would not have characterized themselves as abolitionists, at least when they first picked up the book. This antislavery tract in the form of a novel had the power to make the evils of slavery immediate and palpable and so, like local fugitive slave cases, helped to energize an otherwise emotionally remote subject.

What part Emerson himself had in this dramatic shift in public opinion is hard to pin down. Clearly, he had not been a Wendell Phillips, a William Lloyd Garrison, or even a Theodore Parker. His voice was heard only occasionally. He did not march in the streets in protest. He did not join abolitionist organizations. And though he did write and speak against slavery, these utterances make up but a tiny portion of his work. Yet, as the leading figure in New England intellectual life, as the primary spokesman for idealism in America, and as a figure of enormous popularity and prestige, Emerson spoke words that had an incalculable resonance and residual effect. Whenever he spoke out against slavery and the slave power in the name of a higher law for humanity, he not only lent his name and enormous prestige to the abolitionist cause but reinforced the intellectual and moral underpinnings of the movement. The eagerness with which he was sought out by antislavery groups is one measure of his broad and deep effect. When abolitionists assembled their portraits for an 1857 lithograph print "Heralds of Freedom," Emerson was asked to contribute his likeness. It is a measure of the importance of Emerson's name, and an acknowledgment of his important contributions to the antislavery cause, that they made the request. It is a measure of Emerson's acceptance of the role that had been largely thrust upon him that he consented.[17] The finished print shows William Lloyd Garrison's image surrounded by portraits of six other "heralds." Emerson's likeness hovers directly above Garrison's, as if to suggest that he was the guardian spirit of the group.

NOTES

1. Oliver Wendell Holmes, *Ralph Waldo Emerson* (Boston: Houghton, Mifflin, 1884), p. 304.

2. Len Gougeon, *Virtue's Hero: Emerson, Antislavery, and Reform* (Athens: University of Georgia Press, 1990); *AW*. The present essay is heavily indebted to these two works. For the sake of brevity in the notes that follow, relevant sections of Gougeon's *Virtue's Hero* and his introduction and notes to *AW* are not specifically mentioned, but every note referring to an aspect of Emerson's antislavery activities could begin, "In addition to Gougeon, see . . ." For an early scholarly analysis, see Marjory M. Moody, "The Evolution of Emerson as an Abolitionist," *American Literature* 17 (March 1945): 1–21.

3. Robert D. Richardson, Jr., *Emerson: The Mind on Fire* (Berkeley: University of California Press, 1995): Albert J. von Frank, *The Trials of Anthony Burns: Freedom and Slavery in Emerson's Boston* (Cambridge: Harvard University Press, 1998).

4. Octavius Brooks Frothingham, *Boston Unitarianism, 1820–1850: A Study of the Life and Work of Nathaniel Langdon Frothingham* (New York: Putnam's, 1890), p. 251.

5. Excellent discussions of the relationship between Unitarianism and antislavery can be found in Douglas C. Stange, *Patterns of Antislavery Among American Unitarians, 1831–1860* (Rutherford, N.J.:

Fairleigh Dickinson University Press, 1977); Daniel Walker Howe, *The Unitarian Conscience: Harvard Moral Philosophy, 1805–1861* (Middletown, Conn.: Wesleyan University Press, 1970), pp. 270–305; and Conrad Wright, "The Minister as Reformer: Profiles of Unitarian Ministers in the Antislavery Reform," in his *The Liberal Christians: Essays on American Unitarian History* (Boston: Beacon Press, 1970), pp. 62–80.

6. For descriptions of Emerson's Concord circle of neighbors and friends and their antislavery and reform activities, see Richardson, *Emerson: The Mind on Fire*, pp. 208–14; and the revised and enlarged edition of Walter Harding, *The Days of Henry Thoreau: A Biography* (New York: Dover, 1982).

7. For Emerson's family influences, see *The Selected Letters of Lidian Jackson Emerson*, ed. Dolores Bird Carpenter (Columbia: University of Missouri Press, 1987); *The Selected Letters of Mary Moody Emerson*, ed. Nancy Craig Simmons (Athens: University of Georgia Press, 1993); and Phyllis Cole, *Mary Moody Emerson and the Origins of Transcendentalism* (New York: Oxford University Press, 1998), pp. 220–45.

8. For an analysis of Emerson's early attitudes toward politics, abolition, and other reforms, see Wesley T. Mott, *"The Strains of Eloquence": Emerson and His Sermons* (University Park: Pennsylvania State University Press, 1989), pp. 113–41.

9. Modern commentary noting the ambiguities and complexities of Emerson's thinking about race include Eduardo Cadava, *Emerson and the Climates of History* (Stanford, Calif.: Stanford University Press, 1997); Cornel West, *The American Evasion of Philosophy: A Genealogy of Pragmatism* (Madison: University of Wisconsin Press, 1989), pp. 28–35; and Phillip Nicoloff, *Emerson on Race and History: An Examination of English Traits* (New York: Columbia University Press, 1961).

10. On the Compromise of 1850, the Fugitive Slave Law, and the Northern background, see Holman Hamilton, *Prologue to Conflict: The Crisis and Compromise of 1850* (Lexington: University of Kentucky Press, 1964); and Robert F. Dalzell, *Daniel Webster and the Trial of American Nationalism* (Boston: Houghton Mifflin, 1973). Thomas D. Morris, *Free Men All: The Personal Liberty Laws of the North, 1780–1861* (Baltimore: Johns Hopkins, 1974), is useful for understanding the Northern background of opposition to the fugitive slave laws of 1793 and 1850.

11. For the effects of the Fugitive Slave Law, see Stanley W. Campbell, *The Slave Catchers: Enforcement of the Fugitive Slave Law, 1850–1860* (Chapel Hill: University of North Carolina Press, 1970).

12. Gougeon, *Virtue's Hero,* p. 160.

13. Von Frank's *The Trials of Anthony Burns* is an exhaustive study of Emerson and the Burns case that supersedes everything that has been written on the subject.

14. For the Sumner incident, see David Herbert Donald, *Charles Sumner and the Coming of the Civil War* (Chicago: University of Chicago Press, 1960), pp. 278–311.

15. On Emerson's ideas of manhood, see David Leverenz, *Manhood and the American Renaissance* (Ithaca, N.Y.: Cornell University Press, 1989), pp. 42–71.

16. On Emerson and the Civil War, see Cadava, *Emerson and the Climates of History,* pp. 149–201; and Len Gougeon, "Emerson's Circle and the Crisis of the Civil War," in *Emersonian Circles: Essays in Honor of Joel Myerson,* ed. Wesley T. Mott and Robert E. Burkholder (Rochester, N.Y.: University of Rochester Press, 1997), pp. 29–51.

17. The lithograph is reproduced in *Courage and Conscience: Black and White Abolitionists in Boston,* ed. Donald M. Jacobs (Bloomington: Indiana University Press, 1993), p. 18.

Emerson in the Context of the
Woman's Rights Movement

Armida Gilbert

In order to understand Emerson's developing attitudes toward the woman's rights movement, it is necessary to appreciate the way in which the movement began, grew, and changed and the issues around which the early debates were centered. Before even the earliest stages of the woman's rights movement in America, Emerson had been introduced to the ideas that would inform it, especially through the pioneering work of his friend Margaret Fuller. As explained by her, first in "The Great Lawsuit,—Man Versus Men, Woman Versus Women" in the Transcendentalist literary journal, the *Dial*, in 1843, then in expanded form in the first book written in America to argue for woman's rights, *Woman in the Nineteenth Century*, in 1845, Fuller's ideas, transmitted to Emerson through their frequent conversations and correspondence, came to form the core of his thinking on women. Fuller's carefully reasoned tactics would form the basis for the approaches and arguments that would later be adopted by the nascent woman's rights movement, as Elizabeth Cady Stanton, Susan B. Anthony, and Matilda Joslyn Gage acknowledged in their monumental *History of Woman Suffrage*, when they stated that Fuller's work "gave a new impulse to woman's education as a thinker."[1] Thus Emerson shared essential concepts and patterns of thinking about issues regarding women with the American woman's rights movement from the earliest days of its existence, inspiring suffragists to accept him as one of their champions.

Following on Fuller's prescient presentation of the issues of women's role in society, the woman's rights movement in nineteenth-century America emerged from the crucible of the abolitionist movement, in much the same way that the contemporary women's movement would later spring from the furor of the civil rights movement. The catalyzing event for the woman's rights movement was the 1840 World's Anti-Slavery Convention in London. After women organized and planned the first international convention, a massive undertaking, when they arrived at the site they were informed that they could not be seated at their own conference due to their sex; all women were to be excluded from the platform and convention seating, allowed only to stand voiceless and silent in the aisles and gallery. Outraged, organizers Lucretia Mott and Elizabeth Cady Stanton agreed to hold the first woman's rights convention upon their return to America.[2]

By 1848, these American women had organized their historic first woman's rights convention, held in Seneca Falls, New York. As Julia Ward Howe, later leader of the suffragist American Woman's Party, observed, 1848 was considerably before "the claims of women to political efficiency had begun to occupy the attention . . . of the American public"; full recognition of the "woman question" came only after the Civil War. Word spread quickly among women involved in social reform, however, and another National Woman's Rights Convention was held in Worcester, Massachusetts, in 1850, only two years after the historic Seneca Falls convention. Emerson was invited to the convention and gave it his support; according to Howe, although Emerson was prevented from attending the convention, his absence was due to his deep involvement in editing the *Memoirs of Margaret Fuller Ossoli*, which, as Howe paraphrased Emerson, "he hoped, would be considered as service in the line of the objects of the meeting."[3] That Emerson so closely correlated Fuller and the woman's rights movement reflected her formative influence on his thinking on women's issues from the beginning of his public identification with the movement—indeed, from before the beginning of the movement.

As was the common practice, the convention prepared a Call to Convention, a public declaration of principles that would be signed by the attendees, indicating their agreement with these principles. Emerson signed this statement of support, an unusually bold step for a writer who generally avoided identification with any formal organization for social reform and who tended to be extremely cautious about any public pronouncement. His willingness to be publicly included as a supporter of the convention, then, indicated not only his awareness of the aims of the woman's movement long before most of the country realized its existence but also the strength of his agreement with its beliefs.[4] Much later, in 1876, Thomas Wentworth Higginson recalled Emerson's backing of the convention in a brief article, "Tested by Time," in the suffragist organ the *Woman's Journal,* in which he erroneously referred to this as the "first National Woman's Rights Convention."[5] Apparently, then, nearly thirty years later Higginson was still unaware of the first convention in Seneca Falls in 1848, and it was possible that Emerson, too, was unaware of the Seneca Falls convention. This was especially likely, since it went almost entirely unreported by the press, even in New York State, and news of it spread only by word of mouth among those most intensely interested in the fledgling movement.[6] If Emerson did then believe, as did Higginson, that he was signing the initial declaration of principles for the very first woman's rights convention, his actions became even more daring.

Emerson wrote a public letter to Lucy Stone in the *New York Daily Tribune* on 17 October 1851, apologizing that again his work on the Fuller memoirs would prevent his attendance at that year's Worcester Woman's Rights Convention. He reminded the public that he had signed the previous convention's declaration of principles and stated that he continued to stand by them (*L,* 4:261–62). In his journal, he mused, "I think that, as long as [women] have not equal rights of property & right of voting, they are not on a right footing. But this wrong grew out of a savage & military period, when, because a woman could not defend herself, it was necessary that she should be assigned to some man who was paid for guarding her. Now in more tranquil & decorous times it is plain that she should have her property, &, when she marries, the parties should as regards property, go into a partnership full or limited, but explicit & recorded" as compared to the law and custom of the time, by which the husband took full legal possession of all the woman's property upon marriage, even her clothing. Emerson continued, "I find the Evils real & great. If I go from Hanover street to Atkinson street,—as I did yesterday,—what hundreds of extremely ordinary, paltry, hopeless women I see, whose plight is piteous to think of" (*JMN*, 11:444.) Emerson typically doubted the efficacy of legislation in correcting the "Evils" of women's condition, wishing instead that they could be removed by repairing "the rottenness of human nature" (*JMN*, 11:444), which had initially allowed the rise of such unjust laws.

In 1855, Emerson would appear in person to address that year's woman's rights convention. His address on that occasion was later revised to form the essay "Woman." This lecture has yet to be published. Another source of evidence for Emerson's position on women's rights was an unpublished lecture known as the "Discourse Manqué. Woman," which appears to be drawn almost entirely from the 1855 address.[7]

In both the original lecture and the slightly emended essay form, "Woman" was Emerson's most public and extended statement of his opinion on women's issues, a serious avowal of his dedication to woman's rights. Couched as it was in the terms of the nineteenth-century woman's movement, the essay has continued to be a source of controversy and even chagrin for contemporary readers. Yet Emerson made his partisanship of woman's rights clear from the start, first by staking a claim for the importance of the issue, an opinion he held throughout his life; in his journal in 1868, Emerson stated, "I wish the American Poet should let old times go & write on . . . Woman's Suffrage" (*JMN*, 16:88). Emerson thus declared in the "Discourse Manqué," drawn largely from the 1855 address, that the woman's movement was "no whim, but an organic impulse,—a right and proper inquiry,—honoring to the age"; of the "good signs of the times," he stated, "this is of the best." Emerson went on to contrast the healthful and thoughtful supporters of woman's rights with the presumably unhealthy and thoughtless detractors of the movement, whom Emerson attacked—in very strong language for him—deriding the "cheap shots" at women and their rights and the "monstrous exaggeration" of every sexist writer from Aristophanes to Rabelais and the highly popular Tennyson. As he observed in his journals, even poets promoted a stereotyped and generic view of woman that knew her "only in the plural" (*JMN*, 12:568). They thus became like the "misogynist" he had met who "looked on every woman as an imposter" (*JMN*, 11:455) because real women did not resemble these bland and homogenized stereotypes.

Emerson had deplored this tendency to denigrate women, and particularly their intellectual efforts, for some time. Writing in his journal in 1841, he quoted the mayor of Lowell, Massachusetts, as saying disparagingly of a group of women arriving to testify in a trial, "There go the light-troops!" and criticized, "Neither Plato, Mahomet, nor Goethe have said a severer thing on our fair Eve. Yet the old lawyer did not mean to be satanic" (*JMN*, 8:85). In 1848, in his memoirs of France, he observed, "At the Club des Femmes, there was among the men some patronage, but no real courtesy. The lady who presided spoke & behaved with the utmost propriety,—a woman of heart & sense,—but the audience of men were perpetually on the look out for some equivoque, into which, of course, each male speaker would be pretty sure to fall; & the laugh was loud & general" (*JMN*, 10:268). Similarly, after seeing Isabella Glyn Dallas give her Shakespearean readings, Emerson called her "a woman of great personal advantages & talent—great variety & of style, & perfect self possession" and complained that "her audience was not worthy of her, impertinently read newspapers & had a trick of going out" (*JMN*, 16:201). Even in his analysis of the character of Napoleon Bonaparte in *Representative Men*, Emerson chided Napoleon's "unscrupulous" nature in saying, "Leave sensibility to women" and his "coarse . . . low familiarity" in pulling women's ears and pinching their cheeks (*JMN*, 12:568). The "pitiless" James Fenimore Cooper was another offender, with his boast "I can make any woman blush," which women met with "natural resentment" (*JMN*, 11:446).

Having established the significance of the issue and the superficiality of its opponents' arguments, Emerson consolidated his position by establishing woman's strengths. Unfortunately, the strengths he singled out for praise, however complimentary to nineteenth-century women, would come to seem problematic to late twentieth-century readers. As he had stated in the address to the 1855 Woman's Rights Convention on which the essay "Woman" was based, "Women feel in relation to men as geniuses feel among energetic workers, that tho' overruled & thrust aside in the press, they outsee all these noisy masters" (see also *JMN*, 16:146). This praise of women's "oracular nature," their greater intuitive powers,[8] has reminded many contemporary women of the cliché of "women's intuition." Whenever women used their intelligence more quickly or efficiently than the men around them, it was dismissed as "women's intuition," not recognized as a sign of equal intellectual capacity. In the address, Emerson had clarified this idea by suggesting that what appeared to be women's intuition was actually the result of a quicker thought process: "They learn so fast & convey the result so fast, as to outrun the logic of their slow brother." Also, Emerson did not believe the intuition to be a lower faculty than the intellect, but at least equal, and possibly higher. In addition, he held that men as well as women relied on intuition. In his essay on Emanuel Swedenborg in *Representative Men*, the mystics named, who based their work on the intuitive faculties, were largely male, although Madame Jeanne Marie de la Motte-Guion was also included. That Emerson respected Madame Guyon (the name had variant spellings) was evident in his ownership of Lydia Maria Child's biography of her.[9] Further, during this period, even the strongest suffragists clung to their claim for psychic and spiritual superiority.[10] Fuller's *Woman in the Nineteenth Century* resounded with such rhetoric: "The especial genius of Woman I believe to be . . . intuitive in function."[11] Her influence on Emerson was evident here, as in so many of the other ideas in "Woman," particularly since he had been so recently at work on her *Memoirs*.

Like Fuller, then, Emerson suggested that women's faster thought processes placed them in the vanguard of social reform: "Any remarkable opinion or movement shared by women will be the first sign of revolution" (*W*, 11:406). In this firmer logic, women influenced the progress of society. As Emerson observed in his journal: "[T]hey buy slaves where the women will permit it; where they will not, they make the wind, the tide, the waterfall, the steam . . . do the work" (*JMN*, 10:103; see also *JMN*, 8:307). The French Revolution was another example (*JMN*, 10:296), and in considering Fourier's idea of communal living, Emerson wrote, "The important query is *what* will the women say to the Theory?"[12] Like Fuller and most other nineteenth-century feminists, also, Emerson did not take into account the effect of social conditioning in creating women's "strength" of "sentiment" and "sympathy," as well as in creating the "Gulf betwixt men & women" (*JMN*, 12:307).[13] However, awareness of the effects of gender role conditioning was decades away with the nascent science of sociology, and Emerson's tropes here, however painful to postmodern sensibilities, were no different than those of his female and suffragist contemporaries. In fact, by following the paths of argument laid down by Fuller and her suffragist successors, Emerson proved how closely he adhered to her ideas.

Thus Emerson's views as expressed in the address on which "Woman" was based were what contemporary critics would today term "essentialist," implying an innate, inborn difference between the male and female temperaments that held true across the bounds of cultural and historical conditioning. While today essentialism can be viewed as one among a variety of hotly contended feminist viewpoints, in Emerson's time, given this lack of awareness of social conditioning, it was the norm. It was truly the woman's (singular) movement in the nineteenth century, generally agreed on an essentialist philosophy and a demand for equal legal rights, as compared to today's far more diversely oriented women's (plural) movement, in which a multiplicity of often clashing viewpoints have struggled for expression.[14] Emerson's assumption of intrinsic emotional and physical discrepancies in men and women's strength, then, was aligned to his era. As debatable as it may be in our time, few in the nineteenth century would have disagreed with Emerson's paraphrase of Swedenborg that "the difference of sex [runs] through nature and through thought." The most outspoken suffragists of Emerson's time would have agreed that women were, in his words, "More vulnerable, more infirm, more mortal" than men, in a time when women had an exceptionally high death rate, especially in childbirth. Fuller, in fact, had stated unequivocally in *Woman in the Nineteenth Century* that "woman is the weaker party" (22). Emerson may also well have had the premature demise of his first wife, Ellen, in mind here. Indeed, Ellen Tucker Emerson was, with Fuller, the previously unacknowledged model for Emerson's vision of womanhood, "complete in her perfections" (*JMN*, 5:108), a "mate by spiritual affinities & not by sex" (*JMN*, 3:374). As he mused in his journal, "I can never think of women without gratitude for the bright revelations of her best nature" (*JMN*, 8:381). He continued to contemplate her sayings and examples throughout his life[15] and even continued to commemorate their wedding anniversary after his second marriage. His respect for the literary efforts of women may have arisen from his admiration for her work, and he quoted several of her poems in his journal, kept a special notebook for her verses, and printed them in the *Dial* and in his own volume of poetry, *Parnassus*.

At times Emerson did approach a more androgynous ideal, as when he noted in his journals, "A highly endowed man with good intellect & good conscience is a Man-Woman, & does not so much need the complement of Woman to his being as another. Hence his relations to the sex are somewhat dislocated & unsatisfactory. He asks in woman sometimes the Woman, sometimes the Man" (*JMN*, 8:175, 10:392). He concluded, "Always there is this Woman as well as this Man in the mind" (*JMN*, 8:230), and "there is no sex in thought, in knowledge, in virtue" (*JMN*, 3:192). He also quoted the Hindus as saying, "Man is man as far as he is triple, that is, a man-woman-child" (*JMN*, 16:146). Thus "the finest people marry the two sexes in their own person. Hermaphrodite is then the symbol of the finished soul. . . . in every act shall appear the married pair: the two elements should mix in every act" (*JMN*, 8:380). Elsewhere, he observed the "feminine element" was always to be found in "men of genius" (*JMN*, 10:394), and that "when a man writes poetry, he appears to assume the high feminine part of his nature. . . . a king is dressed almost in feminine attire" (*JMN*, 8:356).[16] Emerson, then, agreed with Fuller that both men and women contained a balance of traits that society called masculine or feminine, but understandably, given that they were already in advance of the awareness of their times, neither he nor Fuller was able to apply this insight further to reach today's hypothesis that social conditioning may create all gender traits.

Perhaps contemporary readers have wished that Emerson could have leapt far enough ahead of the mind-set of his era to be aware of the effects of societal conditioning precisely because, despite Emerson's consonance with the ideas of his era, the lecture and the essay "Woman" constituted a prescient statement of views that would not become current until recent times. When Emerson began to analyze the popular responses to the woman's movement, he sounded remarkably like women who would not be writing until the twentieth century.

An example would be the hoary charge that women had produced no masterworks in the arts and sciences. In the original address on which "Woman" was based, Emerson's response to this charge was that women excelled instead at life. He admired what he called in his journals this "putting of the life into [women's] deed" and used as examples Mary Seton, "who put her arm into the bolt to save Queen Mary," and "the women in the old sieges who cut off their hair to make ropes & ladders" (*JMN*, 10:345).[17] This was in itself an advance on his earlier reflection of the stereotype that women's role was simply to inspire men. Emerson then went a step further and realized that it had not been possible for female genius to be recognized until the new educational opportunities of the latter half of the nineteenth century. Here he anticipated English essayist and novelist Virginia Woolf's classic lecture, "A Room of One's Own," which also refuted this charge by reference to women's historic denial of access to education. In the original address Emerson had also followed the same line of argument as Woolf's essay often titled "Woman in the Professions," pointing out that, in Emerson's words, women "are better scholars than we [men] are at school & the reason why they are not better than we, twenty years later," was not because of an innate intellectual deficit, a stereotype he had himself unthinkingly echoed earlier in his career (*JMN*, 5:190, 9:190), but "because men can turn their reading to account in the professions, & women are excluded from the professions." Similarly, as he controverted the "monstrous exaggeration" of the misogynists, he noted their tendency to resort to stereotypes of women as mentally deficient and of femininity as an illness, anticipating the twentieth-century analyses of Charlotte Perkins Gilman, Simone de Beauvoir, and others. When this skeptical and cynical view of women as constitutionally unfit became a medical system, Emerson realized, women suffered as much as under slavery; both were systems based in a materialistic worldview "selling woman by the pound" (*JMN*, 5:190). Emerson showed interest in anything that undercut these stereotypes, noting, for example, that Theodore Lyman "insisted that he had himself seen hysteria oftener in men than women" (*JMN*, 16:173). Similarly, he refuted the claim that women who asked for autonomy really only wanted to be men: "I cannot even find that a woman wishes to be her lover, though she wishes to be united to him" (*JMN*, 9:195). Woman was not, as the common wisdom insisted, a "homme manqué," an incomplete man, but a complete and self-sufficing being.

Still, contemporary critics have questioned the address and the essay that was based upon it because both were typical of Emerson's penchant in public statements to first summarize all the negative ideas on a topic, then turn to the positive—the technique his friend, the feminist Caroline Dall, called seeming "to lure the conservatives on over his flowers till all of a sudden their feet are pierced by the thorns of reform."[18] In the second half of the essay, if contemporary readers can bear through, they will find Emerson stating an agenda of women's rights that was extremely radical even for the late nineteenth century, much less for its midpoint. He had come a long way from his youthful acceptance, through the mid-1840s, of the common excuse that women did not need rights because men would take care of them, since "every woman is a man's daughter and every man is a woman's son" (*JMN*, 8:411). Possibly seeing the plight of women, such as Concord neighbor Ellery Channing's wife Ellen, whose husbands manifestly did not care and provide for them, had dispossessed Emerson of this chivalric illusion. Emerson

called openly for women to receive their "one half of the world
. . . the right to [equality in] education" and "employment, to
equal rights of property, to equal rights in marriage, to the exercise of the professions; of suffrage." In essence, Emerson was
here setting out the complete agenda of the 1850 Women's
Rights Convention for which he had signed the call, proving that
he was fully aware of his actions in so doing and truly supported
all of these then-radical reforms.

The 1855 address, then, encapsulated Emerson's support for
total equality for women: "Let the public donations to education
be equally shared by them, let them enter a school as freely as a
church, let them have and hold their property as men do theirs."
In a time when colleges were closed to women and the law for-
bade their owning property, Emerson's demands were extremely
progressive. Emerson even went so far as to argue that if suffrage
was denied to women, "You [must] also refuse to tax them,"
based on the American principle of no taxation without representation. That Emerson was aware of this central and most controversial principle of Susan B. Anthony's in only the first decade
of her public work revealed how much he was abreast of the developing suffrage movement and how far ahead of his time he
was, but it was not surprising, given that Anthony also cited
Fuller as her source material. Emerson was certainly aware of
the early feminist activists, praising Lucretia Mott, co-organizer
of the first American woman's rights convention, as a woman
whose "sense, virtue, & good-meaning" guaranteed "victory in
all the fights to which her Quaker faith & connection led her"
(*JMN*, 11:249).

Another reason for the contemporary chagrin over "Woman"
may come from the fact that Emerson, like many among the
relatively few Americans who first became aware of and involved
with the woman's movement in the 1850s, experienced some confusion from listening to the women who constituted both the
pro-suffrage and the equally vocal anti–woman's rights cam-
paigns. Emerson was influenced for a time by women, such as
his own daughter Ellen, who were antisuffrage and at first believed the antisuffrage view that the majority of women did not
want change and that it would thus be forced violently upon

them. Other of the women around him, such as his aunt Mary Moody Emerson, while like Emerson himself repulsed by the materialism and lack of moral judgment in the political and commercial worlds women would be entering, finally persuaded him that change in their status was nonetheless essential. At the time, however, Emerson had not yet come to his later realization that even the most refined and intellectual women desired the vote, as he stated in the 1855 address, "The answer that, silent or spoken, lies in the minds of well meaning persons, to the new claims, is this: that, though their mathematical justice is not to be denied"—a position Emerson held as given, extreme though it was at the time—"yet the best women do not wish these things." Despite this belief, Emerson did not ameliorate the radicalism of his demands for equality, urging that even if the most favored women did not want or even need political parity, it must nevertheless be available for the benefit of the women who lacked their social and economic advantages.

Emerson understood that such women were deprived of intellectual stimulation and were, as he stated in his journals, "Starved for thought & sentiment" (*JMN*, 10:78). Therefore, "intellectual men [were] most attractive to women" (*JMN*, 9:82). Equally serious was the problem of economic powerlessness. Emerson often responded with strong sympathy to the plight of impoverished women.[19] He refused to fall into the trap of blaming the victim, asserting that while a donation "of 100 dollars" would make "little difference" to the lives of an "easy man," "Let it fall into the hands of a poor & prudent woman, and every shilling & every cent of it fully tells, goes to reduce debt" (*JMN*, 8:319), a comment possibly based on observation of his neighbor, the philosopher Amos Bronson Alcott, and his hard-pressed but practical wife, Abigail May. Similarly, he avoided the tendency to blame women more heavily than men for breaches of decorum: "I heard a woman swearing very liberally, as she talked with her companions; but when I looked at her face, I saw that she was no worse than other women; that she used the dialect of her class, as all others do, & are neither better nor worse for it; but under this costume was the same probity, the same repose as in the more civilized classes" (*JMN*, 8:347). He realized that change in women's financially dependent position was essential to their freedom; in his journals he observed: "Society lives on the system of money & woman comes at money & money's worth through compliment. I should not dare to be woman. Plainly they are created for that better system which supersedes money. . . . On [*sic*] our civilization her position is often pathetic. What she is not expected to do & suffer for some invitation to strawberries & cream." At the time he wrote that passage, Emerson consoled himself, "Fortunately their eyes are holden that they cannot see."[20] By the time he was writing the 1855 address, the woman's rights movement had made it plain to Emerson that women did indeed see their subservient economic position and linked it directly to their deprivation of political rights and civic opportunities. This awareness of the result of women's socioeconomic powerlessness and especially of the plight of working-class women was relatively rare even in the woman's movement, as recent histories of the British and American suffrage movements have made clear. For Emerson to display it this early was evidence of how much deep and serious thought he had given the question. While recognizing that economic barriers to women were most burdensome to the underprivileged, Emerson did not see them as lesser beings but insisted that impoverished and working-class women retained their dignity: "In the labours of house & in poverty I feel sometimes as if the handiness & deft apparatus for household toil were only a garb under which the softest Cleopatra walked concealed" (*JMN*, 10:78).[21]

Emerson also recognized that the demands of being solely responsible for child care were heavy for women, asking in his poem "Holidays,"

> Whither went the lovely hoyden?
> Disappeared in blessed wife;
> Servant to a wooden cradle,
> Living in a baby's life. (*W*, 9:136).

Emerson sympathized with the multiple roles into which women were forced and the blame that often accrued to them: "A man is sometimes offended at the superfluous superogatory order & nicety of a woman who is a good housewife. But he must bear with little extremities & flourishes of quality that makes comfort for all his senses throughout his house" (*JMN*, 5:377).

Society did its "worst in intruding into the education of young women, and withers the hope and affection of human nature, by teaching that marriage signifies nothing but a housewife's thrift, and that woman's life has no other end." Such were the difficulties of marriage for women that "the fair girl whom I saw in town expressing so decided & proud choices of influences, so careless of pleasing, so willful, & so lofty a will, inspires the wish to . . . speak to this nobleness" and "to say to her, Never strike sail to any. Come into port greatly, or sail with God the seas. Not in vain you live, for the passing stranger is cheered, refined, & raised by the vision" (*JMN*, 5:445).

Emerson's periodical reading further illuminates his interest in the issue of marriage, an institution with great impact on women's status, particularly in the nineteenth century. He had begun his investigation of these ideas as early as 1817, at the age of fourteen, when he borrowed Hannah More's *Strictures on a System of Female Education*,[22] which emphasized the need to develop woman's intellect as well as her emotions, her logical as well as her affective nature, her sense as well as her sensibility. Further, More argued that marriage should be a union based on educated, mutual understanding, common interests, genuine respect, and sexual equality. Although as a youth he had occasionally mimicked the cynical attitudes of Byron and his ilk toward marriage, Emerson came to respect this idea of "Marriage of the minds" (*JMN*, 12:357). From Verlake he had gained the idea that "A man & a woman" together constituted "the true social unit," including the radical proposition that "the married couple should not take either the name of husband or wife, but a new name common to both" (*JMN*, 8:342).

He continued his exploration of the issue in 1829 by reading one of his major intellectual influences, Sampson Reed, whose unsigned "Introduction to Entomology" contained, of all things, a passage on celibacy.[23] The next year he followed this with reading in the same month two articles, Caleb Reed's unsigned article on the nature of affection and John Hubbard Wilkins's unsigned "On Marriage."[24] In 1831, he returned to Sampson Reed with an unsigned article on "Guardian Angels," which, like the previous articles, stressed the permanence of spiritual ties between the sexes, and in 1832 with Reed's similar piece, "Marriage in the Heavens."[25] In 1834 Emerson also returned to Caleb Reed, whose unsigned article the "Supposed Extinction of Our Proper and Peculiar Loves at Death" reinforced this argument that human affections are eternal.[26] And in 1835, a last unsigned piece by, again, Sampson Reed concerned marriage in heaven.[27] All of these articles on marriage and affectional ties which Emerson devoured in the 1830s were published in the *New Jerusalem Magazine,* an organ of the church founded by the philosopher Emanuel Swedenborg,[28] and conditioned Emerson to its view of marriage as a state of spiritual relation, leading him to argue for "Marriage from Character" (*JMN*, 12:487) or "ideal" marriage (*JMN*, 12:437, 492, 496), rather than seeing marriage as merely a financial and social contrivance, "Marriage empirical" (*JMN*, 12:347, 489, 491). This outlook would predispose him to see women as souls rather than chattel and to assume their equal rights in marriage, for which he would argue so strongly in "Woman."

At first Emerson had considered the "chief institution" of marriage to be either the producer or the product of "good-Order in Society" (*JMN*, 2:209), but before the time of *Representative Men* he was asking, "Is not marriage an open question, when it is alleged, from the beginning of the world, that such as are in the institution wish to get out; and such as are out, wish to get in?" He went on to quote Socrates: "Whether you take a wife or not you will regret it" (*JMN*, 12:535). Emerson continued to try to solve the riddle of marriage, considering not only the ideas of Swedenborg and Percy Bysshe Shelley, whose idea of marriage for love, he noted, removed the scent of the Inquisitor's oppression, but even such unlikely solutions as "For marriage find somebody that was born near the time when you were born" (*JMN*, 8:168).

If marriage were a spiritual state, Emerson observed, its official and legal codification by the state was suspect. "The wave of evil washes all our institutions alike," especially marriage (*JMN*,

8:185), so that "We marry no worse than we eat or dress or speak" (*JMN*, 12:308), but no better either. "None ever heard of a good marriage from Mesopotamia to Missouri and yet right marriage is as possible tomorrow as sunshine. Sunshine is a very mixed & costly thing as we have it, & quite impossible, yet we get the right article every day. And we are not very much to blame for our bad marriages" (*JMN*, 10:351). Emerson seemed almost to be aware of the negative results of social conditioning and gender roles on marriage: "We live amid hallucinations & illusions, & this especial trap is laid for us to trap our feet with, & all are tripped up, first or last. . . . Into the Pandora-box of marriage, amidst dyspepsia, nervousness, screams, Christianity," comes "poetry, & all kinds of music, [and] some deep & serious benefits & some great joys. . . . And in these ill assorted connections there is ever some mixture of true marriage. The poorest Paddy & his jade, if well-meaning & well tempered, get some just & agreeable relations of mutual respect & kindly observation & fostering of each other. & [sic] they learn something, & would carry themselves wiselier if they were to begin life anew in some other sphere" (*JMN*, 10:351–52). The influence of Hannah More's work, with its emphasis on the need for "mutual respect" to constitute a "true marriage," and the Swedenborgian emphasis on the positive effects of marriage on the afterdeath state or "other sphere" were both evident in Emerson's views. Indeed, he echoed both More and Swedenborg frequently in his desire for "the true nuptials of minds" (*JMN*, 8:94) and his argument that "[m]arriage should be by gravitation" (*JMN*, 12:362) of like minds and souls to one another, not by social or material negotiations.

On the other hand, Emerson recognized the dangers of marriage as a social institution rather than a spiritual partnership, since the "low ground" of marriage (*JMN*, 8:293), an "unfit marriage" (*JMN*, 8:69) or "Mezentian marriage"[29] could paralyze individual growth. In addition, the demands of marriage as a social unit mitigated its function as an emotional relationship: "The husband loses the wife in the cares of the household. Later, he cannot rejoice with her in the babe, for by becoming a mother she ceases yet more to be a wife. With the growth of children the relation of the pair becomes yet feebler from the demands children make until at last nothing remains of the original passion out of which all these parricidal fruits proceeded; and they die because they are superfluous" (*JMN*, 5:297).

Yet as long as women lacked autonomy in society, the institution of marriage remained necessary for women's security: "We cannot rectify marriage because it would introduce such carnage into our social relations. . . . Woman hides her from the eyes of men in our world: they cannot, she rightly thinks, be trusted. In the right state the love of one, which each man carried in his heart, should protect all women from his eyes" and make him "their protector & saintly friend, as if for her sake. But now there is in the eyes of all men a certain evil light, a vague desire which attaches them to the forms of many women, whilst their affections fasten on some one. Their natural eye is not fixed into coincidence with their spiritual eye" (*JMN*, 8:95). While "the soul says, The man and woman shall be one flesh and one soul; the body would join the flesh only" (*JMN*, 2:61). Men had not yet learned to deal with their lower instincts: "Jesus said, When he looketh on her, he hath already committed adultery! But he is an adulterer already before yet he has looked on the woman, by the superfluity of animal, & the weakness of thought, in his constitution" (*JMN*, 11:435).

Thus "no man could be trusted" without the institution of marriage: "We cannot spare the coarsest muniment of virtue" (*JMN*, 9:50). Emerson even approached an awareness of how men's repressed desires were often projected psychologically onto women, the phenomenon so notable in the witch trials when women were accused of arousing men's lust simply by walking down the street:

> It happened once a youth & a maid beheld each other in a public assembly for the first time. The youth gazed with great delight upon the beautiful face until he caught the maiden's eye. . . . But he felt by that glance he had been strangely beguiled. The beautiful face had been strangely transformed. He felt the stirring of owls & bats, & horned hoofs, within him. The face which was really beautiful seemed to him have been

usurped by a low devil, and an innocent maiden, for so she still seemed to him, to be possessed. And that glance was the confession of the devil to his inquiry. (*JMN*, 5:8)

Until men could acknowledge and accept responsibility for their own desires, women could not trust their fidelity without the surety of marriage: "Therefore it will not do to abrogate the laws which make Marriage a relation for life, fit or unfit" (*JMN*, 8:95). Emerson summarized, "We need all the conventions of marriage against our evils."[30]

The Swedenborgian view of marriage as a spiritual relationship could help solve some of these problems, which, Emerson wrote, arose "whenever bodily familiarity grows up without a spiritual intimacy," as in marriage for social status or financial support. "Purity in marriage" arose when "the partners are universally near & helpful, & not only near bodily," when "their wisdoms come near & meet. . . . Therefore the remedy of impurity is to come nearer" (*JMN*, 8:392). Thus "what a dupe is the libertine! He thinks he has the sparkle & the color of the cup & the chaste married pair only the lees. They see that he stays always in the basement & never has one glimpse of the high joys of a perfect wedlock" (*JMN*, 5:365).

Ultimately, then, Emerson believed that marriage was worthwhile: "[H]ow little think the youth & maiden who are glancing at each other across a mixed company as with eyes so full of material intelligence . . . of the precious fruits long hereafter to proceed from that gentle external stimulus." Immediately after marriage, "they begin to discover incongruities, defects. Thence comes surprise, regret, strife: But that which drew them first was signs of loveliness, signs of virtue. These virtues appear & reappear, & continue to draw, but the regard changes, quits the sign & attaches to the substance" (*JMN*, 5:297). In other words, the couple would come to appreciate each other's inner, rather than outer, beauty. Such "perfection of the intellect and the heart, from year to year, is the real marriage" (*JMN*, 2:109). This "real marriage" came "to mitigate the disaffection," and life

exorts the resources of each & acquaint[s] each with the whole strength & weakness of the other. All the angels that inhabit this temple of a human form show themselves at the doors & all the gnomes also. By all the virtues that appear, by so much kindness, justice, fortitude &c, by so much are they made one. But all the vices are negations on either part & they are by so much made two. At last they discover that all that first drew them together was wholly caducous, had merely a prospective end like the scaffolding by which a house is built, & the wholly unsuspected & wholly unconscious growth of principles from year to year is the real marriage foreseen & prepared from the first but wholly above their consciousness. This is the boarding school & God. (*JMN*, 5:297–98)

Emerson pondered this "real marriage" deeply in the mid-1830s:

How fast the frivolous external fancying fades out of the mind. . . . Mourn for the rapid ebb of inclination not one moment. . . . The parties discover every day the deep & permanent character each of the other as a root & foundation on which they may safely build their nuptial bower. They learn slowly that all other affection than that which rests upon what they are is superstitious & evanescent . . . there is no luck nor witchcraft nor destiny nor divinity in marriage that can produce affection but only these qualities that by their nature exort it. (*JMN*, 5:208)

A real marriage, then, was built on principle and fostered complete trust and devotion, as Emerson noted in 1841: "We love that lover whose gayest of love songs, whose fieriest engagement of romantic devotion is made good by all the days of all the years of strenuous, long suffering, ever-renewing benefit. The old Count said to the old Countess of Ilchester, 'I know that wherever thou goest, thou wilt both trust & honor me, and thou knowest that wherever I am I shall honor thee'" (*JMN*, 8:134). This "nuptial love releases each from that excess of influence which warped each from his own and gives each again to himself & herself, so that they acquire their own features & proportion again, & new beauty & divinity in each other's eyes." Emerson referred to such successful marriages as a "constitutional nuptial affection" (*JMN*, 12:369), the "joy of the noble in loving" (*JMN*, 12:491).

Ultimately, marriage was subjective (*JMN*, 12:545), and outsiders could not hope to understand or interfere successfully: "When wary fathers & guardians see what potencies mingle in this game of love & marriage, they will hardly dare to advise, dare to dissuade, & incur the life-long responsibilities of making or marring a marriage" (*JMN*, 12:586). Yet Emerson ignored his own advice and entered into many matchmaking attempts with regard to younger male and female acquaintances such as Anna Barker and Samuel Gray Ward. Indeed, the very frequency of Emerson's attempts at devising matrimonial pairs from among his single friends suggests that his opinion of marriage was positive enough for him to attempt to bestow its benefits on the unattached members of his circle. And he noted that women's tendency to date their lives "from their marriage" was "more reasonable" than men's to do so from some "magnified trifle" such as "the foolish games of their college life" (*JMN*, 8:291).

Considering, then, all the social roles, expectations, and institutions that affected women's status, Emerson had made a strong case for equal rights, stating boldly in the 1855 address that women "[h]ave an unquestionable right to their own property. And if the woman demand votes, offices, and political equality with men . . . it must not be refused." The change in number—from the plural of "the best women" to the singular "the woman"—is interesting here, implying that even if only one woman desired the vote, it must be granted her. Further, Emerson determinedly refuted the objections to woman's suffrage. In reply to the common objection to women's political participation, their "want of practical wisdom," he argued wittily that a less than perfect grasp of the issues had never disqualified men from voting. If men voted as they were told by their political bosses and parties without troubling to inform themselves on the issues, women could certainly do no worse. In response to the charge that women lacked worldly experience, Emerson quipped that this was "not a disqualification, but a qualification." In a somewhat ironic tone, he pointed out that there would never be a shortage of voters who would represent "the expediency . . . the interest of trade or of imperative class interest." Even if women did vote from a basis of naïveté and aim "at abstract right

without allowing for circumstances," as many opponents of suffrage argued, they would serve to balance morally the voting
populace who aimed only at material gain or maintaining a
prejudicial status quo without allowing for right or justice. Emerson's implied argument was thus that granting women full political participation would improve the entire nation—again, an
echo of Fuller's tactics, as they were adopted by the suffrage
movement.

Indeed, for Emerson women's civilizing influence was a major reason to give them the ballot. This argument was emphasized in the address to the 1855 Woman's Rights Convention
upon which "Woman" was based. Emerson made the equation
plain: "Woman *is* the power of civilization"; woman "altered &
mended" the "rough & reckless ways of men" (*JMN*, 10:83).
Therefore, given the "election frauds & misdeeds" with which
the land was rife, extending the suffrage to women to "civilize
the voting" was "the remedy at the moment of need." This was a
more specific application of the general principles which Emerson stated in his journals as "the virtue of women [is] the main
girth or bandage of society" (*JMN*, 10:83).

Emerson took this argument further in answering the other
common objection to woman's suffrage, that it would "contami-
nate" women and "unsex" them. He pointed out that this argument "only accuses our existing politics. . . . It is easy to see
that there is contamination enough, but it rots the men now."
Rather than denying the vote to women in order to protect them
from the dirty business of politics, he suggested, the wiser course
was to clean up the political system. Again, Emerson here duplicated Fuller's tactics, as she was wont to argue, as were other suffragists such as Sojourner Truth, that if the system were inimical
and harmful, then the system itself needed to be changed; ban-
ning women from it was only avoiding the problem. In fact, suggesting that to "[i]mprove and refine the men" was to "do the
same by the women," Emerson implied that the better educated,
the more moral men became, the more they became, in his
phrase, "true men," the more they not only would be willing to
give women their "half of the world" but also would insist, like
Emerson himself, on their right to it. Emerson, then, saw a "real

man" as one who was secure enough that he did not need to force others into a subservient position in order to aggrandize his own status. To Emerson, a "real man" was one who actively advocated women's rights and equality; in today's terms, to be a real man was to be a feminist.

Despite his belief in the 1850s that most women did not desire suffrage, then, Emerson nonetheless insisted it be available for those who did. Especially notable in the "Discourse Manqué" was how uncertain Emerson appeared to be about the true desires of women on this issue—notice the hedging language on the part of a writer who was usually so straightforward: "I do not *think* it *yet appears* that women wish this equal share in public affairs" (emphasis added). In the very next sentence, though, when Emerson returned to his call for equal opportunity, he again found his accustomed directness of voice: "But it is they and not we that are to determine it." While Emerson was uncertain of the wishes of the women about him—and he was apparently receiving a great deal of contradictory information at this time—he was certain that the right to choose rested with them, not with men. Emerson explicitly acknowledged women's right to decide for themselves the part they would play on the national and world stage; men's role, in his view, was simply to support them in enforcing their decision against the weight of entrenched prejudice and tradition. As he would write in a letter to Caroline Sturgis Tappan in 1868, "It is of course for women to determine this question! the part of men, if women decide to assume the suffrage, is simply to accept their determination & aid in carrying it out" (*L*, 9:326–27). In his journals he had reached a similar conclusion as early as 1843, the same year Fuller's "The Great Lawsuit," the basis of *Woman in the Nineteenth Century*, appeared in the *Dial:* "To me it sounded hoarsely the attempt to prescribe didactically to woman her duties. Man can never tell woman what her duties are" (*JMN*, 8:381). When "the state & duties of Woman" were only "historically considered," they "had a certain falseness" (*JMN*, 8:372). "Women only can tell the heights of feminine nature, & the only way in which men can help her, is by observing woman reverentially & whenever she speaks from herself & catches him in inspired moments to a heaven of honor

& religion, to hold her to that point by reverential recognition of the divinity that speaks through her" (*JMN*, 8:381). The language of "sacred womanhood" here was a means of expressing respect for women's strengths. "Woman is not," as the nineteenth century often considered her, "a degraded person with duties forgotten, but a docile daughter of God with her face heavenward endeavouring to hear the divine word & to convey it to me" (*JMN*, 8:372).[31] Emerson's was thus a very progressive opinion even for the 1850s, especially in anticipating contemporary feminism's emphasis that women not ask men for rights, thereby implying that those rights were men's property to give to women as a gift, but rather that women should grasp their rights for themselves. As Fuller, again, had stated, these were women's "birthright" (Fuller, 177), and Emerson's trust in Fuller's judgment was again apparent.

In fact, one could argue that Emerson followed Fuller with such implicit faith that he echoed her even in those ideas that contemporary feminism has discarded. Today's critics, who would not condemn Fuller for such concepts, have ignored her profound influence on Emerson when they have attacked him for following her lead. An example would be Emerson's statement that "a masculine woman is not strong, but a lady is,"[32] echoing Fuller's sentiment that a true woman would "never wish to be man-like" (Fuller, 51). Emerson sounded most like Fuller when he argued such ideas as that it was "impossible to separate the interests and education of the sexes." *Woman in the Nineteenth Century* was full of such pleas for the unity of women's and men's interests, as when Fuller stated that women's "interests were identical" with men's, or that "I believe that the development of the one cannot be effected without that of the other" (Fuller, 156). What has sounded to contemporary readers like an implication that women's interests were only important as they affected men was to nineteenth-century readers a daring avowal of the equal significance of women on the world stage, as well as a politic way to appeal to men's self-interest. Emerson emphasized his anticipation of this transformation in attitudes toward women's place when he concluded, perhaps overly optimistically, "[T]he aspiration of this century [for women's equality] will be the code of the next."

Viewing the time line, then, of the development of Emerson's thoughts on women, and particularly on their right to political equality, Emerson was already, at the beginning of the American suffrage movement in the 1850s, convinced of and speaking out for its necessity. While his arguments, influenced by Fuller, were couched like hers in the essentialist nineteenth-century language of sacred womanhood, gentility, and intuitive superiority, his political demands on behalf of woman were as bold as hers.

Emerson's ideas of woman's role were also continually evolving, then. Emerson had come far since the 1830s, when he had attempted to understand gender differences by means of such superficial and unlikely distinctions as "the man loves hard wood, the woman loves pitch pine" (*JMN*, 5:308, 6:228);[33] since the 1840s, when he quoted stereotypes of the nineteenth-century ideal of the passionless woman (*JMN*, 11:25);[34] and even since 1851, when he wrote, "Few women are sane" or "There could be no conversation with women" because they "are always thinking of a husband."[35] By 1855, only a few years later, his ideas of women's capability had broadened to encompass "half of the world."

The next major change in Emerson's developing awareness of women's issues would come once most Americans had become aware of the woman's rights movement, after the Civil War. By this time, encouraged by such women in his circle as Mary Moody Emerson and Louisa May Alcott, Emerson had become aware that the one caveat he had withheld—that women themselves did not desire the vote—was untrue. Emerson commented upon this change himself in the previously mentioned letter to Caroline Sturgis Tappan on 13 November 1868. In response to Tappan's statement that "[a]ll women should feel & cry that they are suffering from being governed without their consent," he explained that previously, he had "believed that women did not wish [to enter into public life], that those whose decision would be final, the thoughtful serene typical minds shrank from it." However, he continued, "I have been much surprised to find that my saints or some of them have a feeling of duty that however odious the new order may appear in some of its details they must bravely accept & realize it" (*L*, 9:326–27). This process of transition in Emerson's views has not been previously recognized.[36] Emerson himself would see this recognition of women's desire for emancipation as the point of his conversion to the woman's cause, even though he had been actively supporting it since 1850, and in the 1860s and 1870s he would become an icon of the suffragist leaders.

Today's readers may be surprised that the suffragists would find any aspect of women's equality "odious." However, many women, like Emerson himself, valued some of the qualities that had arisen from women's socially enforced exile to a passive role in life: unselfishness, spirituality, cooperativeness, gentleness, caring. They feared that when women entered into work and politics, they would be forced to behave as men had been conditioned to so as to survive in the patriarchal outer world and would lose these attributes. Again, Julia Ward Howe, who by the time of Emerson's death had become a distinguished poet as well as a leader of the suffragist American Woman's Party, provided one of the most insightful analyses of this conflict between the appreciation of the more nurturing, "feminine" traits in both women and men and the need for fuller social and political freedom. She especially contrasted Emerson's attraction to the beauty of the feminine character as it had developed in a hothouse environment of artificial restrictions against his recognition of the justice of women's demand for a more equal and active part in defining their own lives. In analyzing this conflict, Howe accurately noted an essential Emersonian debate between Beauty and Justice, or Truth, as Emerson called the principle for which Howe used the term Justice.

In a more abstract fashion, this dialectic between Beauty and Truth rang throughout Emerson's works as it did those of other Romantics such as the English poet John Keats. Emerson respected "Ode to a Grecian Urn" practically alone among Keats's works because it addressed this Romantic problem of the proper relationship of Beauty to Truth. However, although he stated in "The Poet" that Beauty and Truth were equal, Emerson disagreed with Keats as to the exact equivalence of Beauty and Truth (Keats had claimed "Beauty *is* truth, truth beauty"). Emerson believed that Truth was even more important than Beauty.

This decision was notable in, among other indicators, Emerson's placing the chapter "Beauty" in his book *Nature* before that on Truth ("Discipline"), since the chapters were placed, in typical Romantic fashion, in rising order of importance.

Emerson, Howe noted, did not use stereotypical definitions of Beauty as feminine and Justice or Truth as masculine, but recognized that "justice, as well as beauty, was to him a feminine ideal." To Emerson, Beauty and Truth each embodied a "feminine" as well as a masculine "Ideal." Further, Howe recognized Emerson's stand, in declarations such as "Woman," that woman must have the power to decide for herself what her role in society would be: "He believed in woman's power to hold and adjust for herself the scales in which character is weighed against attraction."[37] As Emerson had stated to Caroline Sturgis Tappan, the power of self-determination must be given to women even if their ultimate choice would involve less of "attraction" (Beauty) and more of "character" (Truth) than Emerson's personal aesthetic sense would find pleasing.

Yet Emerson, who himself shrank from the public sphere, admired and appreciated the intensely spiritual unselfishness women had been forced to develop while sequestered as "the angel in the house." He also had, as seen in "Woman," deep doubts about the corruption inherent in participation in the world of politics and commerce. He would have preferred to see women remain, and men become, more inner-directed, aloof from the materialistic concerns of social life. While Emerson's democratic tendencies and his profound respect for the women in his own life forced him to support the movement for women's equality, he had an abiding distrust of the public and especially the political arena, which women were entering by their agitation for suffrage and would be entering even further by gaining the vote. Emerson feared that women, previously excluded and therefore protected from these areas, would make the same mistakes that he saw men as having made, losing their spiritual focus to the necessary compromises of politics (as had Daniel Webster, a prime example) and falling into the lure of materialism when they entered the workplace. Ultimately, Emerson questioned the feasibility of anyone, not only women, being what he had called in the lecture on which "Woman" was based "innocent citizens." To Emerson, the very possibility of being both "innocent" and a participating "citizen" of a flawed—at that time, even slaveholding—political system was highly questionable. Aspirations to innocent citizenhood appeared to him to be laudable in principle but in the practice of the corrupt state regrettably oxymoronic. However, he also recognized that the choice was not his to make, but women's own. If they believed that political and social equality was necessary to their spiritual development, his responsibility was to support them in their struggle. He would no more keep them housebound in order to promote their spiritual beauty any more than he would keep the slaves in captivity in order to enjoy the harmony of their songs for freedom.

Emerson's position was thus characteristic of nineteenth-century feminists, female and male, and the suffragists were outspoken in their praise and gratitude for his efforts on behalf of women's empowerment, education, and equality. The leaders of the suffragist movement specifically addressed Emerson's role, as they saw it, in the woman's rights movement. While Emerson, with characteristic modesty, would not give himself credit for his early support of the woman's rights movement, suffragists such as Julia Ward Howe were adamant concerning his stand.[38] In particular, Howe stressed Emerson's respect for women's intellect, even crediting him with an important role in her own conversion from judging women by their physical attractiveness to considering their true character, the very trait she had emphasized in her analysis of Emerson. As she told it, when Emerson "asked me if I knew Margaret Fuller[,] I told him I thought her an ugly person. He then dwelt upon her mind and conversation."[39] Clearly, Emerson had transcended the Victorian valuing of women solely for their ornamental role, to appreciate them on the same grounds by which he did men—for their intelligence. Emerson recognized the "sad mortifications" of women being judged by society only on their appearance. To him, the key attraction was inner, not outer, beauty, "the beauty of being as it outshines the beauty of seeming" (*JMN*, 5:389). This sort of beauty was available for women of any social class, even if the circumstances of their lives meant they could not afford the outer accouterments of artificial, socially defined beauty: "A woman never so neat & trim does not please by inoffensiveness, while she only complies with the exactions of our established decorum, but is coarse. But, as soon as her own sense of beauty leads her to the same perfect neatness, & we ascribe to her secret neatness, then she is lovely, though sick, poor, & accidentally squalid" (*JMN*, 11:436). Even in admiring the famous actress Elisa Felix, known as Rachel, Emerson admired her "terror & energy . . . defiance or denunciation," and most of all her "highly intellectual air" and "universal intelligence."[40] Indeed, he counted seeing Rachel more highly than hearing a lecture by the renowned scientist Michelet and as one of the high points of his trip to France. Similarly, in his poem "Hermione," although the titular heroine is "not fair" in appearance, her "sceptered genius" is sufficient to enrapture the speaker.[41]

Howe's perception of the value of Emerson as a teacher of women was upheld by Ednah Dow Cheney, a leader of the Massachusetts Woman Suffrage Society and the School Suffrage Association and a prominent writer. Cheney recalled Emerson's total and eager attention to every person he met, however young, making no distinction between male and female.[42] Emerson's journals bear testimony to this respect for his youthful and female audience; in the late 1840s or early 1850s he wrote, "No part of the population interests except the children & the young women" (*JMN*, 10:465).

As Cheney had suggested, Emerson persisted in taking seriously his female audience, despite the fact that they were a hindrance to his public (i.e., male) reputation. As Howe would recall later in an article for the special issue of the *Critic* on Emerson's work, "The distinguished jurist, Jeremiah Mason, said of [Emerson's] lectures: 'I cannot understand them, but my daughters do.' This dictum was at the time considered a damning piece of irony."[43] Indeed, it could be argued that women, especially the suffragists, were among Emerson's earliest and most sympathetic audience because they shared his sense of alienation from the social sphere and were intimately acquainted with society's strictures against nonconformity. Howe continued to emphasize

Emerson's respect for women as an important audience and his "sympathy with the new opportunities accorded to women. He spoke more than once in favor of woman suffrage, and was for many years an honorary member of the New England Women's Club, to whose gatherings he occasionally lent the charm of his presence and his voice."[44] Cheney also recalled Emerson's honorary membership in the New England Women's Club, noting that he became such immediately upon the club's formation in 1865: "He frequently came to its meetings and read some of his most personal and charming papers there," including the first draft of his reminiscences of Mary Moody Emerson, a major figure in his intellectual development.[45]

These public reminiscences of his Aunt Mary were typical of Emerson's respect for the women of his circle. He often quoted their bon mots and insights in his journal, citing most frequently his aunt, the "prophetic" and "profound" Mary Moody Emerson, on whose journal entries he based his poem "The Nun's Aspiration" (*W*, 9:490 n). Aunt Mary was a profound influence on Emerson's formative years, probably the most important person in his life in terms of inspiring and helping to shape his ideas and expectations. After his marriage, another important influence was his second wife, Lidian. The impact of both these women's lives and thought on Emerson deserves further explication in separate studies.

Other women whom Emerson quoted and referred to included his mother, Ruth Emerson, and his daughter Ellen. Emerson especially praised friend and fellow Concordian Elizabeth Hoar, whom he called "immortal . . . an influence I cannot spare" (*JMN*, 8:105), considered a fit contributor to the Transcendentalist literary journal the *Dial*, and wrote of so often that he created his own index of his allusions to her. Emerson also frequently cited the "inspired" Sarah Alden Ripley, whose "high & calm intelligence" (*JMN*, 9:149, 8:94) created in him "some feeling of unworthiness" (*JMN*, 5:481); and the Quaker Mary Rotch. He equally admired Rebecca Black, who shared his Aunt Mary's unconventionality and original thinking. Jane Welsh Carlyle, wife of Thomas Carlyle, he regarded at least as highly as her husband. The same was true of Sophia Ripley, a "true worker" who ran the Brook Farm community together with her husband, George. He also quoted and praised Anna Barker Ward, the "genius" of *Dial* contributor Caroline Sturgis, to whom he referred in his essay "History," as well as Louisa May Alcott, lesser known women, and women no longer remembered today.

Emerson was also concerned with the effect of his lectures on women, especially what would today be called "empowering" women, as one anecdote made clear. Respected author, lyceum lecturer, and women's rights activist Elizabeth Oakes Smith recalled that after one of Emerson's lectures on "Power," he "approached the bright-minded Mrs. C.—I noticed he uttered the one word, 'Well?' interrogatively, and with an almost childish simplicity, to which she replied: 'Oh, Mr. Emerson, you make me feel so powerless, as if I could do nothing.'" At this expected response of stereotypical feminine helplessness, Emerson, in Oakes Smith's words, "Looked grave and turning to me, repeated the enigmatical monosyllable, 'Well?' . . . to which I replied, 'In listening to you, Mr. Emerson, no achievement seemed impossible; it was as though I might remove mountains.' 'Ah, that is well,' he answered cordially."[46]

This response to Emerson by the suffragists has suggested a facet of his work that has been thus far overlooked in the ongoing debate over Emerson's response to women's issues. Like Margaret Fuller before them, the suffragists saw Emerson as one who encouraged women's intellectual independence and honored their literary status on fully equal terms with men. They appreciated his respect for the women and young people in his audience and his efforts to recruit brilliant women for his Concord coterie. They had no difficulty in reconciling his respect for women's spiritual endowments with his awareness of their need for entitlement and empowerment in society, since they themselves performed the same balancing act. While they recognized that he would himself prefer to cultivate both men's and women's souls even at the cost of their social participation, they knew that he understood their need and right to make that decision for themselves and would support their choice.

Further, as more critics of nineteenth-century women writers have begun to recognize, they were deeply aware of stylistic concerns. Dall's "thorns of reform" comment was a fine example. The suffragists comprehended Emerson's typical technique of laying forth all the negative sides of an idea before the positive, and saw that he applied this technique evenhandedly, as much for his criticism of Shakespeare, Milton, and Wordsworth as for women's issues. Indeed, they recognized, as few contemporary readers have, Emerson's strategy in using this advanced argumentation form to lure opponents of his ideas by apparent agreement, then trap them into considering reforms. Julia Ward Howe also stressed that Emerson tended to qualify his public statements, suggesting in her speech at the memorial meeting for the ninety-sixth anniversary of Emerson's birth that "Emerson was as great in what he did not say as in what he said. Second-class talent tells the whole story, reasons everything out; great genius suggests even more than it says."[47] Emerson, in Howe's analysis, inspired the reader to consider for himself or herself the implications of a particular idea. Women could then apply these implications to and for themselves, as Margaret Fuller had done in extending Emerson's concepts of self-reliance, individualism, and the primacy of spiritual or moral character to women and their conditioning in *Woman in the Nineteenth Century*. Thus, Emerson's full ideas on women's rights were not stated publicly but must be inferred from the incidents of his life and his response to women who dared to carry out the radical ramifications of his ideas for women, such as Fuller and Howe. There was no question in their minds that Emerson was, as they would have phrased it, a true friend and proponent of woman's rights.

The suffragists were so intent on clarifying Emerson's support of the woman's rights movement for good reasons. As Emerson had become revered as the Sage of Concord, his opinions carried moral weight. The antisuffrage establishment was eager to claim his allegiance and had shown itself fully capable of distorting his views in order to make it appear so.

A typical example would be the review published in the *Philadelphia Inquirer* of James Elliot Cabot's biography of Emerson. The *Inquirer* had not publicized Emerson's support of the 1850 and subsequent woman's rights conventions, his signature of the declaration of principles, or his delivery of the address at the

1855 convention, with its demands for full political and social equality. When Emerson sent his regrets for the 1869 Woman Suffrage Convention in Newburyport, Massachusetts, however, the *Inquirer* immediately assumed that his failure to appear was due to the fact that "had he put in an appearance he would have been forced to give utterance to his view on the necessity and propriety of women being enrolled in the grand array of voters." Ignoring the fact that Emerson had already appeared at woman's suffrage conventions and had publicly stated those views, the *Inquirer* quoted a few selected phrases from his letter turning down the invitation, then speculated extravagantly in order to interpret them as proving Emerson was antisuffrage. For example, their interpretation of Emerson's statement that "he found so much work that could not be set aside, that he was forced to decline all new tasks not imperative," was that Emerson "does not regard their claims to vote at all pressing." The *Inquirer* then urged the "illogical" suffragists, in light of Emerson's supposed lack of sympathy, to "review their crude and hasty conclusions" in asking for equal rights.[48]

Contemporary readers may question how the *Inquirer* could infer a position in direct opposition to that which Emerson had repeatedly publicly championed. However, there were several reasons that the reading public, both in the nineteenth and twentieth centuries, has been confused about Emerson's stand on the issue despite his eloquent public statements.

First there was the tendency to assume a unilateral attitude among all members of a particular demographic group: that is, all pre-twentieth-century men feared and so hated women; therefore, as a nineteenth-century man Emerson must have been against women's rights. Such assumptions, however, were based on faulty evidence, as the work of early male feminists such as John Stuart Mill, author of the pioneering essay *On the Subjection of Women*, had shown. Premoderns were certainly capable of as wide a range of social responses as postmoderns, and class, gender, race, nationality, religion, and other factors could not be used accurately to predict any individual's opinions. Even among women, as those in Emerson's circle proved, there were pro-suffrage conservative Puritans such as Mary Moody Emerson and antisuffrage liberal Unitarian/Transcendentalists such as his daughter Ellen.

Another factor preventing public recognition of Emerson's position, however forcefully and publicly stated, was the common nineteenth-century problem of the posthumous memoir, or biography. Perhaps the most effective example of this was Rufus Griswold's posthumous biography of Edgar Allan Poe, which introduced the entirely false charge that Poe was a deranged drug addict and alcoholic, slanders that came to be generally accepted as the truth despite their lack of basis in fact. Emerson's early biographer, James Elliot Cabot, certainly did not invent any such untruths, but he did quote only enough of Emerson's correspondence to give the impression that Emerson, like himself, opposed women's rights, while largely ignoring Emerson's public record on the subject.[49]

Indeed, this pattern of late Victorian and fin de siècle writers knowingly or unknowingly distorting the views of their predecessors recurred throughout the nineteenth century. The most famous instance would be Lytton Strachey's *Eminent Victorians,* which poured scorn upon the most renowned nineteenth-century Britons such as Florence Nightingale and Queen Victoria, turning them into caricatures. In Emerson's own circle, Julian Hawthorne's biography of his father, novelist Nathaniel Hawthorne, would severely distort Hawthorne's views of women until they appeared to match Julian's own misogynist attitudes.[50] Given the larger paradigm of the late Victorian writers inaccurately revisioning the Romantics, Emerson came off comparatively well in the distortions introduced by contemporaries such as the *Inquirer* writer and successors like Cabot.

The letter that Cabot quoted to Emerson's detriment was, in fact, Emerson's response to the invitation to address the 1850 Woman's Rights Convention for which he had signed the declaration of principles. Cabot ignored the fact that the letter of 18 September 1850 clearly stated Emerson's support of the women's cause: "The fact of the civil and political wrongs of women I deny not. If women feel wronged then they are wronged. . . . I should vote for every franchise for women . . . if women asked or men denied it." Cabot also did not point out that Emerson at the time was editing *Memoirs of Margaret Fuller Ossoli*, which, as Howe had reported, he considered a service to the suffrage cause. In addition, Cabot failed to mention the 1851 public letter to Lucy Stone reiterating Emerson's support of woman's rights. Since the letter was written before Emerson's recognition in the 1860s that many, if not most, women desired the vote, that caveat was to be expected: "I imagine that a woman whom all men would feel to be the best would decline such privileges if offered, and feel them to be rather obstacles to her legitimate influence." But even this early, Emerson's doubt that he understood the situation correctly was apparent as he continued: "Yet I confess I lay no great stress on my opinion." As mentioned earlier, Emerson also objected to the entry of any thoughtful person, man or woman, into the corrupt political process: "A public convention called by women is not very agreeable to me. . . . I should not wish women to wish political functions, nor, if granted, to assume them." As Emerson stated in his musings on the next year's convention, "I do not think that a woman's convention . . . can much avail" because "[i]t is an attempt to manufacture public opinion" (*JMN*, 11:444). Here Emerson reflected the Transcendentalist conviction that legislation could not improve individuals. Rather, genuine social change could only come about through influencing the private individual; when enough individuals were enlightened, public opinion would of necessity change. Emerson went on to lament, that, "It is not rather a private meeting of private persons sincerely interested, instead of . . . a public meeting." Emerson's own wish to withdraw from public, and especially political, life was his reason for refusing to appear at the convention, just as he had refused to appear at any of the antislavery meetings for many years. By 1855, Emerson would have realized that his preference for social reform to come about through a "rejuvenescence" of human nature created by Ideal Beauty, so that "the Woman's Convention should be holden in the Sculpture Gallery, that this high remedy might be suggested" (*JMN*, 11:444), was overly idealistic, and he would have come to support the women's more practical legislative route to equality.[51]

The *Woman's Journal* took Cabot to task for his distortion of

Emerson's views in the 24 September 1887 issue, calling the biography "a valuable contribution" in most regards, but "unfair" and "misleading" as regarded Emerson's suffrage views. In particular, the author of the notice, H. B. Blackwell, stated that Cabot had failed to include Emerson's later work, especially the address at the 1855 convention, which was considered "so valuable that it has been published by the suffragists as a leaflet."[52]

Cabot's biography did lead many to confuse the few early doubts Emerson had felt regarding the means employed by the woman's suffrage movement to reach the public—but not regarding their goals—with a wider disregard for women's rights. This error was picked up by newspapers such as the *Tribune* and transmitted to the public without question. Since Emerson's essays and letters were unpublished, the public could read only Cabot's biography or the notices given of it in the daily papers and were deceived into believing Emerson was antisuffrage. Therefore, however much letters to the *Tribune* and the *Woman's Journal* sought to reestablish the facts of Emerson's position,[53] the force of this received opinion was great enough that even with the advent of scholarly editions of Emerson's works, it has remained largely unchallenged until now.

Emerson, then, took women's issues very seriously and spent a great deal of time studying and contemplating the roles, rights, and responsibilities of women. As we rediscover the suffragist and women writers of the nineteenth century, so we will continue to rediscover male suffragists such as Emerson. It is our responsibility to see that they are, finally, given the credit that their forward-thinking efforts deserve.

NOTES

1. Elizabeth Cady Stanton, Susan B. Anthony, and Matilda Joslyn Gage, *History of Woman Suffrage* (New York: Fowler and Wells, 1881), 1:40.

2. Ibid., 1:53ff.

3. Julia Ward Howe, *Reminiscences, 1819–1899* (Boston: Houghton, Mifflin, 1899), p. 158.

4. Stanton, Anthony, and Gage, *History of Women Suffrage*, 1:820.

5. Thomas Wentworth Higginson, "Tested by Time," *Woman's Journal* 7 (1 January 1876): 1.

6. Even many historians today remain unaware of the slightly earlier 1850 women's rights convention in Salem, Ohio; see Stanton, Anthony, and Gage, *History of Woman Suffrage*, I:103ff.

7. Both the 1855 address (bMS Am 1280.202 [12]) and the "Discourse Manqué. Woman" (bMS Am 1280.202 [13]) are soon to be published in *The Later Lectures of Ralph Waldo Emerson*, edited by Ronald A. Bosco and Joel Myerson. My source is the clear text of these forthcoming works.

8. For other examples see *JMN*, 5:119, 12:386.

9. *The Biographies of Lady Russell, and Madame Guyon . . .* (Boston: Carter, Hendee, 1832). Listed in Walter Harding, *Emerson's Library* (Charlottesville: University Press of Virginia, 1967), p. 59.

10. The popularity of the spiritualist movement during this period helped to bolster these claims.

11. Margaret Fuller, *Woman in the Nineteenth Century*, ed. Joel Myerson (Columbia: University of South Carolina Press, 1980), p. 102. All subsequent references are to this edition.

12. *JMN*, 9:100. See *JMN*, 9:54, for the answer: "Married women uniformly decide against the communities."

13. See also *JMN*, 3:147, for a meditation on the difficulties of intergender communication under "the terms of intercourse in society."

14. Perhaps I should also observe that while in the late nineteenth century the woman's suffrage movement split over regional and political issues, these controversies occurred largely after Emerson's active involvement in the movement, and so I will not address them here.

15. See, for example, *JMN*, 2:357, 410–11; 3:148–49, 151, 153, 159–62, 181–82, 195, 226–29, 240, 272, 275, 285–86, 289–90, 303 n; 5:19, 119, 188, 190, 264, 456; 6:148–49, 235; 8:29, 339, 381, 498; 12:385. See also the poems to her: "To Ellen at the South," "To Ellen," "Lines to Ellen," "To Eva," "The Amulet," "Thy Eyes Still Shined," probably "Good Hope," and possibly "Security."

16. Emerson repeats this idea in *JMN*, 9:21.

17. It is interesting that Emerson misremembered this deed (actually Katherine Douglas's) as being undertaken to aid another woman, when in actuality Douglas acted to protect James I of Scotland.

18. I am indebted to Helen Deese for providing me with information from her forthcoming edition of the Dall journals. This is from the journal of 23 September 1855.

19. See, for example, *JMN*, 1:49, 10:181. Also see *L*, 3:443.

20. *JMN*, 10:392, 9:108, where the first sentence of the passage is replaced by "*Woman*. It is the worst of her condition that its advantages are permissive."

21. See *JMN*, 2:206, for a further meditation on women's "household toil."

22. Hannah More, *Strictures on a System of Female Education*, 2 vols. (Philadelphia, 1800); see Kenneth Walter Cameron, *Emerson the Essayist* (Raleigh, N.C.: Thistle Press, 1945), p. 241.

23. [Sampson Reed], "Introduction to Entomology (4)," *New Jerusalem Magazine* 2 (May 1829): 274–82. Listed in Kenneth Walter Cameron, *Emerson's Workshop* (Hartford, Conn.: Transcendental Books, 1979), p. 43.

24. [Caleb Reed], "The Love of the World," *New Jerusalem Magazine* 3 (March 1830): 199–206; [John Hubbard Wilkins], "On Marriage," *New Jerusalem Magazine* 3 (March 1830): 217–19 (both listed in Cameron, *Emerson's Workshop*, p. 45).

25. [Sampson Reed], "Guardian Angels," *New Jerusalem Magazine* 5 (November 1831): 112–19; [Sampson Reed], "Marriage in the Heavens," *New Jerusalem Magazine* 5 (May 1832): 321–28 (listed in Cameron, *Emerson's Workshop*, pp. 48, 49).

26. [Caleb Reed], "Supposed Extinction of Our Proper and Peculiar Loves at Death," *New Jerusalem Magazine* 8 (October 1834): 50–53 (listed in Cameron, *Emerson's Workshop*, p. 54).

27. [Sampson Reed], "Changes Effected at Death—Personal Form and Appearance (5)," *New Jerusalem Magazine* 8 (May 1835): 296–300 (listed in Cameron, *Emerson's Workshop*, p. 55).

28. Emerson also owned Swedenborg's *Conjugal Love* (listed in Harding, *Emerson's Library*, p. 262).

29. Named after the king who tied living prisoners to dead (*JMN*, 8:34).

30. *JMN*, 12:368. See *JMN*, 9:191; 12:338, 369, 491 for similar ideas.

31. For other references to sacred womanhood, see *JMN*, 12:224, 358.

32. See also *JMN*, 5:505, for a similar statement.

33. For other examples, see *JMN*, 12:206, 302.

34. For earlier examples of Emerson's repeating negative stereo-

248 Emerson in His Time

types about women, such as their weakness, see *JMN*, 6:186–87, 9:169. Many such quotations are from Plato, whom Emerson later came to rank as a misogynist equal to Mahomet (*JMN*, 9:184).

35. *JMN*, 11:445, 433. See also *JMN*, 9:103, 9:107, 11:444.

36. In fact, the editor of the volume in which this letter appears, Eleanor M. Tilton, in a footnote terms Emerson's statement "evasive" and observes, "In Emerson's own household, only Ellen took his position" (9:327), thus assuming, despite the content of the letter concerning the change in his position, that Emerson was antisuffrage. So pervasive has been the assumption of Emerson's monolithic and static opinion on women's rights that the evidence to the contrary, even in his own words, has been ignored.

37. J[ulia]. W[ard]. H[owe]., "Ralph Waldo Emerson," *Woman's Journal* 13 (6 May 1882): 140.

38. "At more than one woman suffrage meeting, he has entered his protest against the political inequality which still demoralizes society." Howe was certain where Emerson's loyalties lay on the suffrage question: "He was *for us*, knowing well enough our limitations and shortcomings, and his golden words have done much both to fit us for the larger freedom, and to know that it belongs to us" (Howe, "Ralph Waldo Emerson as I Knew Him," *Critic* 42 [May 1902]: 410).

39. Julia Ward Howe, "Reminiscences," in *Concord Lectures on Philosophy*, ed. Raymond L. Bridgman (Cambridge, Mass.: Moses King, 1882), p. 63.

40. *JMN*, 10:269; see also *JMN*, 9:304, for more praise of Rachel's "majestic delivery."

41. See aso *JMN*, 9:190, for a quotation from Plato which suggests that women as well as men can attain Ideal Beauty, "such of them as are of sufficient genius."

42. Ednah Dow Cheney, "Reminiscences," in *Concord Lectures on Philosophy*, ed. Bridgman, p. 74.

43. Howe, "Ralph Waldo Emerson as I Knew Him," 411–15. The importance of this anecdote to nineteenth-century women was evident in the many times they recorded, repeated, and analyzed it. Ednah Dow Cheney, for example, mentioned it in her lecture "Emerson and Boston," printed in *The Genius and Character of Emerson: Lectures at the Concord School of Philosophy*, ed. F. B. Sanborn (Boston: James R. Osgood, 1885), p. 19; and in her *Reminiscences of Ednah Dow Cheney* (Boston: Lea and Shepard, 1902), pp. 232–33.

44. Howe, "Ralph Waldo Emerson as I Knew Him," 413.

45. This may have been the "Ladies Club" to which Emerson gave Cheney tickets for his series of private conversations in Boston in 1872 (*JMN*, 16:440). His respect for her was also emphasized by giving her a copy of his *Poems* (*JMN*, 9:456, 461) and the second series of *Essays* (*JMN*, 9:129), and he owned her *Memoir of Seth W. Cheney* (1881) (listed in Harding, *Emerson's Library*, p. 58).

46. *Selections from the Autobiography of Elizabeth Oakes Smith*, ed. Mary Alice Wyman (New York: Columbia University Press, 1924), p. 145.

47. Laura E. Richards and Maude Howe Elliott, *Julia Ward Howe, 1819–1910*, 2 vols. (Boston: Houghton, Mifflin, 1916), 2:263–64.

48. Anonymous, "Ralph Waldo Emerson and Woman's Suffrage," *Philadelphia Inquirer*, 31 July 1869, p. 4.

49. In the distortion thus introduced, Emerson suffered the same fate he had meted out, innocently and unknowingly, to Margaret Fuller and Henry David Thoreau, when the works he had meant to be tributes to them, *The Memoirs of Margaret Fuller Ossoli* and the essay "Thoreau," instead seriously damaged their posthumous literary reputations.

50. See Katherine Gilbert, "Nineteenth-Century Feminist: The Development of Nathaniel Hawthorne's Anti-patriarchal Attitudes in His Life and Writings Through 1850" (Ph.D. diss., University of South Carolina, 1995).

51. Finally, Cabot failed to note that within the next few years Emerson would have realized not only the need for more practical means to realize women's rights but also that the importance of these issues outweighted his desire for thoughtful seclusion, and he would then appear on the platforms of both woman's rights and antislavery conventions.

52. H. B. B[lackwell], Review of Cabot, *A Memoir of Ralph Waldo Emerson, Woman's Journal* 18 (24 September 1887): 312.

53. Especially in the "Editorial Notes," *Woman's Journal* 18 (22 October 1887): 337.

ILLUSTRATED CHRONOLOGY

Emerson's Life	Historical Events
1803: Ralph Waldo Emerson born.	**1803:** Thomas Jefferson is president. Ohio becomes the seventeenth state. First tax-supported public library founded in Salisbury, Conn. Louisiana Purchase completed.
1805: RWE's brother, Edward Bliss Emerson, born.	
1807: RWE's brother, Robert Bulkeley Emerson, born.	**1804:** Lewis and Clark expedition begins. Elizabeth Marshall, first woman pharmacist, begins practicing in Philadelphia. Nathaniel Hawthorne born.
1808: RWE's brother, Charles Chauncy Emerson, born.	
1811: RWE's sister, Mary Caroline Emerson, born. RWE's father, the Reverend William Emerson, dies.	**1805:** Jefferson's second inaugural. Boston Athenaeum founded.
1812: Enters Boston Latin School.	**1806:** William Gilmore Simms born. Noah Webster, *Compendious Dictionary of the English Language.*
1814: RWE's sister, Mary Caroline Emerson, dies.	
1817: Enters Harvard College.	**1807:** Henry Wadsworth Longfellow and John Greenleaf Whittier born.
1818: Begins occasional school-teaching at Waltham.	**1808:** William Cullen Bryant, *The Embargo.*
1821: Graduates from Harvard College.	**1809:** James Madison inaugurated as president. Oliver Wendell Holmes and Edgar Allan Poe born.
1822: "Thoughts on the Religion of the Middle Ages," RWE's first publication, appears in the *Christian Disciple and Theological Review.*	**1810:** American population is 7,239,881. Margaret Fuller born. Charles Brockden Brown dies.
1824: Begins formal study of religion.	**1811:** Harriet Beecher Stowe and Sara Payson Willis ("Fanny Fern") born.
1825: Registers as a student of divinity at Harvard.	

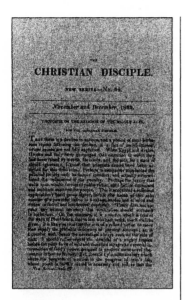

Emerson's first publication, an essay in the Christian Disciple *(1822). From the collection of Joel Myerson.*

1826: Approbated by American Unitarian Association to preach. Sails to Charleston, S.C., and St. Augustine, Fla., to improve health.

1827: Returns to Boston. Meets Ellen Louisa Tucker in Concord, N.H.

1828: Edward is committed to McLean Asylum (released in the fall). Engaged to Ellen Tucker.

1829: Becomes colleague pastor at Second Church, Boston. Ordained at Second Church. Promoted to pastor. Marries Ellen Tucker on 30 September.

1812: War is declared on Britain. Louisiana admitted as a state. American Antiquarian Society founded.

1813: Madison's second inaugural. Game of craps first introduced in New Orleans. *Boston Daily Advertiser* founded.

1814: Francis Scott Key writes "The Star-Spangled Banner." The Treaty of Ghent ends the war with Britain.

1815: Library of Congress acquires Thomas Jefferson's book collection.

1816: Harvard Divinity School organized. Indiana admitted as a state.

1817: James Monroe inaugurated as president. Mississippi admitted as a state. Henry David Thoreau born. William Cullen Bryant, "Thanatopsis."

1818: Illinois admitted as a state.

1819: Alabama admitted as a state. Julia Ward Howe, James Russell Lowell, Herman Melville, and Walt Whitman born. Washington Irving, *The Sketch Book of Geoffrey Crayon.*

1820: American population is 9,638,453. Maine admitted as a state. First high school opened in Boston.

Emerson in 1829, from a miniature by Sarah Goodridge. From Houghton Library, Harvard University.

Ellen Louisa Tucker Emerson in 1829, from a miniature by Sarah Goodridge. From Houghton Library, Harvard University.

1821: Monroe's second inaugural. Missouri admitted as a state. *Saturday Evening Post* founded.

1822: Washington Irving, *Bracebridge Hall.*

1823: Hudson River school of landscape painting formed. James Fenimore Cooper, *The Pioneers.*

1824: Lydia Maria Child, *Hobomok.*

1825: John Quincy Adams inaugurated as president. Unitarian Church organized.

1826: Lyceum movement begins. James Fenimore Cooper, *The Last of the Mohicans.*

1827: Sarah Josepha Hale proposes Thanksgiving as a national holiday. First African-American newspaper, *Freedom's Journal,* founded. Edgar Allan Poe, *Tamerlane and Other Poems.*

1828: First Native American newspaper, *Cherokee Phoenix,* founded. Noah Webster, *American Dictionary of the English Language.*

1829: Andrew Jackson inaugurated as president. First hotel with bathrooms opens in Boston.

Order of Services at the Ordination of Mr. Ralph Waldo Emerson (1829).

1831: Ellen Louisa Tucker Emerson dies of tuberculosis.

1832: Sends farewell letter to Second Church resigning his position. Sails for Europe.

1833: Meets Jane and Thomas Carlyle. Returns to America. Delivers his first public lecture, "The Uses of Natural History," in Boston. RWE's brother, William Emerson (b. 1801), marries Susan Woodward Haven.

1830: American population is 12,866,020. Indian Removal Act signed. Emily Dickinson born.

1831: Antislavery newspaper *The Liberator* founded. Nat Turner's slave rebellion. Edgar Allan Poe, *Poems*.

1832: Pseudoscience of phrenology introduced in America. Louisa May Alcott born.

1833: Jackson's second inaugural. American Antislavery Society founded. Horatio Greenough completes first large marble sculpture by an American, a statue of George Washington. Lydia Maria Child, *An Appeal in Favor of the Class of American Called Africans.*

1834: First valentines commercially manufactured. *Southern Literary Messenger* founded.

1835: Samuel F. B. Morse invents the telegraph. Mark Twain born. William Gilmore Simms, *The Yemassee.*

1836: Battle of the Alamo. Arkansas admitted as a state. First college for women, Mount Holyoke, chartered. First of the school readers by William Holmes McGuffey published.

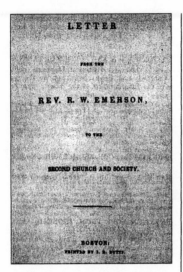

LETTER

FROM THE

REV. R. W. EMERSON,

TO THE

SECOND CHURCH AND SOCIETY.

BOSTON:
PRINTED BY I. R. BUTTS.

Pamphlet printing of Emerson's letter of resignation from the Second Church (1832).

1834: Meets Lydia Jackson of Plymouth. Receives partial inheritance of $11,600 from Ellen Emerson's estate. Edward dies of tuberculosis in Puerto Rico. Moves to Concord, Mass.

1835: Proposes to Lydia Jackson on 24 January (engagement announcement at end of month). Begins first lecture series, "Biography," in Boston. Delivers discourse on Concord's history (published in November). Marries Lydia Jackson (whom he calls "Lidian").

1837: Martin Van Buren inaugurated as president. Michigan admitted as a state. Financial panic hits America. William Dean Howells born.

1838: Establishment of the first transatlantic steamship service. Edgar Allan Poe, *The Narrative of Arthur Gordon Pym, of Nantucket.*

1839: Abner Doubleday lays out the first baseball diamond. First photographs (daguerreotypes) taken in America.

Christopher Pearse Cranch's 1839 caricature of the famous "transparent eye-ball" lines from Nature. *From Houghton Library, Harvard University.*

The Emerson House in Concord, Massachusetts.

1836: Charles dies suddenly in New York. *Nature* published. First meeting of the Transcendental Club. RWE's son, Waldo Emerson, born.

Lidian Jackson Emerson in 1853. From the Concord Free Public Library.

1840: American population is 17,069,453. Republic of Texas recognized as a nation. *National Anti-Slavery Standard* founded. Edgar Allan Poe, *Tales of the Grotesque and Arabesque.*

1841: William Henry Harrison inaugurated as president but dies after only a month in office. John Tyler inaugurated as president. Brook Farm utopian community founded near Boston.

1842: Sons of Temperance founded. Sewing machine patented. Charles Dickens visits America.

1843: Bronson Alcott begins Fruitlands utopian community near Harvard, Massachusetts. First working typewriter patented. Henry James born.

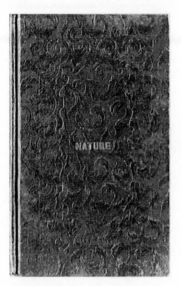

Binding of Emerson's first book,
Nature (1836). From the collection of
Joel Myerson.

Emerson in 1844, from a miniature by
Caroline Neagus Hildreth. From The
Journals of Ralph Waldo Emerson,
ed. Edward Waldo Emerson and Waldo
Emerson Forbes, 10 vols. (Boston:
Houghton Mifflin, 1909–1914), vol. 1,
frontispiece.

Drawing of Concord center in the mid-1840s by J. W. Barber. From Concord Free
Public Library.

1837: Receives remainder of inheritance (another $11,675) from Ellen Emerson's estate. Delivers address "The American Scholar" at Harvard (published 23 September).

1838: Carlyle's *Critical and Miscellaneous Essays* published, edited by RWE. Delivers address at the Harvard Divinity School (published 21 August). Delivers address "Literary Ethics" at Dartmouth College (published 8 September).

1839: RWE's daughter, Ellen Tucker Emerson, born. Jones Very's *Essays and Poems* published, edited by RWE.

1840: First issue of *Dial* appears.

1841: *Essays [First Series]* published on 19 March (and in England on 21 August). Delivers "The Method of Nature" at Waterville College, Maine, on 11 August (published 21 October). RWE's daughter, Edith Emerson, born.

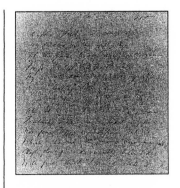

(Bottom left) Broadside printing of Emerson's Concord Hymn *(1837). (Top right) Manuscript of "To Eva" (published 1840), Emerson's poem about his first wife. From the collection of Joel Myerson. (Bottom right) Wrapper from the January 1842* Dial. *From the collection of Joel Myerson.*

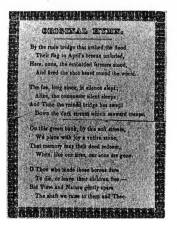

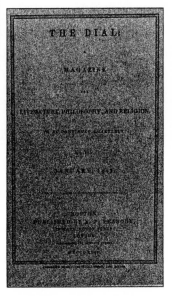

1842: Waldo Emerson dies of scarlatina. Margaret Fuller resigns as editor of *Dial;* Emerson becomes editor.

1843: Carlyle's *Past and Present* published, edited by RWE.

1844: Last issue of *Dial* appears. RWE's son, Edward Waldo Emerson, born. Delivers address "Emancipation of the Negroes in the British West Indies" at Concord Court House (published 9 September and in England in October). *Essays: Second Series* published on 19 October (and in England on 9 November).

1845: Purchases forty-one acres at Walden Pond.

1846: *Poems* published in England on 12 December (and in America on 25 December).

1847: Sails for England.

1848: Arrives in Paris in May. Returns to England in June. Returns to America in July.

1849: *Nature; Addresses, and Lectures* published.

1850: *Representative Men* published on 1 January (and in England on 5 January). Margaret Fuller dies.

1844: Fruitlands community closes. Margaret Fuller, *Summer on the Lakes, in 1843.*

1845: James K. Polk inaugurated as president. Florida and Texas admitted as states. Margaret Fuller, *Woman in the Nineteenth Century.* Edgar Allan Poe, *The Raven and Other Poems* and *Tales.*

1846: Smithsonian Institute authorized by Congress. Mexican War begins. Iowa admitted as a state. Margaret Fuller, *Papers on Literature and Art.* Nathaniel Hawthorne, *Mosses from an Old Manse.* Herman Melville, *Typee.*

1847: Brook Farm community closes. Henry Wadsworth Longfellow, *Evangeline.*

1848: Gold discovered in California. Seneca Falls women's rights convention. Wisconsin admitted as a state. James Russell Lowell, *The Biglow Papers* and *A Fable for Critics.*

1849: Zachary Taylor inaugurated as president. Elizabeth Blackwell is first woman in America to receive M.D. degree. Sarah Orne Jewett born. Edgar Allan Poe dies. Henry David Thoreau, "Resistance to Civil Government" and *A Week on the Concord and Merrimack Rivers.*

Emerson in 1848. From Houghton Library, Harvard University.

(Above) Manuscript letter by Emerson, 11 January 1851, concerning a lecture engagement. From the collection of Joel Myerson. (Below) Whitman's printing of Emerson's letter of 21 July 1855 to him in praise of Leaves of Grass.

1852: *Memoirs of Margaret Fuller Ossoli* published, coedited by RWE.

1853: RWE's mother, Ruth Haskins Emerson, dies.

1856: *English Traits* published on 6 August (and in England on 6 September).

1859: Robert Bulkeley Emerson dies.

1860: *The Conduct of Life* published in America and England on 8 December.

1862: Henry David Thoreau dies. "Thoreau" appears in *Atlantic Monthly.*

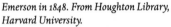

1863: RWE's aunt, Mary Moody Emerson, dies. Thoreau's *Excursions* published, edited by RWE.

1865: Thoreau's *Letters to Various Persons* published, edited by RWE. Edith Emerson marries William Hathaway Forbes.

1866: *Complete Works* published in two volumes in England. Ralph Emerson Forbes, RWE's first grandchild, born. Awarded LL.D. degree by Harvard.

1867: *May-day and Other Pieces* published on 29 June (and in England on 8 June).

Emerson, dressed in his lecturing outfit, in 1857. From the Concord Free Public Library.

CAUTION!!

COLORED PEOPLE
OF BOSTON, ONE & ALL,
You are hereby respectfully CAUTIONED and advised, to avoid conversing with the
Watchmen and Police Officers
of Boston,
For since the recent ORDER OF THE MAYOR & ALDERMEN, they are empowered to act as
KIDNAPPERS
AND
Slave Catchers,
And they have already been actually employed in KIDNAPPING, CATCHING, AND KEEPING SLAVES. Therefore, if you value your LIBERTY, and the Welfare of the Fugitives among you, Shun them in every possible manner, as so many HOUNDS on the track of the most unfortunate of your race.
Keep a Sharp Look Out for
KIDNAPPERS, and have
TOP EYE open.
APRIL 24, 1851.

Sign warning "colored people of Boston" about "slave catchers," written by Theodore Parker. From the Boston Public Library.

1850: American population is 23,191,876. Compromise of 1850 and Fugitive Slave Law enacted. California admitted as a state. Margaret Fuller dies. Nathaniel Hawthorne, *The Scarlet Letter.*

1851: Kate Chopin and Grace King born. James Fenimore Cooper dies. *New York Times* founded. Karl Marx's work begins publication in *New-York Tribune*. Herman Melville, *Moby-Dick.*

1852: Herman Melville, *Pierre.* Harriet Beechert Stowe, *Uncle Tom's Cabin.*

1853: Franklin Pierce inaugurated as president. First elevator with safety devices manufactured. William Wells Brown, *Clotel.*

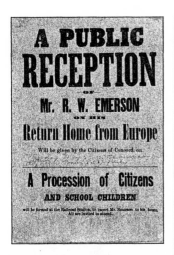

A PUBLIC
RECEPTION
—OF—
Mr. R. W. EMERSON
ON HIS
Return Home from Europe

Will be given by the Citizens of Concord, on

A Procession of Citizens
AND SCHOOL CHILDREN

will be formed at the Railroad Station, to escort Mr. Emerson to his house.
All are invited to attend.

Poster welcoming Emerson upon his return from a trip abroad following the partial burning of his house in 1873. From the Concord Free Public Library.

Emerson in 1857, from a drawing by S. W. Rowse. From The Complete Works of Ralph Waldo Emerson, *ed. Edward Waldo Emerson, 12 vols. (Boston: Houghton Mifflin, 1903–1904), vol. 6, facing p. 168.*

1854: Kansas-Nebraska bill enacted. The slave Anthony Burns is returned to the South. Henry David Thoreau, *Walden.*

1855: Fanny Fern (Sara Payson Willis), *Ruth Hall.* Henry Wadsworth Longfellow, *The Song of Hiawatha.* Walt Whitman, *Leaves of Grass.*

1856: First kindergarten in America opened. Congress passes American copyright law.

1857: James Buchanan inaugurated as president. Central Park is laid out in New York City. Financial panic begins, leading to recession. Herman Melville, *The Confidence-Man.*

1858: Minnesota admitted as a state. Atlantic telegraph cable laid. Oliver Wendell Holmes, *The Autocrat at the Breakfast Table.* Henry Wadsworth Longfellow, *The Courtship of Miles Standish.*

1859: Oregon admitted as a state. John Brown seizes arsenal at Harpers Ferry, Virginia; he is captured and hanged. Washington Irving dies.

1860: American population is 31,443,321. Pony Express mail service begins. Nathaniel Hawthorne, *The Marble Faun.*

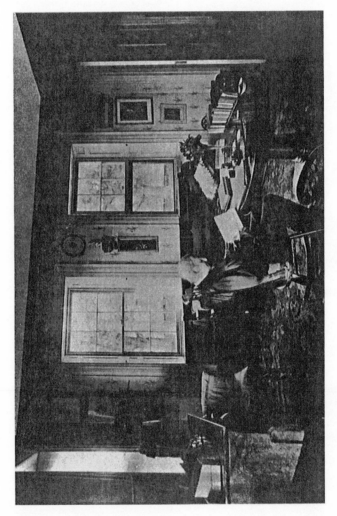

Emerson at the writing table in his study in 1879. From Houghton Library, Harvard University.

1868: William Emerson dies.

1869: *Prose Works* published in two volumes in America.

1870: *Society and Solitude* published in America and England on 5 March.

1871: Begins trip to California in April (returns 30 May).

1872: RWE's house severely damaged by fire. Goes to Europe with Ellen in October. Arrives in Egypt in December.

1873: Returns to Europe in February. Sees Carlyle for the last time. Returns to America in May. Delivers address at the opening of the Concord Free Public Library.

1874: Edward Waldo Emerson marries Annie Shepard Keyes. *Parnassus* (title page dated "1875") published, a poetry collection edited by RWE.

1875: *Letters and Social Aims* (title page dated "1876") published in December (and in England on 8 January 1876).

1876: The "Little Classic Edition" of RWE's works is published in nine volumes.

1878: Delivers address "Fortune of the Republic" on 25 February in Boston (published 10 August).

1861: Confederate States of America formed, with Jefferson Davis as president; American troops fired on at Fort Sumter in Charleston, South Carolina; Civil War begins. Abraham Lincoln inaugurated as president. Kansas admitted as a state.

1862: Lincoln submits Emancipation Proclamation to Congress. Henry David Thoreau dies.

1863: Lincoln issues Emancipation Proclamation; also delivers "The Gettysburg Address." Robert E. Lee's Confederate forces defeated at Gettysburg. Thanksgiving Day made a national holiday. West Virginia admitted as a state.

1864: Nevada admitted as a state. Nathaniel Hawthorne dies.

1865: Lincoln's second inaugural. Civil War ends. Lincoln assassinated; Andrew Johnson inaugurated as president. Thirteenth Amendment, abolishing slavery, passed. Ku Klux Klan founded. Potato chips introduced. Walt Whitman, *Drum-Taps.*

1866: Root beer first commercially manufactured. Herman Melville, *Battle-Pieces and Aspects of the War.* John Greenleaf Whittier, *Snow-Bound.*

1880: Delivers one hundredth lecture before the Concord Lyceum.

1882: Catches cold on 20 April. Ralph Waldo Emerson dies in Concord, Mass., on 27 April. Buried on 30 April in Sleepy Hollow Cemetery, Concord.

1867: Nebraska admitted as a state. Alaskan Territory purchased. First successful typewriter patented. Mark Twain, *The Celebrated Jumping Frog of Calaveras County, and Other Sketches.*

1868: First American kindergarten opens in Boston. Louisa May Alcott, *Little Women.*

1869: Ulysses S. Grant inaugurated as president. Women suffrage granted in Wyoming.

1870: American population is 39,818,449. William Gilmore Simms dies.

1871: National Rifle Association founded. Stephen Crane born.

1872: Jehovah's Witnesses founded. Sara Payson Willis ("Fanny Fern") dies.

1873: Grant's second inaugural. First code of rules for football drafted. Willa Cather and Emily Post born. Mark Twain and Charles Dudley Warner, *The Gilded Age.*

1874: Women's Christian Temperance Union founded. Robert Frost, Ellen Glasgow, Amy Lowell, and Gertrude Stein born.

1875: First baseball glove worn.

1876: General Geroge Armstrong Custer and his men killed at the Battle of Litle Bighorn. Colorado admitted as a state. Mark Twain, *The Adventures of Tom Sawyer.*

1877: Rutherford B. Hayes inaugurated as president. Thomas A. Edison patents the phonograph. Henry James, *The American.*

1878: First bicycles commercially manufactured. Carl Sandburg and Upton Sinclair born. Wiliam Cullen Bryant dies.

1879: First Church of Christ, Scientist, founded by Mary Baker Eddy. Thomas A. Edison perfects the elecric light. Henry James, *Daisy Miller* and *Hawthorne.*

1880: American population is 50,155,783. H. L. Mencken born. Lydia Maria Child dies. Henry Adams, *Democracy.*

1881: James A. Garfield inaugurated as president. Garfield assassinated; Chester A. Arthur inaugurated as president. Joel Chandler Harris, *Uncle Remus, His Songs and His Sayings.* Henry James, *The Portrait of a Lady* and *Washington Square.*

1882: Standard Oil Trust organized. Electric fan invented. Henry Wadsworth Longfellow dies. Walt Whitman, *Specimen Days and Collect.*

We Find What We Seek

Emerson and His Biographers

Ronald A. Bosco

Justifying his selective appropriation of historical fact to suit his artistic purposes while writing *The Crucible*, the American playwright Arthur Miller remarked, "One finds I suppose what one seeks."[1] Miller's comment recognizes the influence that the intellectual and imaginative predispositions of writers and readers exert on historical materials, and it is as instructive for biographical and critical writing as it is for works of fiction or drama that have their source in history. It is especially instructive in accounting for the variety of ways in which biographers and critics have treated Ralph Waldo Emerson's life and thought since the nineteenth century, for Emerson's biographers have never been casual commentators on their subject. Typically, they have approached Emerson with a clearly defined view of his ideas, inner life, social significance, and influence on American culture. Similarly, although scholarly criticism on Emerson has not always concentrated on his biography, critics have invariably selected biographical elements to help make the case for their particular reading of his thought and its relation to his times.

In a chronological sketch of his life the factual Emerson appears to be quickly and easily known; however, at the close of more elaborate biographical and critical studies, readers may well believe that the "essential" or "complete" Emerson remains as much a subject open to interpretation and analysis by today's readers as it was to his contemporaries. In fact, the essential Emerson, which is, of course, the interesting Emerson who fascinates biographers and spurs their critical ingenuity, remains the enigmatic figure foreshadowed in a witticism that circulated in Boston after his return from Egypt in 1873. As Emerson himself reported it, the witticism typically opened with the question, "What do you think the Sphinx said to Mr. Emerson?" "The Sphinx probably said . . . 'You're another,'" was the standard reply (*JMN*, 16:294).

Among major nineteenth-century American writers, Emerson ranks first in terms of both the number and the variety of biographical treatments of his life. The essay that follows is intended to bring order to that number and variety and, in concert with the bibliographic essay included in this volume, to provide readers with starting points for their own consideration of Emerson as a biographical subject. The first section of this essay places Emerson in the context of nineteenth-century approaches to American biographical subjects and recognizes early appropriations of his life as a means to complete an emerging portrait of the ideal American. The second section identifies the several phases through which appropriations of Emerson's biography have passed between the end of the nineteenth century and the present. Finally, drawing on recent biographical and critical scholarship, the third section provides readers with suggestions for several directions in which they may wish to take their own thinking about Emerson's biography.

I

Over the century following the Revolution, Americans mourned the passing of many native heroes and public figures. Late-eighteenth-century and nineteenth-century newspapers, broadsides, and pamphlets reveal unexpectedly long periods of mourning after the passing of political figures such as Benjamin Franklin and George Washington, popular figures such as Davy Crockett and the fallen heroes of the Alamo, and literary figures such as the poet Lydia Howard Sigourney of Hartford, Connecticut, whose immense popularity in her day has been displaced by almost complete obscurity in our own.[2] Perhaps the most sustained national outpouring of grief occurred after the assassination of Abraham Lincoln in 1865. But there is a significant difference between public response to the passing of figures such as these and the forms through which Emerson's passing was acknowledged and his significance to American culture initially appropriated. It is perhaps predictable that in the case of persons like Washington, Franklin, and Crockett emphasis would be placed on a generally uniform set of virtues that each demonstrated in his life and that were worthy of emulation by the Americans he left behind. Only personal history distinguished one hero from another as obituary eloquence was concentrated on celebrating each for his manliness, integrity, force of conviction and perception, and patriotism. In Emerson's case, however, these virtues appear to have been either overlooked or thought of as inappropriate memorials to his character and contribution to American culture. The fact that Emerson was respected as a cultural prophet and visionary, whereas the other heroes mentioned here were men of action, only partially accounts for the difference.

Emerson's final illness occurred over the brief span of about ten days. In contemporary responses to his illness and death, almost all of the personal elements of his life—that is, almost all of the factual information contained in a biographical chronology— were set forth and repeated in newspaper reports and pamphlets of the human interest variety with which we are familiar today. For instance, early on, successive newspaper headlines ran, "Ralph Waldo Emerson Sick," "Mr. Emerson's Condition," "Mr. Emerson Somewhat Better," "No Hope for Emerson," "Mr. Emerson Dead," "Into the Unknown, of Which He Spoke So Grandly, Ralph Waldo Emerson Has Passed," "Ralph Waldo Emerson's Funeral," "Emerson at Rest," and so forth. Several of the accounts appearing under such headings originated in the Boston press and were immediately reprinted in other newspapers; most were eventually supplemented with an editorial on Emerson's significance or with reminiscences by persons who knew him well.

Between 24 and 25 April 1882, when notices of Emerson's final illness first appeared in the *Boston Daily Advertiser, New-York Daily Tribune, New York Evening Post, New York Herald,* and *New-York Times,* and the close of that year, more than two hundred such reports appeared in America and abroad. In them, the facts of Emerson's life and death dominated the prose. These facts included reference to his New England lineage and character, his prominence as an author of many volumes of prose and of occasional poetry, his years of service as a lecturer on the lyceum circuit, and his association with virtually every American luminary of his time and with international figures such as Thomas Carlyle. But in several reports, the facts were momentarily offset by poignant and sometimes hyperbolic expressions of what America's imminent or realized loss of Emerson meant for the nation. When on 27 April, the day that Emerson died, the *Boston Evening Transcript* reported that hope for his recovery had entirely faded, the paper rehearsed one of the more common laments heard in the days immediately following: Emerson was, according to the *Transcript's* reporter, "the teacher, the inspirer, almost the conscience . . . of his countrymen." On the day after his death, the *Boston Daily Advertiser* considerably extended that lament, declaring America's loss of Emerson to be the loss of "the most philosophical mind and temper of this century."

As writers reiterated the details of Emerson's life in the days and months that followed, expressions of his significance that had initially served as formulaic laments were themselves transformed into emphatic statements of fact. Although his poetry had never won him a wide readership, Emerson suddenly became *the* American poet; while throughout his life newspaper reporters complained of his haphazard lecturing style and the difficulty of making sense of many of his pronouncements, Emerson suddenly became *the* American sage; and although he often scorned metaphysicians and systematic thinkers as "gnat[s] grasping the world" (*Natural History of Intellect,* "Powers and Laws of Thought," *W,* 12:12), Emerson suddenly became *the* American philosopher. These transformations occurred very early in the mourning process: Writing in the Chicago *Dial* on 3 May, W. F. Allen stated that Emerson alone had given "tone and shape to American thought," and in an article that appeared in the *Nation* on 4 May, Thomas Wentworth Higginson suggested that Emerson's method of analogical thinking represented a new brand of systematic philosophy.[3]

Appropriation of Emerson's life and thought by biographers and critics has occurred on a massive scale in the century since his death. The several hundred biographies and critical studies referenced in the bibliographies and notes of this volume barely scratch the numerical surface of the many thousands of works devoted in whole or in part to Emerson referenced in the standard secondary sources.[4] As the following brief survey indicates, appropriations that went beyond obituary eloquence also appeared throughout 1882 as complements to the facts about Emerson's life and as justifications for occasional hyperbole concerning how Emerson was to be best remembered. Significantly, these examples serve as early indicators of how Emerson would be appropriated by later generations of readers.

Concentrating on Emerson as poet and philosopher, in *The Character and Genius of Ralph Waldo Emerson* James Little argued that Emerson was America's Shakespeare, and through judicious selections from his writings he showed that Emerson surpassed Socrates and Plato for moral authority and intellectual greatness.[5] Writing under the title "Emerson's Personality" in the *Century Magazine* in July 1882, the poet Emma Lazarus praised Emerson's newness and nationalism as the logical outcomes of American values which shaped him and which his writing reinforced. Although Emerson appears to have written only one complete address which he delivered on three occasions in support of women's rights and to have been a reluctant participant in debates over women's suffrage during his time, in "Ralph Waldo Emerson," an obituary printed in the *Woman's Journal* on 6 May, Julia Ward Howe, the feminist reformer and author of "The Battle Hymn of the Republic," appropriated Emerson as a champion of women's issues.[6] In "A Woman's Estimate of Emerson" appearing in the *Christian Register* on 27 July, Mrs. L. J. K. Gifford carried Howe's claim a significant step further: Arguing that his reliance on intuition in his lectures and writings exhibited a feminine side to his otherwise manly oratory, she predicted that Emerson would long enjoy a following among women.

In "Carlyle and Emerson," published in the *Critic* on 20 May, the American naturalist John Burroughs drew this conclusion from the lifelong friendship between the two men: Whereas Carlyle believed in men and in life as it was really lived, Emerson believed most, if not only, in ideas. In the swirl of appropriation that occurred throughout 1882, many anecdotes of Emerson's behavior and friendships were circulated to provide support for one or another reading of his life and influence, and most seconded Burroughs's portrayal of Emerson as primarily a man of ideas. In one, which appeared in the *Christian Union* on 20 July in a series of "Literary Notes," the pride of Boston's Brahmin class was justified at the same time as Emerson's preoccupation with ideas was lightly, but advantageously, underscored. The anecdote concerns the responses of Emerson and his friend Theodore Parker one day to the news that the world would end at midnight: "'Well,' replied Parker, coolly, 'I am not concerned, I live in Boston.' 'As for me,' added Emerson, equally undisturbed, 'I can get along without it.'"[7] But the extremes to which commentators near and far were inclined to go in appropriating Emerson to their purposes is perhaps no better illustrated than in these remarks made by a visitor to Concord from Calcutta shortly after Emerson's death. Speaking at Concord's School of Philosophy, Protap Chunder Mozoomdar asserted that Emerson as a man of ideas, and the ideas that he advanced, transcended national boundaries:

> Where the blue Narbudda, so still so deep, so pure, flows through the high milk-white walls of the marble hills near Jubbulpoor, in the natural alcoves of the virgin rocks there are devotional inscriptions in Sanskrit. I wish Emerson had composed his essays on nature there. . . . Amidst this ceaseless, sleepless din and clash of Western Materialism, this heat of restless energy, the character of Emerson shines upon India serene as the evening star. He seems to us to have been a geographical mistake. (Quoted in *W,* 8:413)

The early claims cited here for Emerson as *the* American poet, sage, and philosopher complement the claims made for him during the same time as America's foremost Romantic interpreter of nature, champion of individualism, religious thinker, and proponent of social reform. When they are viewed collectively, these claims draw a distinction between Emerson's attractiveness as a biographical subject whose life was devoted to thought and the shaping of his culture and the attractiveness of Washington, whose life demonstrated one form of political activism, or Crockett, whose feats of daring and wilderness survival symbolized a peculiarly rugged, American type of heroism in the nineteenth century. Washington's and Crockett's lives easily became the stuff of national legend and lore, with America's first president declared "the Father of His Country" and the resourceful woodsman named "King of the Wild Frontier." In contrast, Emerson's life was appropriated to complete an emerging portrait of the ideal American which the political activism or rugged heroism of a Washington or a Crockett could only partially represent: Emerson became, in the words of "The American Scholar" (1837), "Man Thinking."

II

For nineteenth-century Americans, the ideal American was a figure who could not be contained or represented in one individual; in effect, their ideal American was an aggregate figure composed of exemplary qualities drawn from more than one life. Had his life served no more lasting purpose than to supply the intellectual dimension that completed the emerging portrait of that ideal American, Emerson would still be an important biographical subject for us to study today. Yet as his contemporaries recognized and rather fully documented in the obituary essays published in 1882, Emerson's life was noteworthy for more than this service alone. First from the pulpit, then from the lecture platform, and finally in the many essays and poems he collected and published during his life, Emerson introduced his fellow Americans to a range of literary, social, political, religious, and philosophical concerns that has not been duplicated by any other person of his own or succeeding generations. It is for his facility in conceptualizing and expressing that wide range of concerns, as well as for his rare intellectual competency, that Emerson's life has so fascinated American biographers and critics. At the same time, the disposition of biographers and critics to treat Emerson's life selectively and to appropriate his ideas and works to their particular purposes has been encouraged by his having provided them with an extraordinarily broad set of concerns and array of personal accomplishments to investigate.

Appropriation of Emerson's life and thought by biographers and critics has gone through roughly four generational phases since 1882. It is fair to say that, on the whole, Emerson has been gifted with a remarkable set of competent and thorough biographers and critics; however, it is also fair to say that although each biographer and critic makes a claim for the objectivity of his or her view of Emerson, none of the biographical or critical studies listed in the bibliographies of this volume is neutral. All betray the interests of authors who have gone to Emerson and found in him a personal quality or an incarnation of American values for which they have sought all along.

Among biographers of his own and immediately succeeding generation, Emerson was uniformly portrayed in positive terms. For example, in reading Moncure Daniel Conway's *Emerson at Home and Abroad* (1882), Alexander Ireland's *Ralph Waldo Emerson: His Life, Genius, and Writings* (1882), James Elliot Cabot's *A Memoir of Ralph Waldo Emerson* (1887), Edward Waldo Emerson's expression of filial devotion to his father's legacy, *Emerson in Concord* (1889), and Oscar W. Firkins's *Ralph Waldo Emerson* (1915), one achieves a firsthand sense of how the words and example of a person like Emerson, who actually had few close personal friends and intimates, nevertheless inspired a generation that included these writers as well as Margaret Fuller, Ellery Channing, and Henry David Thoreau to achieve nineteenth-century Americans' shared dream of personal and cultural fulfillment.

In contrast, biographers and critics from 1915 to the mid-1950s rendered a more varied portrait of Emerson as an individual while, in some cases, also moderating what had become a too idealized version of some aspects of his influence and thought. The force of much of the biography and criticism of this period will be found in a cluster of books that appeared between 1949 and 1953: *The Life of Ralph Waldo Emerson* (1949) by Ralph L. Rusk, *Spires of Form: A Study of Emerson's Aesthetic Theory* (1951) by Vivian C. Hopkins, *Emerson's Angle of Vision: Man and Nature in American Experience* (1952) by Sherman Paul, and *Freedom and Fate: An Inner Life of Ralph Waldo Emerson* (1953) by Stephen E. Whicher.[8] Written by persons who had little quarrel with Emerson's canonization by F. O. Matthiessen in *American Renaissance: Art and Expression in the Age of Emerson and Whitman* (1941), these studies nonetheless acknowledged, for example, that inasmuch as it had been so easily popularized as a defense of the brutal excesses of capitalism in America, Emerson's doctrine of "self-reliance" was not as entirely humane as he or others may have thought.[9] They also argued that Emerson's philosophy was more vague and sentimental ("feel-good") than rigorous, and that rather than being the thoroughly original American thinker celebrated by earlier biographers, Emerson was really a gifted adapter of Platonic idealism, metaphysical speculations drawn from Shakespeare, John Milton, and Thomas Browne, and organic theories of art and history promoted by Samuel Taylor Coleridge, Johann Wolfgang von Goethe, and Friedrich von Schlegel to the conditions American life exhibited during his time. While these views certainly did not diminish Emerson's influence on the development of American intellectuals such as William James, John Dewey, or George Santayana who came after him, or on modern writers such as Robert Frost or Charles Olson who, like Walt Whitman before them, found license for literary experimentation in the theory Emerson advanced in "The Poet" (1844), they provided necessary correction to the sometimes too enthusiastic appropriation of Emerson's ideas and aesthetics by earlier biographers and critics.

Of the studies just mentioned, two exerted an enormous influence on Emerson biography and criticism in the middle of the twentieth century, and their influence continues to the extent that they still condition how his life is received and appropriated today. The studies are Matthiessen's *American Renaissance* and Whicher's *Freedom and Fate*. As Gerald Graff has observed, Matthiessen's book was instrumental in professionalizing American literary study and in identifying Emerson as a dominant force in the emergence of a distinctly American form of thought and literary expression.[10] By representing the 1830s, 1840s, and 1850s as *the* period during which the democratic spirit of America, the quest for a national literary identity, and Americans' belief in the grand scale of their cultural destiny fully merged, and by naming the period—in part, at least—*the Age of Emerson*, Matthiessen showed that the gap between social theory and literary practice had been bridged in America, and that the bridge itself had been built with Emerson's writing and thought. Put another way, Matthiessen showed that to a large extent biographers and critics closer to Emerson's time may have had a better grasp of his significance than did those who between the two world wars found reasons to call his significance into question. In contrast, Whicher's *Freedom and Fate* performed a very different service for Emerson biography and criticism. Using psychological criticism and limiting his discussion to Emerson's life and writings from the 1830s through 1860 as the only portion of his career worthy of attention, Whicher put a rather narrow and, one might well argue, undeserved negative spin on Emerson's significance.

Because it adheres to a chronological approach to Emerson's life and thought, Whicher's position is relatively simple to reconstruct. Whicher acknowledged that Emerson began his career as a champion of individualism, a true believer in the freedom of the individual, and a confirmed idealist. Indeed, initially there is little difference between the person typically portrayed through statements from *Nature* (1836), "The American Scholar," and journals in Emerson biography and criticism and the figure Whicher finds exhibited in Emerson's writings from the 1830s. However, as Whicher turns his attention to Emerson's mature years and considers his writings of the 1840s and 1850s as expressions of a suppressed, tortured interior self that has its origins in the 1830s and earlier, he portrays a figure very different from the one portrayed, for example, by Emerson's contemporaries and earliest biographers. Doubtful that his religious calling is genuine, unsure of his capacity for love or grief, skeptical that the spiritual represents anything more than an ingenious human construction, and conflicted over his relation to the Puritan past that he overtly rejects even as he recognizes its influence on his own psychological and philosophical disposition, Whicher's "inner" Emerson is completely at odds with the one Emerson publicly projected in *Nature* and "The American Scholar." He is a figure who, while living in a period when nature offered Romantics an infinite variety of consolations over the loss of intimates through death, is incapable of consolation after the deaths of Ellen Tucker, his first wife, in 1831; Edward and Charles Emerson, his brothers, in 1834 and 1836, respectively; and Waldo, his son, in 1842. He is a figure who seems no longer to believe in "the perfect system of compensations" for which he once argued as he finds himself adding poverty, materialism, disease, and classism, all of which he observed firsthand in England in 1847 and 1848, to those "lords of life"—temperament, succession, and subjectiveness, and the like—which he had identified in "Experience" in 1844 (*JMN*, 3:316–17; *CW*, 3:47). By the time *Representative Men* appears in 1850, he is a thorough skeptic, effectively ceasing to measure men and their cultures according to his own exacting, idealistic standards of what is desirable, and willing to accept them at face value: as imperfect and limited by circumstance. In *The Conduct of Life* (1860), he finally concedes the necessity of the individual's submission to fate.

Whicher ended his critical treatment of Emerson's "inner life" in *Freedom and Fate* with an interpretation of "Fate," the essay with which *The Conduct of Life* opened, that confirmed his position. In 1957, he published an anthology of readings that, like his book, emphasized the Emerson from *Nature* to "Fate" as the only Emerson worth knowing or studying.[11] Until the late 1980s, Whicher's critical book and anthology completely dominated Emerson biography and criticism. Even though Whicher did not consider *English Traits* (1856) in his construction of Emerson's "inner life," his Emerson is a figure who Philip L. Nicoloff receives and expands on in *Emerson on Race and History: An Examination of English Traits* (1961).[12] In Nicoloff's study, Whicher's dark Emerson concedes that a fundamental, self-destructive materialism exists at the heart of Anglo-Saxon culture, and that inasmuch as materialism can be defined as a racial property, it carries with it the seeds of the potential destruction of American culture. Twenty-five years after Nicoloff's study appeared, Wallace E. Williams re-created Whicher's Emerson at crucial moments in his historical introduction to the Harvard edition of *Representative Men*. There, Williams argued that Emerson's preoccupation with "spotted and defective" men such as Napoleon demonstrated his rejection of the idealism evident in *Nature* and earlier writings and his concession to the essential imperfection of men and culture (*CW*, 4:xxiv–xxv). But perhaps the most complete acceptance of Whicher's Emerson will be found in the work of John Michael. Michael, who views skepticism as the prevailing characteristic of Emerson's personality and thought throughout his life, conveys in Emerson's own terms the conditions under which he and others appropriate Whicher's Emerson as they follow his descent into skepticism. Reading "The Method of Nature" (1841) as Emerson's acknowledgment of the practical limitations of *Nature* and the idealistic system it announces, Michael states:

> The promise of the book, like the promise of . . . man, is finally deceptive, but the desire to find an adequate interpreter, an adequate interpretation, a reliable reflection of the self and of the world, persists and expresses itself in the hopes by which it is repeatedly duped. . . . One is always caught in the crack between the transcendent self and the inhabited world, between that intangible, unutterable consciousness and the material world that appears around it. This, Emerson specifies, is what a person should know. It is what he has come to know.[13]

Whicher's Emerson is also a figure with whom both Gay Wilson Allen and John McAleer had to contend in the major biographies of Emerson they wrote during this period. Allen's *Waldo Emerson: A Biography* (1981) and McAleer's *Ralph Waldo Emerson: Days of Encounter* (1984) both confront this dark figure head-on, but they do not concede that the figure is itself more than one writer's personal construction of Emerson.[14] Instead of concession, Allen and McAleer treat the shifts in Emerson's intellectual views evidenced by his writings of the 1840s and 1850s as mo-

ments during which the mature Emerson reassessed and ultimately reaffirmed the justice of his early, idealistic conceptions
of the individual and American culture. Concentrating on
Emerson's poetic theory as well as on his actual practice in
"Threnody," the elegy he composed after his son Waldo's death,
and in "Days," "Brahma," and "Song of Nature," three of his
best poems, which he printed in *May-Day and Other Poems* (1867),
Allen shows Emerson moving beyond formulaic Romantic consolations when he has to accommodate his personal desires to his
loss of family members and close friends, and resisting rank skepticism or naturalism when he has to face and accommodate himself to the persistence of cultural materialism in America before,
during, and after the Civil War. Concentrating on the importance
of personal relationships to Emerson as means to indulge and express his confidence in the ideal as he exchanged ideas and tested
the limits of art, morals, philosophy, and nature with the likes
of his aunt Mary Moody Emerson, Jones Very, Fuller, Bronson
Alcott, and Thoreau, McAleer portrays Emerson surviving the
negative side of personal experience and culture not just by having access to the printed wisdom of Socrates, Plato, and Shakespeare but also, and more important, by possessing the friendship
of persons such as these who, Emerson believed, could have spoken with Socrates, Plato, and Shakespeare as equals. These persons, as McAleer's study persuasively shows, were Emerson's real
teachers, and against the imperfection of men and the sense of
fatalism to which the times seemed to be directing him, they provided Emerson with elevating lessons. Their lessons were the
friendship and example they extended to him; through these,
they enlarged Emerson's capacity for feeling and sentiment as
they illuminated his personal world with "their habitual grandeur of view" ("Character," *W*, 10:101).

For several reasons, Whicher's Emerson continues to exert influence on the shape of Emerson biography and criticism to this
day. First, because that figure has achieved canonical stature
equivalent to that of any other appropriation of Emerson, biographers and critics are obliged to state clearly the relation between their own Emerson and Whicher's. Second, because
Whicher's is a very narrow and incomplete Emerson constructed

through reference to, at best, only the middle third of his life, it has reinforced the disposition of many biographers and critics to concentrate only on these years—the years in which *Nature, Essays: First* and *Second Series, Representative Men, English Traits,* and *The Conduct of Life* appeared—as most important literarily and personally to account for in studies of Emerson's life and thought. And third, as Leonard Neufeldt observed some time ago, Whicher's Emerson is "efficient" in that his is a more modern (one might also say tragic) than romantic story, and for a practiced psychological critic, his is a story easy to tell and to teach.[15] Indeed, the longevity and influence of Whicher's Emerson is evident in the introduction to Emerson printed in the most recent edition of *The Norton Anthology of American Literature* (1998). There, the many lectures Emerson delivered between the 1850s and the 1870s are dismissed along with *Society and Solitude* (1870), *Parnassus* (1875; a poetry anthology on which Emerson had worked on and off for nearly fifty years), *Letters and Social Aims* (1876), and a host of essays published in the *North American Review,* the *Atlantic Monthly,* and elsewhere as "a slow anticlimax" to the writings and intellectual ferment of Emerson's earlier years.[16] The *Norton Anthology*'s Emerson is barely distinguishable from the one anthologized by Whicher in 1957. Emerson's literary and intellectual legacy anthologized here opens with *Nature* and closes with "Fate" and "Thoreau" (1862). The only justification the editor mentions for extending representation of Emerson's achievement two years beyond "Fate" is that the later essay is "the source for many of Thoreau's sayings, which otherwise would [be] lost."[17] In effect, Whicher's Emerson still prevails: "Thoreau" is not anthologized to extend Emerson's reputation but to preserve some of the sayings of its subject.

Yet in the 1980s and 1990s, the biographies by Allen and McAleer have been joined by other biographical and critical treatments of Emerson to restore a degree of completeness to the intellectual and personal dimensions of his life. The most interesting and original writing on Emerson today is being carried out in the spirit of recovery and reinvention. Supported by scholarly editions of his *Journals and Miscellaneous Notebooks,* completed in 1982; *Sermons,* completed in 1992; *Topical Notebooks,* completed in 1994; and *Antislavery Writings,* published in 1995,[18] several works have undertaken detailed study of Emerson's early years as a minister and lecturer; brought Emerson's domestic life and influences and his position in American intellectual and social history into contemporary discussions of gender, race, and class; tested his durability against the doctrines of deconstructionism and postmodernism; and initiated serious review of the major writings of Emerson's later years.[19] As admirably demonstrated by the example of Robert D. Richardson, Jr.'s, recent intellectual biography, *Emerson: The Mind on Fire* (1995), today's scholars are allowing Emerson a voice in the important conversations of our day, and while doing so, they are illustrating for us how a century ago Americans could so easily have imagined that this cultural priest and visionary was the reincarnation of Shakespeare in their age.[20] By enlarging this one "man's nature [as an] . . . advertisement . . . of the character of his fellows" ("Politics," *CW,* 3:125), and by universalizing his biography as an expression of his culture's dreams, current biographers and critics are giving us the most thoroughly Emersonian Emerson to date.

III

Even as his recent biographers and critics are providing us with a more complete and reliable Emerson than has been seen in a while, much more remains to be done. Several directions available to the present and next generation of Emerson's biographers and critics have been hinted at in this essay. One of the most obvious and promising courses open to them is to extend serious study of Emerson into the writings of his later career. This portion of his life and achievement has been virtually lost to the present generation, largely as a consequence of Whicher's influence. Since nearly half of the works included in the forthcoming edition of Emerson's later lectures come from this period and show Emerson dealing extensively with subjects drawn from philosophy, science, morals, and American social history, biographers and critics will soon have at their disposal new resources through which to approach this period of his life, assess his reputation, and rule on the extent to which biographical and critical neglect of the later Emerson has been fair.[21] Reading these lectures against Emerson's journals and notebooks, they may well be surprised by what they find. For instance, in contrast to Nathaniel Hawthorne, whose story "Rappaccini's Daughter" (1844) discloses one nineteenth-century writer's distrust of science as a corruptive influence on the human spirit, Emerson, in several lectures and journals from the 1850s, 1860s, and 1870s, embraces science as both a confirmation of his idealism and a means to expand on his earlier confidence that "the order of nature" ensures that the human race possesses the capacity to offset the effects of materialism and reject fatalism. In a journal entry dated 1871, Emerson explicitly addressed this point:

> I do not know that I should feel threatened or insulted if a chemist should take his protoplasm or mix his hydrogen, oxygen & carbon, & make an animalcule incontestably swimming & jumping before my eyes. I should only feel that it indicated that the day had arrived when the human race might be trusted with a new degree of power, & its immense responsibility; for these steps are not solitary . . . but only a hint of an advanced frontier supported by an advancing race behind it. . . .
>
> All science must be penetrated by poetry. I do not wish to know that my shell is a strombus, or my moth a vanessa, but I wish to unite the shell & the moth to my being: to understand my own pleasure in them; to reach the secret of their charm for me. (*JMN*, 16:232, 251)

Another promising direction in which future Emerson biographers and critics may wish to go is suggested by Gerald Graff's work noted earlier: to study Emerson further for the influence his writing and thought have exerted on the professionalization of literary study and, one might add, creative writing in America.[22] On the other hand, while reading this essay some may have wondered whether that remark by the visitor to Concord from Calcutta about Emerson's having been "a geographical mistake" was hyperbole delivered for effect or an honest statement of opinion.

Along with "Persian Poetry," which Emerson first published in 1858 and collected in *Letters and Social Aims* in 1876, the recently published Emerson notebook "Orientalist" provides a useful starting point for serious inquiry (*W*, 8:235–65; *TN*, 2:39–141). Indeed, as the following reading shows, our access now to a work such as "Orientalist" provides us with new ways of extending discussion of Emerson's poetics and nationalism beyond "Fate" and the effective end of his career in the early 1860s alleged by Whicher and others.

While all of Emerson's recently published topical notebooks invite new biographical and critical readings of his poetics and views on rhetoric, nature, fate, and philosophy, "Orientalist" stands apart from most of them as a completely unexpected resource. In part because of its unusual range (it is a notebook in which Emerson recorded his thoughts while he studied Eastern culture as well as translated a substantial amount of Persian poetry from German sources and drafted several versions of "Brahma" and other of his poems) and in part because it dates from the 1850s and 1860s, "Orientalist" provides a wealth of unexplored information on the directions Emerson's idealism and nationalism took during his middle and later years. Here one will find Emerson's summary testimony to the East as a principal intellectual and imaginative influence on his brand of idealism throughout his life; here, too, one will find Emerson actively engaged in reconstructing the Eastern origin of ideas and values which he and his heroes such as Plato, Shakespeare, and Montaigne have assimilated, and finding in that reconstruction a degree of personal satisfaction and illumination which he expressed in a near-devotional epigraph he inscribed in Latin at the beginning of the notebook: "Ex oriente lux"—"Light out of the east."

Emerson's "Orientalist" is a natural complement to the scholarly attention devoted today to postcolonial and transnational studies. This notebook and "Persian Poetry" underscore his conviction that nature and fate transcend all forms of temporal or national expression and his belief that the nonmaterial, the spiritual content of experience, is, as he stated so clearly in "The Method of Nature," the only and ultimate value. In the imaginative freedom, occasional primitivism, wonder at nature's prospect, and comprehensive unity of Brahman faith which he found celebrated in the panegyrics, epics, and sensual lyrics of Anvari, Firdousi, Saadi, and especially Hafiz, Emerson appears to have achieved relief from crassness, brutality, and vulgarity as he encountered them in nineteenth-century material culture. And contrary to Whicher's thesis, in the 1850s and 1860s Emerson seems still able to realize the idealism of *Nature* and "The Method of Nature" in poems such as "Saadi," where he represents the ideal empowering the poet as simultaneously "joy-giver and enjoyer" once he heeds the muse's counsel against humanity's fatal limitation: its preoccupation with the flesh, with the material world. Emerson's idealism is also evident in "Brahma," where it is expressed in that one line which re-creates the power of the infinite and the constancy of "the order of nature": "I keep, and pass, and turn again." In "Orientalist" as a whole, moreover, readers will find that Emerson's creative acts of initial and revisionary translation are themselves manifestations of "the spiritual act," not merely its representation or repetition. His repeated reworking of Hafiz's intoxicating rhythms, his evident pleasure in re-creating Anvari's and Firdousi's exoticism and in emulating their spontaneity in verses of his own, and his embracing of Eastern mysticism and mythology are Emerson's conscious reenactments of Eastern "Light." Through his assimilation of its visionary aesthetics, religion, and philosophy, Emerson seems to be saying that the East has the power to nourish otherwise impoverished individuals and nations and to transmute, as he implies in the couplet he used as the epigraph for "Persian Poetry," materialism into wisdom (*W*, 8:235).

Emerson's own facility in appropriating ideas from the long span of Western and Eastern thought justifies the disposition of his many biographers and critics to appropriate his life and message to their particular ideological and psychological purposes. And because biography is a written form of personal relationship established among a writer, a subject, and a reader, we should have reason to believe that *our* biography of Emerson has not yet been written. If we choose to write that biography, it may well be that through our own appropriations of his life and thought Emerson will perform services for us today comparable to those for which biographers and critics have turned to him over the past century. While we certainly do not need more facts about Emerson's life, since the facts reported in the thoroughly annotated volumes of his published journals, notebooks, letters, and primary works will take the better part of anyone's career to master, what the facts of those volumes disclose about the essential Emerson—about the growth of his mind and art, about his connections with and responses to the people, events, and dreams of his time, and about the extent to which his life may be read as an archetype for the spiritual journey of all thoughtful Americans—has hardly been exhausted. Because the greatest virtue of Emerson as a thinker and as a biographical subject is his ability to transcend time and place and speak directly to Americans in terms they can understand and judge the value of for themselves, Emerson needs to be discovered, thought about, and written about by every American generation, including our own. The day that any generation is content to accept the published record as the complete report of the essential Emerson, Emerson and that part of America he created will cease to exist.

NOTES

1. *The Crucible: Text and Criticism*, ed. Gerald Weales (New York: Viking, 1971), p. 41.

2. Lydia Howard Sigourney (1791–1865) was a prolific writer of historical verse, occasional poetry and fiction, and essays on popular topics of the day. During her career, she published over sixty books, most of which are now forgotten. Virtually every newspaper in America announced her death in headlines that proclaimed her literary immortality.

3. For complete bibliographic details on newspaper accounts cited in this and following paragraphs, as well as for additional works published in this genre between late April and the end of 1882, see Robert E. Burkholder and Joel Myerson, *Emerson: An Annotated Secondary Bibliography* (Pittsburgh: University of Pittsburgh Press, 1985), pp. 204–35.

4. See Burkholder and Myerson, *Emerson: An Annotated Secondary Bibliography*, which accounts for Emerson biography and scholarship

published before 1980, and their *Ralph Waldo Emerson: An Annotated Bibliography of Criticism, 1980–1991* (Westport, Conn.: Greenwood Press, 1994).

5. James Little, *The Character and Genius of Ralph Waldo Emerson, with Selections from His Works. An Address* (Manchester, England: n.p., 1882).

6. For details of Emerson's position with respect to women's rights, see the essay on Emerson and women in this volume and Emerson's "Address at the Woman's Rights Convention, 20 September 1855," forthcoming in *The Later Lectures of Ralph Waldo Emerson, 1843–1871*, ed. Ronald A. Bosco and Joel Myerson. Emerson drew on his 1855 "Address" for a lecture he delivered on 2 December 1860 in Boston and for another he delivered on 26 May 1869 before the New England Woman's Suffrage Association; however, the "Address" itself was not published until 1884—two years after Emerson's death and nearly thirty years after its original delivery—when it appeared as "Woman" (see *W*, 11:403–26).

7. As quoted in Burkholder and Myerson, *Emerson: An Annotated Secondary Bibliography*, p. 228.

8. Ralph L. Rusk, *The Life of Ralph Waldo Emerson* (New York: Scribner's, 1949); Vivian C. Hopkins, *Spires of Form: A Study of Emerson's Aesthetic Theory* (Cambridge: Harvard University Press, 1951); Sherman Paul, *Emerson's Angle of Vision: Man and Nature in American Experience* (Cambridge: Harvard University Press, 1952); and Stephen E. Whicher, *Freedom and Fate: An Inner Life of Ralph Waldo Emerson* (Philadelphia: University of Pennsylvania Press, 1953).

9. F. O. Matthiessen, *American Renaissance: Art and Expression in the Age of Emerson and Whitman* (New York: Oxford University Press, 1941).

10. Gerald Graff, *Professing Literature: An Institutional History* (Chicago: University of Chicago Press, 1987), p. 219.

11. *Selections from Ralph Waldo Emerson*, ed. Stephen E. Whicher (Boston: Houghton, Mifflin, 1957).

12. Philip L. Nicoloff, *Emerson on Race and History: An Examination of English Traits* (New York: Columbia University Press, 1961).

13. John Michael, *Emerson and Skepticism: The Cipher of the World* (Baltimore: Johns Hopkins University Press, 1988), pp. 156–57.

14. Gay Wilson Allen, *Waldo Emerson: A Biography* (New York: Viking, 1981); and John McAleer, *Ralph Waldo Emerson: Days of Encounter* (Boston: Little, Brown, 1984).

15. Leonard Neufeldt, *The House of Emerson* (Lincoln: University of Nebraska Press, 1982), p. 12.

16. *The Norton Anthology of American Literature*, 2 vols., ed. Nina Baym et al. (New York: Norton, 1998), 1:1072.

17. Ibid., 1:1202 n. Whicher also included "Thoreau" in his anthology, explaining that although Emerson had "an inadequate appreciation of Thoreau's importance as a writer and a social critic," the essay is "probably the best thing he ever did" in the biographical genre; see *Selections from Ralph Waldo Emerson*, p. 498 n.

18. *Emerson's Antislavery Writings*, ed. Len Gougeon and Joel Myerson (New Haven, Conn.: Yale University Press, 1995).

19. The following studies provide useful starting points for those interested in pursuing these avenues of current scholarship. For Emerson's early years as a minister and lecturer, see Wesley T. Mott, *"The Strains of Eloquence": Emerson and His Sermons* (University Park: Pennsylvania State University Press, 1989); Susan L. Roberson, *Emerson in His Sermons* (Columbia: University of Missouri Press, 1995); and David Robinson, *Apostle of Culture: Emerson as Preacher and Lecturer* (Philadelphia: University of Pennsylvania Press, 1982). To examine the ways that Emerson has been brought into contemporary discussions of gender, race, and class, see Phyllis Cole, *Mary Moody Emerson and the Origins of Transcendentalism: A Family History* (New York: Oxford University Press, 1998); Len Gougeon, *Virtue's Hero: Emerson, Antislavery, and Reform* (Athens: University of Georgia Press, 1990); David Leverenz, *Manhood and the American Renaissance* (Ithaca, N.Y.: Cornell University Press, 1989); and Christina Zwarg, *Feminist Conversations: Fuller, Emerson, and the Play of Reading* (Ithaca, N.Y.: Cornell University Press, 1995). For Emerson's durability both within and outside of contemporary preoccupation with deconstruction and postmodernism, see Evelyn Barish, *Emerson: The Roots of Prophecy* (Princeton, N.J.: Princeton University Press, 1989); Sacvan Bercovitch, *The Rites of Assent: Transformations in the Symbolic Construction of America* (New York: Routledge, 1993); Stanley Cavell, *Conditions Handsome and Unhandsome: The Constitution of Emersonian Perfectionism* (Chicago: University of Chicago Press, 1990); and Merton M. Sealts, Jr., *Emerson on the Scholar* (Columbia: University of Missouri Press, 1992). For studies that concentrate on the recovery of Emerson's later writing and thought, see Ronald A. Bosco, "His Lectures Were Poetry, His Teaching the Music of the Spheres: Annie

Adams Fields and Francis Greenwood Peabody on Emerson's 'Natural History of the Intellect' University Lectures at Harvard in 1870," *Harvard Library Bulletin*, n.s., 8 (Summer 1997): 1–79; David M. Robinson, *Emerson and the Conduct of Life: Pragmatism and Ethical Purpose in the Later Work* (Cambridge: Cambridge University Press, 1993); and Lawrence Buell, "Emerson's Fate," Len Gougeon, "Emerson's Circle and the Crisis of the Civil War," and Ronald A. Bosco, "The 'Somewhat Spheral and Infinite' in Every Man: Emerson's Theory of Biography," all in *Emersonian Circles: Essays in Honor of Joel Myerson*, ed. Wesley T. Mott and Robert E. Burkholder (Rochester, N.Y.: University of Rochester Press, 1997), pp. 11–28, 29–52, and 67–103, respectively.

20. Robert D. Richardson, Jr., *Emerson: The Mind on Fire* (Berkeley: University of California Press, 1995).

21. For *The Later Lectures of Ralph Waldo Emerson, 1843–1871*, see note 6.

22. See D. G. Myers, *The Elephants Teach: Creative Writing Since 1880* (Englewood Cliffs, N.J.: Prentice Hall, 1996), pp. 31–33, where an argument is made for crediting Emerson with the professionalization of creative writing in American higher education.

Bibliographical Essay

Joel Myerson

Ralph Waldo Emerson was an extremely popular author in his lifetime.[1] Beginning with *The Conduct of Life* in 1860, his books were brought out by the prestigious Boston publisher Ticknor and Fields (which later became Houghton, Mifflin). This firm also published such New England writers as Nathaniel Hawthorne, Henry Wadsworth Longfellow, James Russell Lowell, and Henry David Thoreau, and it made a conscientious effort to package and market them as the "standard" American authors. Accordingly, all of Emerson's works were kept in print, and an eleven-volume collected edition of his writings was published within two years of his death.

The control of Emerson's writings was kept within the family. As Emerson's intellectual powers waned after 1872, his published works more and more became collaborations with his daughter Ellen and James Elliot Cabot, who would later become his literary executor and biographer.[2] The two helped Emerson put together *Letters and Social Aims* (1876); Ellen and her sister, Edith Emerson Forbes, assisted their father in assembling the anthology of his favorite poetry, *Parnassus* (1875). After Emerson's death, Cabot took the lead in putting together, both from previously published and from manuscript works, *Miscellanies* (1884), *Lectures and Biographical Sketches* (1884), and *Natural History of Intellect* (1893). The centenary of Emerson's birth was marked by the publication of *The Complete Works of Ralph Waldo Emerson*, edited and with annotations by his son Edward.[3]

Emerson's writings have fared even better in the twentieth century. Ralph L. Rusk's edition of *The Letters of Ralph Waldo Emerson* set high standards for editorial accuracy and annotational quality, standards that were maintained by Joseph Slater in his edition of Emerson's correspondence with Carlyle and Eleanor M. Tilton in her supplementary edition to Rusk.[4] Beginning in 1959, a series of editions of Emerson's works started coming out that forever changed the scholarly approach to him by making available for the first time his lectures, journals, notebooks, and sermons. The editors of Emerson's *Early Lectures*, *Journals and Miscellaneous Notebooks*, *Poetry Notebooks*, *Topical Notebooks*, and *Complete Sermons* added twenty-seven new volumes of Emerson's works to his literary canon. All these editions achieved the highest standards of textual accuracy (and reporting of Emerson's revisions in the manuscripts) and are fully annotated, to the point of showing the usages Emerson made of his ideas and phrases between his journals and other writings.[5]

Anyone wishing to read all of Emerson's work is faced with the daunting prospect of some fifty volumes of primary texts. Fortunately, there are some ways to access this material easily. In addition to the many general anthologies of Emerson's published writings, there are good one-volume selections from his antislavery works, literary criticism, journals, and letters.[6] Also, there are a number of concordances (none, alas, complete) to help readers find specific references in Emerson's writings to people, places, and concepts.[7] And editors are still working on Emerson: a new, textually accurate and fully annotated edition of Emerson's *Collected Works* is ongoing,[8] and editions of his *Later Lectures* and the correspondence among his brothers are forthcoming.[9]

BIBLIOGRAPHIES

American Literary Scholarship. 1963–present. Durham, N.C.: Duke University Press, 1965–.

Burkholder, Robert E., and Joel Myerson. *Emerson: An Annotated Sec-*

ondary Bibliography. Pittsburgh: University of Pittsburgh Press, 1985.

——. "Ralph Waldo Emerson." In *The Transcendentalists: A Review of Research and Criticism*, ed. Joel Myerson, pp. 135–66. New York: Modern Language Association, 1984.

——. *Ralph Waldo Emerson: An Annotated Bibliography of Criticism, 1980–1991*. Westport, Conn.: Greenwood Press, 1994.

Charvat, William. *Emerson's American Lecture Engagements: A Chronological List*. New York: New York Public Library, 1961.

Emerson Society Papers. Annual bibliography of Emerson studies.

Myerson, Joel. "Ralph Waldo Emerson." In *Prospects for the Study of American Literature*, ed. Richard Kopley, pp. 6–20. New York: New York University Press, 1997.

——. *Ralph Waldo Emerson: A Descriptive Bibliography*. Pittsburgh: University of Pittsburgh Press, 1982.

——, ed. *Emerson and Thoreau: The Contemporary Reviews*. New York: Cambridge University Press, 1992.

Pütz, Manfred. *Ralph Waldo Emerson: A Bibliography of Twentieth-Century Criticism*. New York: Peter Lang, 1986.

COLLECTIONS OF ESSAYS

Bode, Carl, ed. *Ralph Waldo Emerson: A Profile*. New York: Hill and Wang, 1969.

Buell, Lawrence, ed. *Ralph Waldo Emerson: A Collection of Critical Essays*. Englewood Cliffs, N.J.: Prentice-Hall, 1993.

Burkholder, Robert E., and Joel Myerson, eds. *Critical Essays on Ralph Waldo Emerson*. Boston: G. K. Hall, 1983.

Cady, Edwin, and Louis J. Budd, eds. *On Emerson: The Best from American Literature*. Durham, N.C.: Duke University Press, 1988.

Donadio, Stephen, Stephen Railton, and Ormond Seavy, eds. *Emerson and His Legacy: Essays in Honor of Quentin Anderson*. Carbondale: Southern Illinois University Press, 1986.

Konvitz, Milton R., ed. *The Recognition of Ralph Waldo Emerson*. Ann Arbor: University of Michigan Press, 1972.

Levin, David, ed. *Emerson: Prophecy, Metamorphosis, and Influence*. New York: Columbia University Press, 1975.

Mott, Wesley T., and Robert E. Burkholder, eds. *Emersonian Circles:*

Essays in Honor of Joel Myerson. Rochester, N.Y.: University of Rochester Press, 1997.

Myerson, Joel, ed. *Emerson Centenary Essays.* Carbondale: Southern Illinois University Press, 1982.

Porte, Joel, ed. *Emerson: Prospect and Retrospect.* Cambridge: Harvard University Press, 1982.

Sanborn, F. B., ed. *The Genius and Character of Emerson: Lectures at the Concord School of Philosophy.* Boston: James R. Osgood, 1885.

Sealts, Merton M., Jr., and Alfred R. Ferguson, eds. *Emerson's "Nature"—Origin, Growth, Meaning.* New York: Dodd, Mead, 1969. 2d enl. ed., Carbondale: Southern Illinois University Press, 1979.

BIOGRAPHIES

Allen, Gay Wilson. *Waldo Emerson: A Biography.* New York: Viking, 1981.

Baker, Carlos. *Emerson Among the Eccentrics: A Group Portrait.* New York: Viking Press, 1996.

Barish, Evelyn. *Emerson in Italy.* New York: Henry Holt, 1989.

———. *Emerson: The Roots of Prophecy.* Princeton, N.J.: Princeton University Press, 1989.

Cabot, James Elliot. *A Memoir of Ralph Waldo Emerson.* 2 vols. Boston: Houghton, Mifflin, 1887.

Cole, Phyllis. *Mary Moody Emerson and the Origins of Transcendentalism: A Family History.* New York: Oxford University Press, 1998.

Conway, Moncure Daniel. *Emerson at Home and Abroad.* Boston: James R. Osgood, 1882.

Cooke, George Willis. *Ralph Waldo Emerson: His Life, Writings, and Philosophy.* Boston: James R. Osgood, 1881.

Emerson, Edward Waldo. *Emerson in Concord.* Boston: Houghton, Mifflin, 1889.

Emerson, Ellen Louisa Tucker. *One First Love: The Letters of Ellen Louisa Tucker to Ralph Waldo Emerson.* Ed. Edith W. Gregg. Cambridge: Harvard University Press, 1962.

Emerson, Ellen Tucker. *The Letters of Ellen Tucker Emerson.* Ed. Edith E. W. Gregg. 2 vols. Kent, Ohio: Kent State University Press, 1982.

————. *The Life of Lidian Jackson Emerson.* Ed. Delores Bird Carpenter. Boston: Twayne, 1980.

Emerson, Lidian Jackson. *The Selected Letters of Lidian Jackson Emerson.* Ed. Delores Bird Carpenter. Columbia: University of Missouri Press, 1987.

Emerson, Mary Moody. *The Selected Letters of Mary Moody Emerson.* Ed. Nancy Craig Simmons. Athens: University of Georgia Press, 1993.

Engstrom, Sallee Fox. *The Infinitude of the Private Man: Emerson's Presence in Western New York, 1851–1861.* New York: Peter Lang, 1997.

Firkins, O. W. *Ralph Waldo Emerson.* Boston: Houghton, Mifflin, 1915.

Garnett, Richard. *Life of Ralph Waldo Emerson.* London: Walter Scott, 1888.

Gonnaud, Maurice. *An Uneasy Solitude: Individual and Society in the Work of Ralph Waldo Emerson.* Trans. Lawrence Rosenwald. Princeton, N.J.: Princeton University Press, 1987 [Paris: Didier, 1964].

Haskins, David Greene. *Ralph Waldo Emerson: His Maternal Ancestors.* Boston: Cupples, Upham, 1886.

Holmes, Oliver Wendell. *Ralph Waldo Emerson.* Boston: Houghton, Mifflin, 1884.

Ireland, Alexander. *In Memoriam: Ralph Waldo Emerson.* London: Simpkin, Marshall, 1882. New edition as *Ralph Waldo Emerson: His Life, Genius, and Writings.* London: Simpkin, Marshall, 1882.

Kleinfield, H. L. "The Structure of Emerson's Death." *Bulletin of the New York Public Library* 65 (January 1961): 47–64.

McAleer, John. *Ralph Waldo Emerson: Days of Encounter.* Boston: Little, Brown, 1984.

Pommer, Henry F. *Emerson's First Marriage.* Carbondale: Southern Illinois University Press, 1967.

Richardson, Robert D., Jr. *Emerson: The Mind on Fire.* Berkeley: University of California Press, 1995.

Rusk, Ralph L. *The Life of Ralph Waldo Emerson.* New York: Scribner's, 1949.

Sanborn, F. B. *The Personality of Emerson.* Boston: George E. Goodspeed, 1903.

Scudder, Townsend. *The Lonely Wayfaring Man: Emerson and Some Englishmen.* London: Oxford University Press, 1936.

[Thayer, James Bradley]. *A Western Journey with Mr. Emerson.* Boston: Little, Brown, 1884.

von Frank, Albert J. *An Emerson Chronology.* New York: G. K. Hall, 1994.

Woodberry, George Edward. *Ralph Waldo Emerson.* New York: Macmillan, 1907.

RELIGION

Ahlstrom, Sydney E. *A Religious History of the American People.* New Haven, Conn.: Yale University Press, 1972.

Bercovitch, Sacvan. *The Puritan Origins of the American Self.* New Haven, Conn.: Yale University Press, 1975.

Jackson, Carl T. *The Oriental Religions and American Thought: Nineteenth-Century Explorations.* Westport, Conn.: Greenwood Press, 1981.

Kazin, Alfred. *God and the American Writer.* New York: Knopf, 1997.

Persons, Stow. *Free Religion: An American Faith.* New Haven, Conn.: Yale University Press, 1947.

UNITARIANISM

Ahlstrom, Sydney E., and Jonathan S. Carey, eds. *An American Reformation: A Documentary History of Unitarian Christianity.* Middletown, Conn.: Wesleyan University Press, 1985.

Allen, Joseph Henry, and Richard Eddy. *A History of the Unitarians and Universalists in the United States.* New York: Christian Literature Company, 1894.

Cooke, George Willis. *Unitarianism in America.* Boston: American Unitarian Association, 1902.

Howe, Daniel Walker. *The Unitarian Conscience: Harvard Moral Philosophy, 1805–1861.* Cambridge: Harvard University Press, 1970.

Hutchison, William R. *The Transcendentalist Ministers: Church Reform in the New England Renaissance.* New Haven, Conn.: Yale University Press, 1959.

Robinson, David. *The Unitarians and the Universalists,* Westport, Conn.: Greenwood Press, 1985.

Wider, Sarah Ann. *Anna Tilden, Unitarian Culture, and the Problem of Self-Representation*. Athens: University of Georgia Press, 1997.

Wright, Conrad. *The Beginnings of Unitarianism in America*. Boston: Starr King Press, 1955.

———. "The Early Period (1811–1840)." In *The Harvard Divinity School: Its Place in Harvard University and in American Culture*, edited by George Hunston Williams, pp. 21–77. Boston: Beacon Press, 1954.

———. *The Liberal Christians: Essays on American Unitarian History*. Boston: Beacon Press, 1970.

———. *The Unitarian Controversy: Essays on American Unitarian History*. Boston: Skinner House, 1994.

———, ed. *A Stream of Light: A Sesquicentennial History of American Unitarianism*. Boston: Unitarian Universalist Association, 1975.

Wright, Conrad Edick, ed. *American Unitarianism, 1805–1865*. Boston: Northeastern University Press, 1989.

TRANSCENDENTALISM

Albanese, Catherine. *Corresponding Motion: Transcendental Religion and the New America*. Philadelphia: Temple University Press, 1977.

Asselineau, Roger. *The Transcendentalist Constant in American Literature*. New York: New York University Press, 1980.

Barbour, Brian M., ed. *American Transcendentalism: An Anthology of Criticism*. Notre Dame, Ind.: University of Notre Dame Press, 1973.

Boller, Paul F. *American Transcendentalism, 1830–1860: An Intellectual Inquiry*. New York: Putnam, 1974.

Buell, Lawrence. *Literary Transcendentalism: Style and Vision in the American Renaissance*. Ithaca, N.Y.: Cornell University Press, 1973.

———. "The Transcendentalists." In *Columbia Literary History of the United States*, gen. ed. Emory Elliott, pp. 364–78. New York: Columbia University Press, 1988.

Christy, Arthur. *The Orient in American Transcendentalism*. New York: Columbia University Press, 1932.

Flower, Elizabeth, and Murray G. Murphey. "Transcendentalism."

In their *A History of Philosophy in America.* 2 vols., 1:397–435. New York: Putnam, 1977.

Francis, Richard. *Transcendental Utopias: Individual and Community at Brook Farm, Fruitlands, and Walden.* Ithaca, N.Y.: Cornell University Press, 1997.

Frothingham, Octavius Brooks. *Transcendentalism in America: A History.* New York: Putnam, 1876.

Grusin, Richard. *Transcendentalist Hermeneutics: Institutional Authority and the Higher Criticism of the Bible.* Durham, N.C.: Duke University Press, 1991.

Gura, Philip F., and Joel Myerson, eds. *Critical Essays on American Transcendentalism.* Boston: G. K. Hall, 1982.

Hochfield, George. "New England Transcendentalism." In *American Literature to 1900,* edited by Marcus Cunliffe, pp. 135–68. New York: Peter Bedrick Books, 1987.

Kaplan, Nathan, and Thomas Katsaros. *The Origins of American Transcendentalism in Philosophy and Mysticism.* New Haven, Conn.: College and University Press, 1975.

Kern, Alexander C. "The Rise of Transcendentalism, 1815–1860." In *Transitions in American Literary History,* edited by Harry Hayden Clark, pp. 247–314. Durham, N.C.: Duke University Press, 1954.

Koster, Donald N. *Transcendentalism in America.* Boston: Twayne, 1975.

Miller, Perry, ed. *The Transcendentalists: An Anthology.* Cambridge: Harvard University Press, 1950.

Mott, Wesley T., ed. *Biographical Dictionary of Transcendentalism.* Westport, Conn.: Greenwood Press, 1996.

——. *Encyclopedia of Transcendentalism.* Westport, Conn.: Greenwood Press, 1996.

Myerson, Joel. *The New England Transcendentalists and the Dial: A History of the Magazine and Its Contributors.* Rutherford, N.J.: Fairleigh Dickinson University Press, 1980.

——, ed. *The American Transcendentalists.* Detroit: Gale Research Company, 1988.

——. *The Transcendentalists: A Review of Research and Criticism.* New York: Modern Language Association, 1984.

Packer, Barbara. "The Transcendentalists." In *The Cambridge History of American Literature,* edited by Sacvan Bercovitch, vol. 2,

Prose Writing, 1820–1865, pp. 329–604. Cambridge: Cambridge University Press, 1995.

Pochmann, Henry A. *New England Transcendentalism and St. Louis Hegelianism*. Philadelphia: Carl Schurz Foundation, 1948.

Rose, Anne C. *Transcendentalism as a Social Movement, 1830–1850*. New Haven, Conn.: Yale University Press, 1981.

Simon, Myron, and Thornton H. Parsons, eds. *Transcendentalism and Its Legacy*. Ann Arbor: University of Michigan Press, 1966.

Versluis, Arthur. *American Transcendentalism and Asian Religions*. New York: Oxford University Press, 1993.

Vogel, Stanley M. *German Literary Influences on the American Transcendentalists*. New Haven, Conn.: Yale University Press, 1955.

Whicher, George F., ed. *The Transcendentalist Revolt Against Materialism*. Boston: D. C. Heath, 1949. Rev. ed., Gail Kennedy, ed., *The Transcendentalist Revolt*. Boston: D. C. Heath, 1968.

CONCORD, MASSACHUSETTS

Brooks, Paul. *The People of Concord: One Year in the Flowering of New England*. Chester, Conn.: Globe Pequot Press, 1990.

Engel, Mary Miller. *I Remember the Emersons*. Los Angeles: Times-Mirror, 1941.

Fischer, David Hackett, ed. *Concord: The Social History of a New England Town, 1750–1850*. Waltham, Mass.: Brandeis University, 1983.

Jarvis, Edward. *Traditions and Reminiscences of Concord, Massachusetts, 1779–1878*. Ed. Sarah Chapin. Amherst: University of Massachusetts Press, 1993.

Oehlschlaeger, Fritz, and George Hendrick, eds. *Towards the Making of Thoreau's Modern Reputation: Selected Correspondence of S. A. Jones, W. A. Hosmer, H. S. Salt, H. G. O. Blake, and D. Ricketson*. Urbana: University of Illinois Press, 1979.

Remembrances of Concord and the Thoreaus: Letters of Horace Hosmer to Dr. S. A. Jones. Ed. George Hendrick. Urbana: University of Illinois Press, 1977.

Scudder, Townsend. *Concord: American Town*. Boston: Little, Brown, 1947.

Stearns, Frank Preston. *Sketches from Concord and Appledore*. New York: Putnam, 1895.

Stoehr, Taylor. *Nay-Saying in Concord: Emerson, Alcott, and Thoreau.* Hamden, Conn.: Archon Books, 1979.

Swayne, Josephine Latham. *The Story of Concord Told by Concord Writers.* Boston: E. F. Worcester, 1906. 2d rev. ed., Boston: Meador, 1939.

Wheeler, Ruth. *Concord: Climate for Freedom.* Concord, Mass.: Concord Antiquarian Society, 1967.

PHILOSOPHY

Bauerlein, Mark. *The Pragmatic Mind: Explorations in the Psychology of Belief.* Durham, N.C.: Duke University Press, 1997.

Cavell, Stanley. *Conditions Handsome and Unhandsome: The Constitution of Emersonian Perfectionism.* Chicago: University of Chicago Press, 1990.

———. *In Quest of the Ordinary: Lines of Skepticism and Romanticism.* Chicago: University of Chicago Press, 1988.

———. *Philosophical Passages: Wittgenstein, Emerson, Austin, Derrida.* Cambridge, Mass.: Blackwell, 1995.

———. *The Senses of Walden: An Expanded Edition.* San Francisco: North Point Press, 1981.

———. *This New Yet Unapproachable America: Lectures After Emerson After Wittgenstein.* Albuquerque, N.M.: Living Batch Press, 1989.

Goodman, Russell B. *American Philosophy and the Romantic Tradition.* New York: Cambridge University Press, 1990.

Howe, Daniel Walker. *Making the American Self: Jonathan Edwards to Abraham Lincoln.* Cambridge: Harvard University Press, 1997.

———. *The Unitarian Conscience: Harvard Moral Philosophy, 1805–1861.* Cambridge: Harvard University Press, 1970.

Kateb, George. *The Inner Ocean: Individualism and Democratic Culture.* Ithaca, N.Y.: Cornell University Press, 1992.

Patterson, Anita Haya. *From Emerson to King: Democracy, Race, and the Politics of Protest.* New York: Oxford University Press, 1997.

Shi, David E. *The Simple Life: Plain Living and High Thinking in American Culture.* New York: Oxford University Press, 1985.

West, Cornel. *The American Evasion of Philosophy: A Genealogy of Pragmatism.* Madison: University of Wisconsin Press, 1989.

LITERARY HISTORY

Andrews, William L., ed. *Literary Romanticism in America*. Baton Rouge: Louisiana State University Press, 1981.

Bercovitch, Sacvan. *The Rites of Assent: Transformations in the Symbolic Construction of America*. New York: Routledge, 1993.

Blasing, Mutlu Konuk. *American Poetry: The Rhetoric of Its Forms*. New Haven, Conn.: Yale University Press, 1987.

Bloom, Harold. *Agon: Towards a Theory of Romanticism*. New York: Oxford University Press, 1982.

———. *The Breaking of the Vessels*. Chicago: University of Chicago Press, 1982.

———. *Figures of Capable Imagination*. New York: Seabury Press, 1976.

———. *Poetry and Repression: Revisionism from Blake to Stevens*. New Haven, Conn.: Yale University Press, 1976.

Brantley, Richard E. *Coordinates of Anglo-American Romanticism: Wesley, Edwards, Carlyle and Emerson*. Gainesville: University Presses of Florida, 1993.

Buell, Lawrence. *New England Literary Culture from Revolution Through Renaissance*. New York: Cambridge University Press, 1986.

Carafiol, Peter. *The American Ideal: Literary History as a Worldly Activity*. New York: Oxford University Press, 1991.

———. *Transcendent Reason: James Marsh and the Forms of Romantic Thought*. Tallahassee: University Presses of Florida, 1982.

Chai, Leon. *The Romantic Foundations of the American Renaissance*. Ithaca, N.Y.: Cornell University Press, 1987.

Cowen, Michael H. *City of the West: Emerson, America, and Urban Metaphor*. New Haven, Conn.: Yale University Press, 1967.

Fredman, Stephen. *The Grounding of American Poetry: Charles Olson and the Emersonian Tradition*. New York: Cambridge University Press, 1993.

Gilmore, Michael T. *American Romanticism and the Marketplace*. Chicago: University of Chicago Press, 1985.

Grey, Robin. *The Complicity of Imagination: The American Renaissance, Contests of Authority, and Seventeenth-Century English Culture*. New York: Cambridge University Press, 1997.

Gura, Philip F. *The Wisdom of Words: Language, Theology, and Litera-*

ture in the New England Renaissance. Middletown, Conn.: Wesleyan University Press, 1981.

Gustafson, Thomas. *Representative Words: Politics, Literature, and the American Language, 1776–1865.* New York: Cambridge University Press, 1992.

Hedges, William L. "From Franklin to Emerson." In *The Oldest Revolutionary: Essays on Benjamin Franklin,* edited by J. A. Leo Lemay, pp. 139–56. Philadelphia: University of Pennsylvania Press, 1976.

Hertz, David Michael. *Angels of Reality: Emersonian Unfoldings in Wright, Stevens, and Ives.* Carbondale: Southern Illinois University Press, 1993.

Howe, Irving. *The American Newness: Culture and Politics in the Age of Emerson.* Cambridge: Harvard University Press, 1986.

Johnson, James L. *Mark Twain and the Limits of Power: Emerson's God in Ruins.* Knoxville: University of Tennessee Press, 1982.

Kazin, Alfred. *An American Procession: The Major American Writers from 1830 to 1930—The Crucial Century.* New York: Knopf, 1984.

Kramer, Michael P. *Imagining Language in America from the Revolution to the Civil War.* Princeton, N.J.: Princeton University Press, 1992.

Kronick, Joseph G. *American Poetics of History: From Emerson to the Moderns.* Baton Rouge: Louisiana State University Press, 1984.

Lease, Benjamin. *Anglo-American Encounters: England and the Rise of American Literature.* Cambridge: Cambridge University Press, 1981.

Leverenz, David. *Manhood and the American Renaissance.* Ithaca, N.Y.: Cornell University Press, 1989.

Marr, David. *American Worlds Since Emerson.* Amherst: University of Massachusetts Press, 1988.

Matthiessen, F. O. *American Renaissance: Art and Expression in the Age of Emerson and Whitman.* New York: Oxford University Press, 1941.

Miller, Perry. "From Edwards to Emerson." In *Errand into the Wilderness,* pp. 184–203. Cambridge: Harvard University Press, 1956.

———. *The Raven and the Whale: The War of Words and Wits in the Era of Poe and Melville.* New York: Harcourt, Brace, 1956.

New, Elisa. *The Regenerate Lyric: Theology and Innovation in American Poetry.* New York: Cambridge University Press, 1993.

Parini, Jay, ed. *The Columbia History of American Poetry.* New York: Columbia University Press, 1993.

Parrington, Vernon Louis. *The Romantic Revolution in America, 1800–1860.* New York: Harcourt, Brace, 1927.

Peach, Linden. *British Influence on the Birth of American Literature.* London: Macmillan, 1982.

Pearce, Roy Harvey. *The Continuity of American Poetry.* Princeton, N.J.: Princeton University Press, 1961.

Poirier, Richard. *Poetry and Pragmatism.* Cambridge: Harvard University Press, 1992.

Railton, Stephen. *Authorship and Audience: Literary Performance in the American Renaissance.* Princeton, N.J.: Princeton University Press, 1991.

Reising, Russell J. *The Usable Past: Theory and the Study of American Literature.* New York: Methuen, 1986.

Reynolds, David S. *Beneath the American Renaissance: The Subversive Imagination in the Age of Emerson and Melville.* New York: Knopf, 1988.

Reynolds, Larry J. *European Revolutions and the American Literary Renaissance.* New Haven, Conn.: Yale University Press, 1988.

Rowe, John Carlos. *At Emerson's Tomb: The Politics of Classic American Literature.* New York: Columbia University Press, 1997.

Rowland, William G., Jr. *Literature and the Marketplace: Romantic Writers and Their Audiences in Great Britain and the United States.* Lincoln: University of Nebraska Press, 1996.

Ruland, Richard. *The Rediscovery of American Literature: Premises of Critical Taste, 1900–1940.* Cambridge: Harvard University Press, 1967.

Shucard, Alan. *American Poetry: The Puritans Through Walt Whitman.* Boston: Twayne, 1988.

Spencer, Benjamin T. *The Quest for Nationality: An American Literary Campaign.* Syracuse, N.Y.: Syracuse University Press, 1957.

Spengemann, William C. *A Mirror for Americanists: Reflections on the Idea of American Literature.* Hanover, N.H.: University Press of New England, 1989.

Stafford, John. *The Literary Criticism of "Young America": A Study in the Relationship of Politics and Literature, 1837–1850.* Berkeley: University of California Press, 1952.

Waggoner, Hyatt H. *American Poets from the Puritans to the Present.* Boston: Houghton Mifflin, 1968.

Weisbuch, Robert. *Atlantic Double-Cross: American Literature and British Influence in the Age of Emerson.* Chicago: University of Chicago Press, 1986.

Wilson, R. Jackson. *Figures of Speech: American Writers and the Literary Marketplace, from Benjamin Franklin to Emily Dickinson.* New York: Knopf, 1989.

Wolfe, Cary. *The Limits of American Literary Ideology in Pound and Emerson.* New York: Cambridge University Press, 1993.

Ziff, Lawrence. *Literary Democracy: The Declaration of Cultural Independence in America.* New York: Viking, 1981.

BOOKS ON RALPH WALDO EMERSON

Bishop, Jonathan. *Emerson on the Soul.* Cambridge: Harvard University Press, 1964.

Brantley, Richard E. *Anglo-American Antiphony: The Late Romanticism of Tennyson and Emerson.* Gainesville: University Presses of Florida, 1994.

Brown, Lee Rust. *The Emerson Museum: Practical Romanticism and the Pursuit of the Whole.* Cambridge: Harvard University Press, 1997.

Cadava, Eduardo. *Emerson and the Climates of History.* Stanford, Calif.: Stanford University Press, 1997.

Cameron, Kenneth Walter. *Emerson the Essayist.* 2 vols. Raleigh, N.C.: Thistle Press, 1945. Rpt., Hartford, Conn: Transcendental Books, 1972.

———. *Emerson's Reading.* Raleigh, N.C.: Thistle Press, 1941. Rev. ed., Hartford, Conn.: Transcendental Books, 1962.

———. *Emerson's Workshop: An Analysis of His Reading in Periodicals through 1836 . . .* Hartford, Conn.: Transcendental Books, 1964.

Carpenter, Frederic Ives. *Emerson and Asia.* Cambridge: Harvard University Press, 1930.

Cayton, Mary Kupiec. *Emerson's Emergence: Self and Society in the Transformation of New England, 1800–1845.* Chapel Hill: University of North Carolina Press, 1989.

Cheyfitz, Eric. *The Trans-Parent: Sexual Politics in the Language of Emerson.* Baltimore: Johns Hopkins University Press, 1981.

Duncan, Jeffrey L. *The Power and Form of Emerson's Thought.* Charlottesville: University Press of Virginia, 1973.

Ellison, Julie. *Emerson's Romantic Style.* Princeton, N.J.: Princeton University Press, 1984.

Field, Susan L. *The Romance of Desire: Emerson's Commitment to Incompletion.* Madison, N.J.: Fairleigh Dickinson University Press, 1997.

Geldard, Richard G. *The Esoteric Emerson: The Spiritual Teachings of Ralph Waldo Emerson.* Hudson, N.Y.: Lindisfarne Press, 1993.

Gelpi, Donald L. *Endless Seeker: The Religious Quest of Ralph Waldo Emerson.* Lanham, Md.: University Press of America, 1991.

Gougeon, Len. *Virtue's Hero: Emerson, Antislavery, and Reform.* Athens: University of Georgia Press, 1990.

Hallengren, Anders. *The Code of Concord: Emerson's Search for Universal Laws.* Stockholm: Almqvist and Wiksell, 1994.

Harding, Walter. *Emerson's Library.* Charlottesville: University Press of Virginia, 1967.

Harris, Kenneth Marc. *Carlyle and Emerson: Their Long Debate.* Cambridge: Harvard University Press, 1978.

Hodder, Alan D. *Emerson's Rhetoric of Revelation: Nature, the Reader, and the Apocalypse Within.* University Park: Pennsylvania State University Press, 1989.

Hopkins, Vivian C. *Spires of Form: A Study of Emerson's Aesthetic Theory.* Cambridge: Harvard University Press, 1951.

Hudnut, Robert K. *The Aesthetics of Ralph Waldo Emerson: The Materials and Methods of His Poetry.* Lewiston, N.Y.: Edwin Mellen Press, 1996.

Hughes, Gertrude Reif. *Emerson's Demanding Optimism.* Baton Rouge: Louisiana State University Press, 1984.

Hutch, Richard A. *Emerson's Optics: Biographical Process and the Dawn of Religious Leadership.* Washington, D.C.: University Press of America, 1983.

Jacobson, David. *Emerson's Pragmatic Vision: The Dance of the Eye.* University Park: Pennsylvania State University Press, 1993.

Kateb, George. *Emerson and Self-Reliance.* Thousand Oaks, Calif.: Sage, 1995.

Lange, Lou Ann. *The Riddle of Liberty: Emerson on Alienation, Freedom, and Obedience.* Atlanta: Scholars Press, 1986.

Leary, Lewis. *Ralph Waldo Emerson: An Interpretive Essay.* Boston: Twayne, 1980.

Loewenberg, Robert J. *An American Idol: Emerson and the "Jewish Idea."* Lanham, Md.: University Press of America, 1984.

Lopez, Michael. *Emerson and Power: Creative Antagonism in the Nineteenth Century.* DeKalb: Northern Illinois University Press, 1996.

Loving, Jerome. *Emerson, Whitman, and the American Muse.* Chapel Hill: University of North Carolina Press, 1982.

Makarushka, Irene S. *Religious Imagination and Language in Emerson and Nietzsche.* New York: St. Martin's, 1994.

Michael, John. *Emerson and Skepticism: The Cipher of the World.* Baltimore: Johns Hopkins University Press, 1988.

Mitchell, Charles E. *Individualism and Its Discontents: Appropriations of Emerson, 1880–1950.* Amherst: University of Massachusetts Press, 1997.

Mott, Wesley T. *"The Strains of Eloquence": Emerson and His Sermons.* University Park: Pennsylvania State University Press, 1989.

Neufeldt, Leonard. *The House of Emerson.* Lincoln: University of Nebraska Press, 1982.

Newfield, Christopher. *The Emerson Effect: Individualism and Submission in America.* Chicago: University of Chicago Press, 1996.

Nicoloff, Philip L. *Emerson on Race and History: An Examination of English Traits.* New York: Columbia University Press, 1961.

O'Keefe, Richard R. *Mythic Archetypes in Ralph Waldo Emerson: A Blakean Reading.* Kent, Ohio: Kent State University Press, 1995.

Packer, B. L. *Emerson's Fall: A New Interpretation of the Major Essays.* New York: Continuum, 1982.

Packer, Barbara. "Ralph Waldo Emerson." In *Columbia Literary History of the United States,* gen. ed. Emory Elliott, pp. 381–98. New York: Columbia University Press, 1988.

Paul, Sherman. *Emerson's Angle of Vision: Man and Nature in American Experience.* Cambridge: Harvard University Press, 1952.

Perry, Bliss. *Emerson Today.* Princeton, N.J.: Princeton University Press, 1931.

Poirier, Richard. *The Renewal of Literature: Emersonian Reflections.* New York: Random House, 1987.

Porte, Joel. *Emerson and Thoreau: Transcendentalists in Conflict.* Middletown, Conn.: Wesleyan University Press, 1966.

———. *Representative Man: Ralph Waldo Emerson in His Time.* New York: Oxford University Press, 1979.

Porter, Carolyn. *Seeing and Being: The Plight of the Participant Observer in Emerson, James, Adams, and Faulkner.* Middletown, Conn.: Wesleyan University Press, 1981.

Porter, David. *Emerson and Literary Change.* Cambridge: Harvard University Press, 1978.

Rao, Adapa Ramakrishna. *Emerson and Social Reform.* Atlantic Highlands, N.J.: Humanities Press, 1980.

Roberson, Susan L. *Emerson in His Sermons.* Columbia: University of Missouri Press, 1995.

Robinson, David. *Apostle of Culture: Emerson as Preacher and Lecturer.* Philadelphia: University of Pennsylvania Press, 1982.

———. *Emerson and the Conduct of Life: Pragmatism and Ethical Purpose in the Later Work.* New York: Cambridge University Press, 1993.

Rohler, Lloyd. *Ralph Waldo Emerson: Preacher and Lecturer.* Westport, Conn.: Greenwood Press, 1995.

Rosenwald, Lawrence. *Emerson and the Art of the Diary.* New York: Oxford University Press, 1988.

Scheick, William J. *The Slender Human Word: Emerson's Artistry in Prose.* Knoxville: University of Tennessee Press, 1978.

Sealts, Merton M., Jr. *Emerson on the Scholar.* Columbia: University of Missouri Press, 1992.

Sowder, William L. *Emerson's Impact on the British Isles and Canada.* Charlottesville: University Press of Virginia, 1966.

Stack, George J. *Nietzsche and Emerson: An Elective Affinity.* Athens: Ohio University Press, 1992.

Staebler, Warren. *Ralph Waldo Emerson.* New York: Twayne, 1973.

Teichgraeber, Richard F., III. *Sublime Thoughts/Penny Wisdom: Situating Emerson and Thoreau in the American Market.* Baltimore: Johns Hopkins University Press, 1995.

Thurin, Erik Ingvar. *Emerson as Priest of Pan: A Study in the Metaphysics of Sex.* Lawrence: Regents Press of Kansas, 1981.

———. *The Universal Autobiography of Ralph Waldo Emerson.* Lund, Sweden: C. W. K. Gleerup, 1974.

Van Cromphout, Gustaaf. *Emerson's Modernity and the Example of Goethe.* Columbia: University of Missouri Press, 1990.

Van Leer, David. *Emerson's Epistemology: The Argument of the Major Essays.* New York: Cambridge University Press, 1986.

Wagenknecht, Edward. *Ralph Waldo Emerson: Portrait of a Balanced Soul.* New York: Oxford University Press, 1974.

Waggoner, Hyatt H. *Emerson as a Poet.* Princeton, N.J.: Princeton University Press, 1974.

Whicher, Stephen E. *Freedom and Fate: An Inner Life of Ralph Waldo Emerson.* Philadelphia: University of Pennsylvania Press,1953.

Williams, John B. *White Fire: The Influence of Emerson on Melville.* Long Beach: California State University, Long Beach, 1991.

Yannella, Donald. *Ralph Waldo Emerson.* Boston: Twayne, 1982.

Yoder, R. A. *Emerson and the Orphic Poet in America.* Berkeley: University of California Press, 1978.

Zwarg, Christina. *Feminist Conversations: Fuller, Emerson, and the Play of Reading.* Ithaca, N.Y.: Cornell University Press, 1995.

NOTES

1. Emerson's life as a professional author may be followed in Joel Myerson, *Ralph Waldo Emerson: A Descriptive Bibliography* (Pittsburgh: University of Pittsburgh Press, 1982); and Myerson, "Ralph Waldo Emerson's Income from His Books," in *The Professions of Authorship: Essays in Honor of Matthew J. Bruccoli,* ed. Richard Layman and Joel Myerson (Columbia: University of South Carolina Press, 1996), pp. 135–49.

2. See Nancy Craig Simmons, "Arranging the Sibylline Leaves: James Elliot Cabot's Work as Emerson's Literary Executor," *Studies in the American Renaissance 1983,* ed. Joel Myerson (Charlottesville: University Press of Virginia, 1983), pp. 335–89.

3. See *W.*

4. See *L; CEC;* and *The Correspoondence of Emerson and Carlyle,* ed. Joseph Slater (New York: Columbia University Press, 1964).

5. See *EL; JMN; The Poetry Notebooks of Ralph Waldo Emerson,* ed. Ralph H. Orth et al. (Columbia: University of Missouri Press, 1986); *TN;* and *CS.* Also of value is Ronald A. Bosco, "His Lectures Were Poetry, His Teaching the Music of the Spheres: Annie Adams Fields

and Francis Greenwood Peabody on Emerson's 'Natural History of the Intellect' University Lectures at Harvard in 1870," *Harvard Library Bulletin*, n.s., 8 (Summer 1997): 1–79.

6. See *AW; Emerson's Literary Criticism*, ed. Eric Carlson (Lincoln: University of Nebraska Press, 1979); *Emerson in His Journals*, ed. Joel Porte (Cambridge: Harvard University Press, 1982); and *The Selected Letters of Ralph Waldo Emerson*, ed. Joel Myerson (New York: Columbia University Press, 1997).

7. See George Shelton Hubbell, *A Concordance to the Poems of Ralph Waldo Emerson* (New York: H. W. Wilson, 1932); Eugene F. Irey, *A Concordance to Five Essays of Ralph Waldo Emerson* (New York: Garland, 1981); and Mary Alice Ihrig, *Emerson's Transcendental Vocabulary* (New York: Garland, 1982). A more complete concordance by Irey, keyed (as are all the others) to the 1903–1904 edition of Emerson's *Complete Works*, is available at the Web site maintained by the Thoreau Institute, www.walden.org.

8. See *CW*. The volumes published are *Nature, Addresses, and Lectures* (1971); *Essays: First Series* (1979); *Essays: Second Series* (1983); *Representative Men* (1987); and *English Traits* (1994).

9. *The Later Lectures of Ralph Waldo Emerson, 1843–1871*, ed. Ronald A. Bosco and Joel Myerson, is a multivolume edition to be published by the University of Georgia Press. Bosco and Myerson are also editing the correspondence of Charles, Edward, and William Emerson and their brother Waldo for publication by Oxford University Press.

Contributors

RONALD A. BOSCO, Distinguished Service Professor of English and American Literature at the University at Albany, SUNY, has been an editor of the Emerson papers at the Houghton Library of Harvard University since 1977. With Joel Myerson, he has recently completed *The Later Lectures of Ralph Waldo Emerson, 1843–1871*, and he and Myerson are now at work on an edtion of the Emerson brothers' correspondence.

GARY COLLISON, Professor of English at Penn State University–York, has published articles on Theodore Parker, the Harvard Divinity School, and other subjects realted to New England Transcendentalism. He is author of *Shadrach Minkins: From Fugitive Slave to Citizen* (Harvard, 1997).

ARMIDA GILBERT is currently preparing a book on Emerson and women. She has presented papers on the subject at professional conferences and is currently teaching at East Georgia College.

WESLEY T. MOTT is Professor of English at Worcester Polytechnic Institute and Secretary of the Ralph Waldo Emerson Society. He has written and edited five books about Emerson and New England Transcendentalism.

JOEL MYERSON, Carolina Distinguished Professor of American Literature at the University of South Carolina, has published nearly sixty books about the American Romantic period, including twenty volumes of the annual *Studies in the American Renaissance* (1977–1996). A former President of the Association for Documentary Editing, the Ralph Waldo Emerson Society, and the Thoreau Society, he is currently editing *Transcendentalism: A Reader* for Oxford University Press.

DAVID M. ROBINSON is Oregon Professor of English and Distinguished Professor of American Literature at Oregon State University. He is the author of *Apostle of Culture: Emerson as Preacher and Lecturer* (Pennsylvania, 1981), *The Unitarians and the Universalists* (Greenwood, 1985), and *Emerson and the Conduct of Life* (Cambridge, 1993). He has directed a number of National Endowment for the Humanities Summer Seminars for School Teachers on the New England Transcendentalists and is currently serving as President of the Ralph Waldo Emerson Society.

WILLIAM ROSSI is Associate Professor of English at the University of Oregon. He is coeditor of *Journal: 1853* in *The Writings of Henry D. Thoreau* (Princeton, forthcoming), and is working on a study of Thoreau's environmental writing and the mid-nineteenth-century evolutionary debates.

Index

Socrates, 281
Spenser, Edmund, 30
Stäel, Madame de, 69
Stanton, Elizabeth Cady, 211–12
Stein, Gertrude, 63
Stevens, Wallace, 63
Stewart, Dugald, 71
Stoics, 72, 92
Stone, Lucy, 213, 244
Stowe, Harriet Beecher, 47, 206
Strachey, Lytton, 243
Sturgis, Caroline. *See* Caroline
 Sturgis Tappan
Sumner, Charles, 202, 205, 206
Swart, Koenraad W., 77
Swedenborg, Emanuel, 37, 69, 72,
 84, 116, 216, 225–26, 228

Tappan, Caroline Sturgis, 33,
 35–36, 234, 240
Tate, Allen, 64
Tennyson, Alfred, Lord, 215
Thackeray, William Makepeace,
 32
Thénard, Louis, 15
Thome, James J., 189–90
Thompson, George, 186
Thoreau, Cynthia Dunbar, 186
Thoreau, Helen, 186
Thoreau, Henry David, 3, 24, 33,
 34, 42, 52, 61–62, 63, 64, 66,
 101–2, 162, 180, 182, 194,
 203, 249, 276, 281. *See also*
 Ralph Waldo Emerson,
 "Thoreau"
Thoreau Institute, 63–64
Thoreau, Maria, 186
Tiananmen Square, 64
Tilton, Eleanor M., 248
Tocqueville, Alexis de, 79
Tolstoy, Leo, 64

Transcendental Club, 24, 33, 185
Transcendentalism, 69, 70, 71, 73,
 74–75, 82, 84, 86, 89–90, 91,
 105, 133, 151, 158–62, 166,
 180
Truth, Sojourner, 231
Turner, Frederick Jackson, 83,
 85–86
Twain, Mark, 4, 63
Tyndall, John, 100–109

Unitarianism, 70, 73, 110, 112,
 151–77, 183–85

Van Buren, Martin, 187
Van Cromphout, Gustaaf, 96–97
Verlake, 224
Versluis, Arthur, 165
Very, Jones, 33, 281
Victoria, Queen, 243
Vietnam War, 64, 67
von Frank, Albert J., 83, 182–83

Ward, Anna Barker, 230, 240
Ward, Samuel Gray, 230
Ware, Henry, Jr., 157, 185
Ware, Henry, Sr., 154
Warner, Charles Dudley, 4
Washington, George, 99, 270–71,
 275
Webster, Daniel, 73–74, 197, 200,
 201, 236
Westminster Review, 129
Whewell, William, 119
Whicher, Stephen E., 277–83,
 285–86, 289
Whitefield, George, 154
Whitman, Walt, 3, 47, 49, 63, 277
Wilkins, John Hubbard, 225
Williams, Wallace E., 280
Woman's Journal, 244–45